THE VICE GUIDE TO SEX AND DRUGS AND ROCK AND ROLL COMES FROM THE FOLLOWING 89 ISSUES:

PREMIER ISSUE
Oct. 94 - Vol.0 No.0
Drawn & Quarterly/ Johnny Rotten/ Low Art/ Black Barbers

Nov. 94
Vol.1 No.1
The State of Hip Hop/ Art and War/ Queer Flick Fest/ Erotic City

Dec. 94
Vol.1 No.2
Sex Workers Resist/ Canada Customs vs. Tom of Finland

Jan. 95
Vol.2 No.1
Montreal Vandals/ Oliver Stone/ Media Sabotage/ Board to Death

Feb. 95
Vol.2 No.2
Blaxploitation/ Black gays/ Black Cartoonists/ Heroin Addicts

Mar. 95
Vol.2 No.3
Paris/ David Koresh's Girlfriend/ Bosnia/ Rave Culture for Sale

Apr. 95
Vol.2 No.4
Natives & Sovereignty/ Local Hip Hop/ Tattoos / Last Poets

May 95
Vol.2 No.5
Hate Literature/ Beastie Boys/ Peter Bagge

June 95
Vol.2 No.6
The Police and the Shoplifters They Kill/ Jazz Fest Blues/ Rock Sluts

Jul./Aug. 95
Vol.2 No.7
Motorhead/ Prostitutes/ Japanimation/ Separation

Sep. 95
Vol.2 No.8
"Dropping Out" by Noam Chomsky/ Nusrat Fateh Ali Khan

1st NATIONAL
Oct. 95
Vol.3 No.1
Crispin Glover/ Wu-Tang Clan/ Dan Clowes/ Lowriders

Nov. 95
Vol.3 No.2
Life in Prison/ Flaming Lips/ Stripping

Dec./Jan. 95
Vol.3 No.3
Rocket From the Crypt/ Joyriding/ Snowboarding/ Girls and Guns

Feb. 96
Vol.3 No.4
Napalm Death/ Police Violence/ Louis Farrakhan

March. 96
Vol. 3 No.5
Ian Mackaye/ The Cows/ Cuba/ GG Allin/ Mad Professor

April 96
Vol.3 No.6
Princess Superstar/ Goodie Mob/ Tampons/ Curtis Mayfield

May 96
Vol.3 No.7
Raekwon/ Skate Chicks/ Cartel/ Jad Fair/ Sepultura

June 96
Vol.3 No.8
Korean Gangsters/ Delinquent Habits/ Kozik/ Crack/ Butthole Surfers

1st INDEPENDENT
Jul./Aug. 96
Vol.3 No.8b
Russia/ A Tribe Called Quest/ Fluff/ Kung-Fu/ Kiss

Sep. 96
Vol.3 No.9
Hollywood/ Mexican Gangs/ De La Soul/ Jesus Lizard/ The Wienermobile

Oct. 96
Vol.3 .No.10
Sex&Cars/ Guide to Drugs/ Jeru the Damaja/ The Descendents

Nov. 96
Vol.3 No.11
Ghostface Killah/ Hard Core Logo/ Guide to Beats/ Norwegian Metal

Dec./Jan. 96
Vol.3 No.12
Rocks Stars/ Mobb Deep/ DJ Shadow/ Michelle Yeoh

Feb. 97
Vol.4 No.1
Tricky/ Women in Hip Hop/ Sex Drugs/ Corruption in Canada's Military

March 97
Vol.4 No.2
Sneaker Pimps/ Thai Prostitutes/ Afrika Bambaata/ Candy Guide/ Fluffy

April 97
Vol.4 No.3
Xena/ Helmet/ ATR/ Flyer Art/ An Interview with God

May 97
Vol.4 No. 4
Squatting/ KRS-one/ Jello Biafra/ The Chemical Brothers

June 97
Vol.4 No.5
Crime Pays/ Canada Skates/ Melvins/ Break-dancing School/ DJ A Trak

July 97
Vol.4 No.5b
FLQ Terrorism/ Company Flow/ Kung-Fu Guide/ Satanic Orgies

Aug./Sep. 97
Vol.4 No.7
Ween/ Alkaholiks/ Interview with Black Guy/ The Cramps

Oct. 97
Vol.4 No.8 & 9
Pizzicato Five/ Ron Jeremy/ Crime Quiz/ Japan/ Graffiti

Nov. 97
Vol.4 No.10
Kool Keith/ Religious Hard Core/ Che Guevara vs. Muhammad Ali

Dec./Jan. 97
Vol.4 No.11
The Goddess/ Hash/ Sex and Fashion/ NOFX/ Gravediggaz/ Phone Fraud

Feb. 98
Vol.5 No.1
France is Going Bald/ Sex Rhymes/ Spice Girls vs. Nashville Pussy

March 98
Vol.5 No.2
Vaginas/ DJ Premier/ Prison Weddings/ Twisted Sister

Apr. 98
Vol.5 No.3
Cappadonna/ DNA/ Keoki/ Gummo/ Pimps/ Buffalo Daughter

May 97
Vol.5 No.4
Guy on Acid for a Year/ Fugazi/ Goodie Mob/ Massive Attack

June 97
Vol.5 No.5
Money Mark/ Mods/ Chicks with Dicks/ Violence/ Turnstylez Crew

July/ Aug. 98
Vol.5 No.6
A Tribe Called Quest/ Horny Retards

Sep. 98
Vol.5 No.7
The Biz/ Nazis vs. Tibetan Monks/ Peep Shows

1st GLOSSY
Oct. 98
Vol.5 No.8
Panther Update/ Hangovers and Heroin/ Outkast

INVESTMENT
Nov. 98
Vol.5 No. 9
Students Who Whore/ Madman from Sudan/ Kurtis Mantronik

Dec./Jan. 98
Vol.5 No.10
Watching Pornos/ RZA/ The Preps Must Die/ Black Sabbath

Originally VICE was a local newspaper called *VOICE OF MONTREAL* and it stayed that way from October 94 (Vol.0 No.0) to a year later (Vol.3 No.1) when it became simply *VOICE* and was distributed internationally. In July of 96 the "o" was dropped and it became *VICE*. Then, in October 98, for our four year anniversary, the newspaper became a glossy magazine (Vol.5 No.8).

July 1999 New York

Feb. 99
Vol.6 No.1
Hillbillies/ in the Punjab/ Turbonegro/ Prince Paul/ Women on Death Row

March 99
Vol.6 No.2
Kruder & Dorfmeister/ Interview with Potato/ Peanut Butter Wolf

April 99
Vol.6 No.3
Eminem/ Planet V/ Gaza Strippers/ Black People vs. White People

May 99
Vol.6 No.4
Moscow Clubs/ Star Wars vs. Tunisia/ The Damned/ Scratch Acid

June 99
Vol.6 No.5
Barbie Polaroids/ PMS/ Drum n' Bass for TV/ Banned Dildos

NEW YORK
July/ Aug. 99
Vol.6 No.6
Summer Violence/ The Ronettes

Sep 99
Vol.6 No.7
Ravers in the Bathroom/ Art Pranks/ Breakbeat Era/ Living Legends

Oct. 99
Vol.6 No.8
Gay Midget Wrestlers/ Teenage Girl Gangs/ Q-Bert/ Pharoahe Monch

1st PERFECT BOUND
Nov. 99
Vol.6 No.9
The Worlds Biggest Slut/ The Shanghai Club Scene/ Supersuckers/ Lord Sear

Dec./Jan. 99
Vol.6 No.10
VICE Guide to Eating Pussy/ Retards and Hip Hop/ Kid Koala

Feb. 2000
Vol.7 No.1
Not Cuban Whores/ Blackalicious/ Retards/ Paki Supremacy

March 00
Vol.7 No.2
Film Stuff/ Rock Stars/ Porn/ Rap Snacks/ Torture

April 00
Vol.7 No.3
Andrew WK/ Moustache Clubs/ Dead Sumo Wrestlers/ Blow Jobs

May 00
Vol.7 No. 4
Satpal Ram/ Rape Stories/ Jurassic 5/ Ali G

June 00
Vol.7 No.5
Gay Slobs/ A Bank Robber and his Wife/ Pimpadelic/ Terrorism

INDEPENDENT AGAIN
July/ Aug. 00
Vol.7 No.6
Japanese Porn/ Kid 606/ Chicks on Speed/ Swayzak/ Balloon Sluts

Sep. 00
Vol.7 No.7
East Timor and the NYPD/ Prison Recipes/ RA/ Abe Lincoln the Fag

Oct. 00
Vol.7 No.8
Lolita Storm/ 1950s Motorcycle Gangs/ Chinese Art vs. Dead Cows

Nov. 00
Vol.7 No.9
Sex + Punishment/ 555 Soul Ad/ Ben Sherman Ad/ Transfer Ad

Dec./Jan. 00
Vol.7 No.10
The Gays/ Bratmobile/ Carl Craig/ Cocaine/ Capone 'n Noreaga

Feb. 01
Vol.8 No.1
Lots and lots of Arrows/ High School Confessions

March 01
Vol.8 No.2
Anal Sex/ Black Elvis/ Add N to X/ Beatnuts

Apr. 01
Vol.8 No.3
Prison Fashion/ The Gossip/ Irak/ People on Drugs/ Crime

May 01
Vol.8 No. 4
Asia Argento/ Electroclash/ Dealing/

June 01
Vol.8 No.5
Internal Ejaculation/ White Stripes/ 80s Anti-Drug Films

July/ Aug. 01
Vol.8 No.6
The First Photo Issue feat. pre Sept 11th shots of Afghanistan

Sep. 01
Vol.8 No.7
Prescription Drugs/ Aesop Rock/ Hobbit Killers/ Female Ejaculation

OVERSIZED

Oct. 01
Vol.8 No.8
Afghanistan (Masoud)/ Papa M/ The Avalanches/ Cars

Nov. 01
Vol.8 No.9
Liquid Acid/ Garfield/ American Foreign Policy/ Fischerspooner

Dec./Jan.01
Vol.8 No.10
Hate/ AIDS proof whores/ The Strokes/ Ghostface/ David Cross

Feb. 02
Vol.9 No.1
Terry Richardson/ Guilty Pleasures/ Skins/ Zwan/ Corporate Crimes

March 02
Vol.9 No.2
Latinos/ El-P/ TIGA/ The Yeah Yeah Yeahs/ Racism

April 02
Vol.9 No.3
Kid 606/ Dirty Bombs/ Bush's Home Movie/

May 02
Vol.9 No. 4
Sex Machines/ Outsider Videos/ UK Garage/ DJ Quik/ Conspiracy Theories

June 02
Vol.9 No.5
Bands That Suck/ Gold Chains/ Warp Records/ Comet Gain/ Lazy Artists

July 02
Vol.9 No.6
Second Photo Issue feat. The Streets

One of 4 covers

1st AUGUST ISSUE
Aug. 02
Vol.9 No.7
Iraq/ Skinheads/ Dead Nerds/ E-40/ Black Dice

Sep. 02
Vol.9 No.8
Goth Jocks/ Larry Clark vs. Harmony Korine/ Gator/ Cage/

Oct.02
Vol.9 No.9
80s Issue Journey/ Paper Rad/ Chromeo/ Vice City/ Finding Yourself

Nov. 02
Vol.9 No.10
Violence Issue Gaspar Noe/ Fat Joe/ Finsbury Park Mosque

Dec./Jan 03
Vol.9 No.11
Special Issue Guest Edited by Severely Handicapped Adults

Feb. 03
Vol.10 No.1
Happiness Issue Celebrity letters/ Cheerleaders/ No More AIDS or War

March 03
Vol.10 No. 2
The West issue Dave Eggers/ Marines/ Saddaam/ Islam/ Country

April 03
Vol.10 No.3
11 Artists/ Parisian Dandies/ Dancehall Queens/ Crushes

May 03
Vol.10 No.4
Bullshit guide/ Media Bias/ Bullies/ Psychos/ TV Carnage

THE VICE GUIDE TO SEX AND DRUGS AND ROCK AND ROLL

THE VICE GUIDE TO SEX AND DRUGS AND ROCK AND ROLL

Suroosh Alvi, Gavin McInnes, and Shane Smith

WARNER BOOKS

An AOL Time Warner Company

Copyright © 2003 by VICE Magazine Publishing USA, Inc.
Copyright © 2002 by VICE Holding, Inc.
All rights reserved.

A previous edition was published in Canada by HarperCollins.

Warner Books, Inc., 1271 Avenue of the Americas, New York, NY 10020

Visit our Web site at www.twbookmark.com.

 An AOL Time Warner Company

Printed in the United States of America

First Printing: September 2003
10 9 8 7 6 5 4 3 2 1

ISBN: 0-446-69281-6
LCCN: 2003107691

Cover design by Gavin McInnes

This book is dedicated
to John Coinner
1968–1999

UPDATE

The VICE Guide to Sex and Drugs and Rock and Roll is a compilation of the best articles *VICE* Magazine published between October of 1994 and May of 2003. The problem is it's a monthly news magazine, so a lot of the more time-specific articles didn't make it. Even some of the ones that did make it are reliant on the date they were originally published. When we wrote about Afghanistan in "The *VICE* Guide to Evil," it was still an unknown shithole and, as this book goes to print, it is still illegal to dance in New York. Everything else was, is, and always will be totally fucking true.

CONTENTS

EDUCATION

THE PHOTOGRAPHERS AND ILLUSTRATORS BEHIND THE VICE GUIDE TO SEX AND DRUGS AND ROCK AND ROLL

We don't have enough space to talk about all the writers in this book. Besides, they already get a whole page or so to show you what they're about. If you need to know more about contributors like David Cross, Sarah Silverman, Rat Scabies, Andrew WK or the book's editor Sharky Favorite you can google them. If there's nothing there then fuck them, they're irrelevant (just kidding). What we do have room for is some of the photographers and illustrators that made this book way more than just a greatest hits compilation. And they are...

TERRY RICHARDSON
Photographer for the SEX Chapter

Terry's life is a book in itself. He grew up as the son of a successful fashion photographer until Angelica Houston broke up the marriage. Then his adolescence went from skateboarding around Hollywood and playing in punk bands to: poverty, violence, abandonment, drugs, squatting, then ... getting discovered, fashion, international stardom, Gucci, Vogue, extreme wealth, Milan, marriage, heroin, Paris, cancer, divorce, death, Narcotics Anonymous and ping pong. The best part is, after all this chaos, he's still a little skateboard punk from California photographing super models for a billion dollars a day going "wow, is she ever a babe eh you guys?"

VICE CONTRIBUTIONS: Shot a ton of covers, "Table of Content" shots, fashion shoots and shots for features.

DAVID CHOE
Illustrator for the DRUGS Chapter

David Choe is a street kid from Oakland that steals everything he can find and gets into fights. He also makes stunning art books he calls *Slow Jams* that are filled with gorilla robot sculptures and comics and stories and paintings and cartoons and porno collages. When he anonymously sent us a box of his stuff back in the spring of 1999 they kind of dominated the magazine for a really long time. Not anymore though. Now he lives in Africa and sits on his ass all day.

VICE CONTRIBUTIONS: Illustrated a ton features and the V6N4 cover and he wrote a bunch of stuff too.

BRIAN DEGRAW
Illustrator for the ROCK AND ROLL Chapter

All we know about this guy is that he used to play in a band with Harmony Korine, he's been having art shows from the Lower East Side to Tokyo for the past ten years, he threw his bike through the front window of the Virgin Megastore in London (and went to jail for it), he got third degree sunburns on his legs after passing out in the park, his apartment burnt down (apparently related to passing out again) and the guy can FUCKING DRAW.

VICE CONTRIBUTIONS: He was there for us when we needed someone to talk to.

RYAN McGINLEY
Photographer for the CRIME Chapter

Ryan is one of those fucked up vandal wastoids that got shit together and become a famous artist. The fist night we met him he was pissing on the TV Screen at Karaoke Village. Today he's in Milan doing a solo show and will be having another one at The Whitney (the fucking Whitney) as soon as he gets back to New York. We tried to tell him all this was thanks to us but it ended up in a fistfight wherein he won. Oh yeah, the Polaroids here might be shoplifting Polaroids anonymously, er, misplaced by a local drugstore. See if you can guess which one is staged.

VICE CONTRIBUTIONS: Shot a ton of covers, "Table of Content" shots, fashion shoots and shots for features.

BRUCE LaBRUCE
Photographer for the SPECIAL PEOPLE Chapter

It's hard to find someone that personifies the brand more than Bruce (except for the part where he's a fag). He's covered in tattoos, makes pornos regularly, takes great photographs, sounds like a total nazi and travels the world getting so fucked up he has no idea where he is. The last time we hung out with him in New York we had a four-hour debate about the failings of Pierre Trudeau and then got so drunk the night ended in a slapping contest. That's the kind of guy he is; an intellectual fuck up.

VICE CONTRIBUTIONS: No covers but he did tons of photographs for features and a bunch of features for photographs and sometimes he'd even do both. What a guy.

MIN KIM
Illustrator for the EDUCATION Chapter

Min Kim is impossible to explain. Some people call her an alien baby because she is naïve and innocent yet somehow of interplanetary omnipotence. When she has dreams about death, people die. When she has dreams about fire, entire blocks burn down. I know it sounds like hippy dippy bullshit but I've seen it happen. She's spooky. Look at her drawings. When she was a kid growing up in rural Korea she would stay up all night drawing and then sleep all day in school (even though it led to regular beatings with a bamboo branch). Today she reads 14th Century poetry and often draws for 23 hours in a row. You figure it out.

VICE CONTRIBUTIONS: Covers for V8N2 and V8N6.

Suroosh, Gavin and Shane circa 1985

... and today.

VICE—THE WHOLE STORY

ON THE BEGINNING:

Suroosh Alvi: There was an eight-to-ten-year period before the magazine started that I refer to as "the dark years." I think I'm finally ready to come clean on all that. Going back to July '94, when I was in a treatment center . . .

Gavin McInnes: For what, Suroosh?

SA: For a little problem I had with heroin.

GM: What a relief to finally hear you say that in an interview.

SA: In a nutshell, I went to treatment, I relapsed, I hit rock bottom, went back out there—using again, doing bad things to support the habit. I got on a waiting list to go back into a treatment center for another round. While I was waiting, biding my time for two weeks before going in, my dad asked me to come along with my family to the mosque for a religious holiday.

In the prayer hall I was literally on my knees begging for mercy. I remember saying, "If there's an Allah out there, fucking help me out now, and make this obsession with heroin go away." That was really a turning point in my life because it actually worked. And then after coming out of rehab, I met someone in NA who asked me, "Have you ever thought about writing? Because I know a place that's looking for an editor." He walked me down the next day and they hired me. I kept a journal in rehab, and I wrote about how it would be cool to work for a magazine. I wrote that and Allah made it happen. If I hadn't been a heroin addict, *VICE* wouldn't exist. It's all been predetermined, apparently.

Anyway, the first issue hit the streets in October of '94. It came out after a bit of a revolving door at our publisher at the time. This other guy was supposed to be the editor, but he quit and got heavily into cocaine and kind of fell by the wayside.

GM: That was back when it was a free English newspaper in a French province that didn't need it.

ON SUROOSH AND GAVIN MEETING:

SA: I needed someone to do comics for the first issue and my friend Rufus suggested him. Gavin was doing a comic book called *Pervert* at the time and had brought in a strip about smack that I thought was great because I had just gotten out of treatment. So Gavin hooked up the other comic artists and got me some numbers and I asked him to come on board.

GM: But then you hired some gay dude to be the assistant editor instead of me because it was a welfare make-work program. I had to go on welfare to get the job off him. The secret is you fill out the forms with your left hand so they think you're retarded.

ON HATE LITERATURE:

SA: I remember I was living in my parents' basement and I was really into *Answer Me*, Jim Goad's magazine. I had piles upon piles of, I guess, hate literature, they call it—*Sewer Cunt* from Denmark, *Fuck Magazine*, *Murder Can Be Fun*—and I just sat and I read it for two weeks.

GM: You think being a junkie and dying so many times gave you this sort of dark outlook?

SA: Maybe. I remember after reading this shit for like two weeks, it definitely twisted my brain a bit. Everything else was so boring to read, and this stuff actually felt alive because it was seething with hate. It was easy to identify with because I was in a shitty place at the time.

ON SHANE COMING ABOARD:

Shane Smith : I had just come back from Hungary, where I had been living for a couple of years. Gavin and I had been friends since we were little kids in Ottawa. We were in a few punk bands together. Leatherassbuttfuk was one. Anyway, he told me they were looking for someone to help with the mag. I met Suroosh when Gavin and I were on acid, and I was trying to tell him that we were going to take over the world, but I couldn't because I was too high. So I was going, "I can't get it out. I can't get it out." Then I said he was my new best friend and showed him how to throw a googlie because since he was from Pakistan he must love cricket. That's how I bonded with him.

Back then we were always in production, which seemed to consist of staying awake for days and days and trying to find shit that we had misplaced. Towards the end we'd occasionally break down and celebrate too early.

One day they sent me to pick up the cover photo, which was a picture of Lemmy from Motörhead, at the film developer, and then I was gonna go with a friend who worked with us to try and get some advertising from this woman who owned a bar. I ended up at the bar too soon and I barely remember the rest. I do remember being so drunk that I went into the stockroom by mistake on my way to the bathroom. Since I was there I decided to put some bottles of whiskey down my leg. Meanwhile, people who worked there were coming in and out of the storeroom looking at me. So I walked out, calm as you please, with three bottles of whiskey down my pants—cling-clang, cling-clang. . . . They went up and grabbed my buddy, who said he didn't know who I was. So I escaped to a porn booth (a tiny room where a dollar coin provides two minutes of limitless pornography) on St. Catherine St. and decided to make myself a little bar in the booth. I was drinking booze and having a gay old time until I ran out of change and was forced to go to the front to get more. When I came back someone had taken my booth so I freaked out and kicked the door down, whereupon I got arrested.

They took me to jail, and I was sitting there waiting to be booked. At this point the sun's coming up, and these guys are going, "Where the fuck is Shane? We sent him to get the cover, like, a day ago." Meanwhile I'm at the police station sitting there waiting to get arrested, and I go, "Why am I sitting here waiting to get arrested? I have to get back to work." They were changing shifts and I didn't have my cuffs on so I just left. I walked out and sort of arrived at the office at eight in the morning going, in triumph, "I made it! I got out of jail, you guys!" They were like, "Where's the cover, you asshole?"

SA: We were still at our desks from the night before and you came in reeking of booze. We were pissed off.

ON *VOICE* SPREADING OUT FROM MONTREAL:

GM: Eventually we went international. The titles went *Voice of Montreal*, then *VOICE* because it was all of Canada, and then *VICE*.

ON THE IMPORTANCE OF RELATIONSHIPS:

SS: This is how we got our first color cover (points to an ad in an old issue). I sold an ad to my friend Dave Porter, who was an A & R guy . . .

GM: Which goes to prove that marketing and getting ads and selling the magazine has more to do with who you know—friends cutting favors and whatnot—than the merit of the mag.

SS: It also helps to eat them out and mail them drugs.

ON COUGARS AND MAILING DRUGS:

SS: The first major ad that I sold was to a big beer company, the worst ad campaign ever. But it paid for the whole issue, the cover and everything.

SA: The only reason you got that was because the woman in charge of the campaign wanted to get you in the sack.

SS: Yeah, the woman in charge of the campaign was a cougar (an upwardly mobile, single, hipster, thirty-something woman in marketing), and all the cougars in Toronto want to screw, and you have to play the game and then you fucking get the ads.

GM: We ate our way to the top. The whole world of marketing is female. They say women are in the workforce, but they're not. They're just in the marketing force. It goes men at the top, then women buying the ads. And they want to fuck. So we would fuck them—even the old, balding dogs with horrible tits. It was straight-up sexual harassment but it worked for both sides.

And then there'd be the odd male guy in marketing and we would send him drugs—GHB or ecstasy. It was the modern version of taking the client to the strip club or Studio 54. We'd take him out for a good time, but in his mind. I remember there was a story once when we were regularly sending GHB to this guy and his secretary thought, "Oh, I'd like to try this," and instead of putting it in water first she took it raw and it burned her mouth.

SS: Sending drugs in the mail was commonplace until we found out it was a felony.

ON MAKING SHIT UP FOR CONTENT:

GM: I think it's worth mentioning that Shane wrote a first-person story about being in a horrible prison in Bangkok.

SS: (laughing) I don't know, you guys used to say we needed a story so I'd just make something up. I knew it was a story that I had heard from somebody and I just co-opted it.

GM: You probably rented that movie *Bangkok Hilton*, because I know we used the cover of the box for the photo.

SS: Probably. I probably watched it when I was stoned and thought it was me so I wrote it first-person: "I'm eating millipedes now. . . ."

ON GOING NATIONAL:

SS: We went national by accident. This guy named Kevin from Cargo Records said they'd ship us nationally, so we went to Toronto and sold ads. It was gonna be the first national issue. And two days before we were gonna go they said, "Sorry, we can't do it." So we had to set up a whole distribution and circulation—the works—overnight. We called friends and bartered ads with people at radio stations. That was the way we became a free distribution magazine.

GM: Any major move we've done has been by accident. It's always been some sort of Band-Aid solution where we stayed up all night and called people and said, "Can you help us out?" If we ever tried to do a real thank-you list it would be fucking endless.

ON LEAVING IMAGES INTERCULTURELLES:

SA: The Haitian publishers who gave us *Voice of Montreal* were choking us to death. They weren't even giving us any money to buy pencils, let alone pens.

GM: We suspect they were getting grants for our wages and just keeping it all.

SA: Yeah, so we each borrowed $5,000 from our parents and moved to the other side of Old Montreal, and that's where we really got strong. It was just the three of us, with no more ball and chain with the Third-World publishers. We had to fend for ourselves.

ON *VOICE* BECOMING *VICE*:

GM: We changed our name so our old owner wouldn't sue us for leaving. We were scared of him and his lawyer wife so we became *VICE* and paid him $500 a month for, like, three years.

People kept asking us why we changed the name, and we didn't want to say we were scared of getting sued back then—now it's become commonplace—but we were so scared that we said, "Oh, we went down to the States and the *Village Voice* saw that we were called *VOICE* and threatened to sue us."

The Canadian media loves David and Goliath stories, and they fuckin' jumped on it. We were in *Maclean's*, we were on CBC news, we were in every local paper, every national paper. The lie just snowballed out of control.

SS: That's when we realized the power of publicity. If you can get some sort of angle—even if you make it up—it's just media logrolling, because magazines and TV just want to talk about their peers.

SA: But I think the reason those lies were so successful was because even *we* believed them after a while.

GM: Lying became part of who we were back then. I guess a magazine started by a junkie is inevitably going to be duplicitous.

ON AMMA:

GM: Yeah, we've always used the magazine as a way to get laid, especially *VICE* girls (a "girl of the month" feature in old issues).

SS: We even got some orgies out of it.

GM: Well, in the case of Amma, she came to Montreal and the way we got her was our printing guy was telling us about this slut from Malta he was disgusted by and we were like robots after his stories. We just kept repeating, "Must . . . have . . . her, must . . . have . . . her." We set up this *VICE* girl shoot and got together that night. Shane and I took to fucking her regularly in a porn booth and at the office.

One time we were fucking her and Shane was lying on his back, and I couldn't get anywhere because they were like a sandwich. There was nowhere for me, and I knew it wouldn't fit in her bum because we had all tried that and it didn't go. But I was like, "Oh, I can get it in there if I really go for it." It was like fitting an elephant into a phone booth. So I'm pushing and pushing and then it just goes "blooooooooink"—right in—and Shane's stroking her hair going, "It's okay, it's okay . . ."

SS: And she goes, "Uuuuuuuuuuuunh . . . yeaaah."

GM: She never used to like that so I was confused. Then I look down at her asshole and I'm like, "Look at that beautiful pink assho . . . hey, wait a minute. How come I can see the asshole? I thought I was *in* the asshole." And then I feel down and I have a condom on, and I'm like, "What is this? I didn't have a condom on when I went into her ass." Then I realize I pushed so hard I forced my dick into Shane's condom with Shane's dick and we were both in her vagina. I was so horny I almost kept going but it was a bit too homo to be penis-rubbing like that.

ON THE SERIAL KILLER AD:

SS: It was a good time for the magazine and we had no fear. We'd put in whatever we wanted. I remember we were ready to do our first trade show and then they said we were no longer invited because of this Serial Killer ad that showed a picture of pubic hair. It was something we never even thought about.

We had to manually rip out the page on five thousand copies in order to still be invited. That was followed by a big fiasco at our old alma mater—Gavin's and mine—Carleton, University when the gay and lesbian center had banned *VICE* from campus because of the same ad. And then the student newspaper got the gay and lesbian center magazine banned from the campus as well because they wrote about it and printed the same picture. There was just this frenzy of censorship.

GM: It exposed the liberal academics for what they really are—Stalinist Nazis that want to push around people they assume have inferior intellects. They act like heroes championing the underdog but they're really just classists.

SS: So this became a huge issue in Canada. By accident, we had become champions of free speech fighting the PC dickheads. All of a sudden we were on TV every day talking about censorship because of a little bit of pubic hair. And it was great publicity, which just led to more fucking popularity, more money, more everything.

GM: I remember asking the guy at Carleton, "What's the problem with it?" And he goes, "Well, it's using sex and not sexuality to sell ads," and I just gave up. These people aren't interested in logic.

SA: But in reality the PC lobby in America isn't so different. In Canada they were afraid of a bit of nudity and pubes and in America it's the race card. You can't say "nigger." Apparently it's okay for us to say "nigga," though. I mean, how fucking gay is that?

ON THE MESC BINGE:

GM: It was hard to put out a magazine with so few people and the $200-a-week salary we were making back then. You'd need drugs to stay up all night and then more drugs to release the pressure after the issue came out. The best pressure reliever around at the time was Montreal's version of mescaline (horse tranquilizer).

There was this girl named Brenda who was our mescaline dealer. One night, Shane and I went to this punk bar to meet up with her, wearing three-piece suits as a joke.

Eventually she gave us each a dose and we put it in our beer and drank it. And then—and this was the stupidest fucking thing—Shane and I stole some from her beer (using straws) when she wasn't looking. She was doing ten times the normal dose at the time and we barely had a tolerance.

SA: Meanwhile, we were in production and the magazine had to go to the printer the next day. I left the office at about two in the morning, and as I was driving up St. Laurent in Montreal I saw Gavin and Shane sitting on a bench. I pulled over and walked up to them. Shane looked at me with no recognition in his eyes whatsoever. I thought he was just fucking with me, and Gavin, meanwhile, had his head back on the bench and his eyes closed. His tie was wrapped around his neck and his pager was lying on the ground. I went to hand him his pager, and when he opened his eyes it was pretty clear that neither one of them recognized me at all.

The next four hours were totally insane. They couldn't walk or function in any way. Gavin was literally speaking in tongues and trying to deconstruct every little thing that he saw. His brain was taking things in at a thousand miles a minute and working on all these different levels. And Shane was crying about something and telling me he died.

I called some friends to walk Shane home and I took Gavin back to my place and put him in my bed so I could make sure he wouldn't choke on his puke or something. I remember him getting up in the middle of the night to use the bathroom, but instead of walking out he hopped around my bed in the dark like a ninja, still wearing his suit and not making a sound.

The next morning I was a good guy and let them sleep it off. I went to the office thinking they would show up maybe a couple of hours late. But they never showed up. What I later found out is that when they woke up they called each other—as you are wont to do the day after bringing it on with your buddies—and then went back to the bench to look for some mescaline they had lost the night before. And that's a great statement on drugs: They'll put you on the edge of death, and the next day you're like, "Where can I get more?"

ON ROBBIE DILLON:

GM: Robbie Dillon was a Montreal loan shark ex-con who came in off the street and had this idea for an article about how to survive in prison. We ended up building a strong relationship with him because he wrote the only serious content in our magazine for months.

SS: Well, the best Robbie Dillon story is when he wrote this amazing article for us about the biggest drug bust in Canadian history. It was reported that the government had found 27 tons of hash, but we found out that it was actually 35 tons. The other eight tons were a pay-off to the stoolie, and the cops were packing his fridge and his couch and everything with it. So this was a huge scoop for us. We made it the cover story and it was all set to go when Robbie came in and said, "You can't run the article." And we were like, "What are you talking about? Fuck you. We already spent the money on the printing. It's gone."

Then he pulled out a shoebox of cash and was like, "Oh, it cost a lot of money? How about this?" And it was more money than we'd ever seen in cash in one place in our lives (which wasn't that much—we were broke). So he gave it to us and we divided it up, spent it, and ran "Interview with a Potato" or something like that instead. No big deal.

About two months later we all went to a strip club/brothel called Grand Prix that was run by the cops, and on the way home later that night Robbie goes, "So it's a good thing you guys didn't run that story because then I would've had to, you know, burn down the printing house and have you guys whacked." We could tell he wasn't kidding and it was petrifying.

SA: I just remember driving back that night in total silence.

GM: At the time I would never talk to someone again if they so much as disagreed with me. And here we were hanging out with someone who almost killed us.

SA: But Robbie really brought us hard-hitting journalism.

GM: You know what else he brought to us? We were getting all lost in contracts and signatures and we learned that if someone wants to fuck with you, they'll fuck with you whether you have a contract or not. So Robbie taught us to trust everyone implicitly, and if they fuck you over you go and get them. So when those dudes tried to steal $25,000 from *VICE* fashion in the UK, we started calling these people we know in Wales who beat the shit out of people for money. Word magically got back to the guy that we were making these calls, and we got all our money back. Robbie taught us that.

ON PEEP SHOWS:

SS: Peep shows (porn booths) were the best part of living in Montreal. We would always go out for breakfast with bunches of people and eat and talk and then when everyone went home to go back to bed, we'd go to the peep show around the corner, whack off, and go to work.

SA: We'd each be allowed to spend one loony (Canadian dollar coin) so that we'd all be done at the same time.

GM: Shane always cheated and stayed in longer. We had this running joke that he'd go in, neatly fold his pants and shirt, put oil all over his body, light some candles, and just totally make love to himself.

SS: Well, I'd put a couple extra bucks in and get into it. Then I'd come out and go, "I don't know what happened. The thing just kept going." I remember there was this one peep show where you could spend a little bit more money and get this beautiful leather chair with this *Star Trek* panel that would come up with a widescreen TV and Surroundsound. You could really go to town in there, boy.

ON BEING FREE:

SS: We sort of stumbled into this way of distribution that now has been heralded as a kind of revolution in publishing. Initially we just wanted to get every copy into the right pair of hands, each issue was that precious to us because we had put so much into it. What ended up happening was that not only did we have a hundred percent pick up rate, usually within hours of dropping off the mags, but it was totally niche specific, so the response rate was insane. One big reason for this fanatical fan base was that our content was not influenced by the hugely conservative distribution companies that run all magazine circulation in North America. Because we were free we didn't have to kow tow to their censorship and editorial pressure. We are one of the only magazines in the world that totally control our own content. Not to mention our model is very profitable and doesn't waste sixty percent of printed issues, like newsstand does. I guess it's another example of organic growth and tuning bad shit into good shit.

ON GOING GLOSSY:

SS: I would like to say we went glossy because we wanted to get bought by a billionaire, and Richard Szalwinski was interested in us at the time. But what really happened was there was a strike at our printer and the type of newsprint paper we used was gone. We called up a buddy of ours at a skateboard magazine called *Concrete Powder*, and he told us how to go glossy. So we tried it, and when we got it back it was like the coming of the Holy Grail. It was the most beautiful thing we had ever seen.

It did two things. It got us out of that shitty, "stay small," indie mentality, and it really impressed investors. We were fucked, we had to find a solution, we found the solution, and it ended up being one of the launching pads for *VICE* to become a real magazine.

ON RICHARD SZALWINSKI:

SA: The first time we met Richard Szalwinski (*VICE*'s first real investor) he was in a large, flowing, white robe, with a perfect tan. I reached out to shake his hand and he grabbed my balls instead.

GM: So we got bought by Richard, who was this eccentric dot.com millionaire, and we were so wowed by his cash after being on welfare and scraping by that we had a massive party and Shane and I did way too much coke and had a horrible time.

SS: Yeah, it was this big party where we were gonna gloat about how rich we'd become overnight. And it was literally overnight. He told us to give him a one-page thing detailing what we wanted for him to buy into the mag, and it was our own ignorance that led us to value ourselves at $4 million, which was way too much. Anyway, that day he gave us the checks. So we went out and ran around in circles in the grass screaming at the top of our lungs. We didn't even know what to do with all that money. In fact, Gavin and I ended up buying a house in Costa Rica, where we had been vacationing every year. Up until then everyone down there knew us as the guys in bare feet with a bottle of rum. We would just stumble around and stay in hostels and piss our pants. Then all of a sudden we were down there, like, "Will you mow our lawn if we give you an 8-ball?"

So everybody hated us because we went from being these local guys in the bar to starting our lives for real, and the Canadian reaction was like a bunch of junkies when you get clean. They want to drag you back down with them. They all came to the party, though, hugging us and saying shit like, "You guys made it!" But like Gavin said, we were on way too much coke to tell anyone to fuck off.

GM: Yeah, and we had come up with this amazing idea of the three of us renting big cartoon costumes but not wearing the heads. So you're this big puffy guy with a tiny little peanut head. It's not fun to have a costume on when you're having a bad trip. You're all trying to be serious and everything with a gigantic Garfield body.

SS: Suroosh was having a blast.

SA: Yeah, I was on the dance floor in my cow costume with two girls on each arm grinding into me. I remember wondering, "Where's the other guys?"

GM: There's your antidrug commercial right there.

ON GOING ONLINE:

SA: We went from being a tiny company to having a staff of 25 people just for our e-commerce website in Montreal and two warehouses filled with streetwear in Quebec and Vermont, and we were just spending millions of dollars. It was over the top. And at that point I remember thinking, "This is not fun. This is not why we started this magazine."

We were rookies, but we understood the basic concept that you should be making more than you're spending. It didn't matter, though. We were willing to throw that principle out the window because there was so much cash flowing down the pipeline. They said we were going to make all these millions if we just followed their plan. But nothing really added up in the end. We never had any faith in the Internet and they mocked us for being skeptical.

ON THE STORES:

SA: During our honeymoon phase with Normal (Richard Szalwinski's company) we opened up this store in Toronto and everyone had money and our company was mushrooming. We would have meetings with Richard where he would make Shane drink an entire bottle of Jack Daniel's and then we'd sit there for two hours talking about business.

SS: I was going to invest my money in a Toronto store so I didn't blow it all on booze and drugs and whores, but when Richard found out, he insisted it be a *VICE* store.

SA: For about three years everything moved way too fucking fast.

ON THE DOWNFALL:

SA: At the height of *VICE* and Normal, when dot.com fervor was at its zenith, we went to a trade show and set up a booth. We had built-in digital screens with plush burgundy velour sofas and beds with a bar and it was pretty ridiculous. It made no sense and it was the epitome of excessive spending. It really represented what was wrong with that era and also our whole Normal experience. For me personally, that was my most unhappy time in the whole seven years—doing this dot.com thing that felt so wrong. But we did it because we were told we would make $30 million. I guess I was willing to sacrifice happiness for greed. It made us feel dirty.

SS: Yeah, but the peak of the insanity was when I went to Europe with the CEO on a mission to aggregate youth culture. We were literally buying up the phenomenon that was streetwear—stores, magazines, clothing companies, the works. We actually had letters of intent to buy companies that were fucking ten times our size. So we were just spending money like crazy over there in Europe with the CEO. Meanwhile, Suroosh would call me and say, "We can't get paper clips over here. They're repossessing everything." So I asked the CEO, "Hey, what's going on?" and he'd be like, "Oh, don't worry. It's just paperwork. It's just a bureaucracy. Let's have another bottle of champagne and buy another company." And the day I got back to the States, I got an e-mail from Richard saying, "It's over."

ON GOING TO NANTUCKET:

SS: So Gavin, Suroosh, and I got in a car and drove up to Nantucket to find Richard. We called him the day before and told him we just wanted to hang out.

His girlfriend was so happy that there would be other people there because they'd just been hiding out, kind of like in a bunker or something.

GM: He picked us up in a Mercedes-Benz convertible with no steering or brakes.

SS: I remember he got mad at me for bringing up business. He just didn't want to talk about it. Meanwhile, the company was fucking going down the toilet. What did he think, we were gonna go up there and play fucking croquet?

GM: We asked him how much time we had and he said he wasn't sure our desks would be there on Monday.

SS: So we were like, "Ho-leeeeeeeeeee shiiiiiiiittt!!!" and drove back screaming. We looked at the books and realized we were owed about $900,000 in unpaid invoices. It was a shocking realization of just how inefficient we had become. That was the big slap in the face that made us say, "Okay, let's just shut everything down, get over to Brooklyn, and try to make things profitable again."

GM: And we didn't want to kill any of the projects we already had going. We had to take this top-heavy business plan—the clothing line, stores, all that shit—and keep it going on no money. We had gone from stinking rich to flat broke in a matter of days.

ON REBUILDING:

SS: After two years of rebuilding hell everything came out okay. Of course, a few things were battered beyond repair. The clothing line was a bust, but the stores became profitable again. We signed a film deal and that led to VICE Films which is now four separate movies in production. We're doing a TV show for Showtime with David Cross (see p. 291). We've made some amazing partnerships in Japan and Europe as well as Australia that work to not only publish the mag in those areas but also to develop the other media channels that we're involved in. VICE Records made The Streets huge in America and are doing that with lots of other artists like The Stills and Chromeo. There's a DVD division starting up. A VICE pub in london... I'm sure by the time this book comes out there will be a whole slew of other things happening. It's a really good time for us now. The secret is to always make sure what you're doing turns a profit, even if it's ten cents. If people are getting paid and a good-quality product is coming out and it's not losing money, that's a success.

SA: One thing I need to get across about the magazine is how the whole thing has been completely organic from day one. We learned as we went along. There's a basic philosophy that's been there from the beginning that's still there today. I don't know what it is, but trust me, there is definitely a philosophy behind all this. As we progressed as editors and writers, we learned what made the magazine tick and then we would pursue that vein. Like miners.

We learned *VICE* had to be a well-balanced combination of smart and stupid content—stupid done in a smart way and smart done in a stupid way. We decided it had to be free but it had to turn a profit. It had to be brutally honest and punk rock and unlike anything that came before it. And most of all, it had to be about our favorite things: sex and drugs and rock and roll. And it is.

SEX

**From February 2002, Vol. 9, No. 1

THE VICE GUIDE
TO GUILTY PLEASURES

by Lesley Arfin and **VICE** *Staff*

A.R.E. Weapons

This band is so cool that it's basically uncool to like them, which is why they are commonly referred to as "Gay R.E. Weapons." Everyone loves to hate on them because admitting you like them is admitting you're a scenester, and no one ever wants to say that—at least not out loud. Secretly they are your favorite, you dance around to them naked, and you love their shows because you know all your friends will be there.

Honorable mentions: Airplane food, the Academy Awards, As Four bags, acting like you're still asleep when the car pulls in so your parents have to carry you to bed.

Beastie Boys

Let's face it, you cut school in tenth grade to stand in line for the Tibet benefit they

threw at The Academy. You had their stickers on your Trapper Keeper. You called dibs on Ad-Rock while your best friend planned to marry Mike D.

Honorable mentions: Being haunted by your love, Britney Spears, Broadway musicals, *Beverly Hills 90210*, big boobs.

Chat Rooms

When the Internet first happened, chat rooms were the place to be. The only place to be, actually. Like a total geek, you'd enter the "Sonic Youth" or "Rave till Dawn" room and make friends that you planned to meet at the mall food court or something. Then you saw them and discovered they were ugly. Thus, no one ever mentioned chat rooms again—but you still do it. Cyber-flirting is fun. You can have an affair without all the horribly complicated bullshit fucking entails.

Honorable mentions: Corndogs, cyber porn, cumming too soon.

Dope, a.k.a. heroin

The drug everyone loves to hate cuz it's only, like, the best drug in the world. People diss dope when they're just too pussy to try it. "I'd like it too much, man"—really logical. I'm not going to Bermuda for my holiday in case I like it too much and end up moving there.

Honorable mentions: Doing another bump of coke when you know you've had enough, Dinosaur Jr., dildos.

Entertainment Weekly

Hidden beneath all those copies of *Purple*, hipsters are secretly reading *EW*. No one wants to admit they're fascinated with celebrity, yet who can resist the clever "quote corner" or the behind-the-scenes *Lord of the Rings* exposé?

Honorable mentions: Eating your boogers, Eminem, early Rod Stewart.

Friends

The best show on TV. Sometimes you feel like they really are your only friends. It's corny to say you like it but for reals, the show is fucking funny and it makes you feel all warm and fuzzy inside.

Honorable mentions: Folk music, flavored condoms, the Food Channel, flags, fags.

Gwen Stefani

You say she's cheesy but when she's on TV you can't keep your eyes off her. How about that video she did with Eve when she's wearing the little sailor suit thing? Hellooooo. She also makes that pouty face that you kinda wanna slap and kiss at the same time. "Hey Baby" is a good jam too.

Honorable mentions: Gay porn, granny porn, God, Googleing ex-boyfriends.

Harry Potter

When you buy a Harry Potter book, you tell people it's a birthday present for your aunt. I know I do. I was fully anti-Potter until one rainy day when I picked up the first book and literally read the entire thing in one sitting. Now I go to HP conventions in a cape and have a cat named Dumbledore.

Honorable mentions: Hearing neighbors fuck, happy hardcore, Hot Topic, hacky sack, "hot lunch," having people with disabilities as friends just to make others uncomfortable.

Indigo Girls

Come on! "Closer to Fine" is the best sing-a-long song ever. True they are crunchy lesbian-coffeehouse-alterna-rock, and I know you hide the CD when people come over, but it's time we make these girls cool again. Call it "ironic" if you need a cover-up.

Honorable mentions: *InStyle* magazine, imagining what your funeral would be like if you killed yourself.

Journey

Depending on where irony is at when you're reading this, Journey is either a guilty pleasure or just a pleasure.

Honorable mentions: Jazz music, Jr. Miss section at Kmart, jerking off to pictures of shemales.

King

Known to his fans as simply "King," Stephen King is a guilty-pleasure god. I liked him so much more when I found out how many drugs he used to do. He doesn't even remember writing *Cujo*. Nice!

Honorable mentions: K-holes, keggers.

Loving the Ass

Putting it in the hiney is fun. It's rude and harsh and God hates it. It's a life-saver too. If you can't get it up just smell her crack and you'll get a boner no matter what. We call it "the poor man's Viagra." Smelling your own ass is another very private, guilty pleasure you shouldn't tell anyone about. Smelling your farts is one too.

Honorable mentions: Lexxus, love, Larry from *Three's Company*.

MTV awards shows

Do you really care who won for "Best Visual Effects"? No, you just want to see what J.Lo is wearing, or who's gonna do something "wacky" this year.

Honorable mentions: Magik, Morrissey, malt liquor, McDonald's.

Nigger

Being able to say the N-word is definitely a guilty pleasure. There's very few people allowed to add the "er" at the end but if you're alone, you can put your face into your pillow and say it as loud as you want.

Honorable mentions: Not pulling back your foreskin to pee, Nazis (as a sexual fantasy).

Oprah's Book Club

Despite what Jonathan Franzen says, OBC pretty much rules. You might feel gay admitting that this is where your book recommendations come from, but hey, at least she had housewives all over the country reading Toni Morrison.

Honorable mentions: The Olsen twins.

Popping zits

Okay, hear me out. To those of you who don't know, popping zits is totally disgusting and horrible and anyone who could possibly enjoy it is fucked up. However, to those who do know, holy shit. Popping zits is, like, just one step lower than an orgasm. I literally have to compromise with my boyfriend, popping zits on his back if I promise him a blowjob.

Honorable mentions: Pretending your boyfriend or girlfriend is someone else when you're doing it, pissing in the pool, pretending to work but just looking at porn.

Quake

Violence for pussies. One of my ex-boyfriends used to wear a headset so that only he would experience Quake's inner sanctum.
Honorable mentions: Quaaludes.

Reading people's diaries

The fact that diaries are soooo private and soooo secret only makes you want to read them more. Finding where someone keeps their diary is basically like discovering a small pile of rubies (don't tell a soul).
Honorable mentions: Romantic comedies, rape (as a sexual fantasy).

Singing in the mirror

Sometimes you stand there with your toothbrush in your mouth posing for the most irreverent *SPIN* cover of all time. Sometimes you're just playing air guitar during Hüsker Dü's "Diane" (your friends didn't know you could play guitar!— "How long have you had a band!?" they ask incredulously). Sometimes you're just smoking an invisible cigarette in your new video, hollerin', "Say nigga ride or die or ride or die." Another guilty mirror pleasure is looking at your reflection when you cry. Sometimes it freaks you out so much that you stop crying, but if you really push the martyr factor you can keep the tears going for as long as you want.
Honorable mentions: *Star Search*, skater boys, The Strokes, Speedos, *Saved by the Bell*, *SNL*, *Sex in the City*, Spandex, Skrewdriver, secretly fantasizing about killing your grandmother with a soil rake.

Tennis

Tennis is like one notch above ice-skating as far as gayness is concerned. So why is it that people (mostly guys) are super into it? It's probably those little white tennis skirts and all the grunting.
Honorable mentions: Teen movies, *Temptation Island*, Tupac, tuna fish, telling your mom it really hurts when it's not even bleeding.

USA

A year ago, a dude rollerskating in Central Park wearing American-flag shorts would get laughed out of town. Now American flags are cool. It's become a "rooting for the underdog" flag, like the Confederate flag.
Honorable mentions: Umlauts, unicorns.

V.C. Andrews

This one is for the ladies. V.C. Andrews was the ultimate preteen author because (unlike Judy Blume) her books were total trash. The main character was always finding out that her husband was really her father, and in *Flowers in the Attic* you

weren't supposed to get turned on when the brother and sister did it but you couldn't help it.
Honorable mentions: *Viz* comics, video games, *The Vagina Monologues*.

Whippits
Otherwise known as "hippie crack" or "dessert crack." Either way, it's the best high a thirteen-year-old can get.
Honorable mentions: Wanting glasses and/or braces, White Castle, whiteboy dreads, *Who Wants to Be a Millionaire*, whiteout (sniffing it), wanting to fuck your friend, waking up at 4 PM on Sunday, jerking off, and then going back to sleep.

Xanadu
Again, not very embarrassing to be accused of liking this film cuz it's awesome, but there was a time when you were supposed to be "over" *Xanadu*, maybe during high school, but you so weren't.
Honorable mentions: X is a hard one. Xylophones clearly aren't a guilty pleasure.

Yahoo pictures
The inevitable side effect of cyber-flirting is having to show a picture of yourself. At photos.yahoo.com you can assemble your best nudes (you can even Photoshop the zits off your ass), your best party pictures, and your favorite porn shots and pretend you just threw them up there without thinking.
Honorable mentions: Yellow-dog contracts, Yes, Yaz, Ya Kid K.

Zoo babies
The zoo is bad because gorillas get so bored they barf into their hands and eat it (remember that?), but how can you resist those babies? As Andrew W.K. says, "A baby crocodile!? How cool is that!?" The baby pandas are too much, man. Girls pinch your arm and go "eeeeeeh" till it hurts when they see them.
Honorable mentions: Long Island and New Jersey rock station Z100, zebra-striped guitars.

**From Vol. 6, No. 10, December 1999

THE VICE GUIDE TO EATING PUSSY

by Gavin McInnes

Men suck at eating pussy. Not because they don't like it but because it's really fucking hard. You have to learn it. Giving good head is the key to just about everything in life (including getting good head later on), so it's time we broke it down. Like this.

The secret to giving good head is to read the signs. You could be the best sexual mechanic in the world, but if you can't read the emotional road signs, you're going to end up wandering around in a desolate labial wasteland until, eventually, you drop from exhaustion, hot tears of confusion streaming down your face.

Think of eating the puss as your way of saying, "Although I am about to rock your insides with 3,000 pounds of explosives, here's a little intimate treat session to show you how I really feel." Instead of a screamed "OH MY GOD!!" like her baby has been trapped under a car (which is what fucking should do), cunnilingus elicits a more splendiferous "ooohmygodohmygodohmygod." Kind of like being massaged with exotic fruits by a muscular Arab oil sheik. A good *mange* (that's French for "eat," you brutes) is like a thousand years of Saturdays or a "Calgon, take me away" ad.

Break it down!

Be Down

Don't go down unless you're down. Unlike fellatio, cunnilingus can never be done as a favor. Doing it when you don't want to will only bring on the dry heaves. Eat like a pig at the trough and a lot of stupid mistakes get forgiven.

Don't Say Hi to Dry

A dry pussy is an unhappy pussy. If your fingers graze a dry bush, go back to the kissing and hugging for a while. Just make sure you actually dip your finger between the lips. Sometimes moisture gets trapped between the labia and a little fingerial coaxing is all that's needed to get the honey dripping.

Once you're sure the beaver is wet, give it a few light, teasing strokes with your finger. There's nothing worse than rushing into this, so make sure she's really begging for it before you get under the covers.

Extra tip: Be like Prince and bring up a wet finger that both of you can share like a 1950s milkshake with two straws.

Important: Don't play your trump card too soon by putting your fingers all the way inside. This can detract from the upcoming penetration and kill the tease factor. Try to remember that 78 percent of a woman's pleasure is about yearning. Poking it in too soon is sure to put out the fire.

Submarine Mission for You, Baby

Once she's lathered up, it's time to go down. Get your fingers out of there and don't touch anything for a bit. Let your lap do a bit of grinding and get some last-minute necking in like you're going away on vacation.

Though it's very tempting on your way down to pull the blankets over your head like the little mole-man that you are, this is a very bad idea. It gets super hot down there and whipping the duvet off your head and gasping for air ten seconds before she comes is pretty much going to kill the mood.

Start by kissing her boobs and stomach and slowly working your way down. Don't get carried away with those stupid tits, though. That's something you should have taken care of before the pants even came off. Right now it's all about the stomach and inner thighs. A little bit of gentle biting is good, but a sure winner is to start at the knee and move toward the muff in a slow, shark-like swoop. Nibble your way right up to the edge of her cunt, then skip across it and head for the other knee.

Repeat. Doing this a few times will get her really hot and save you a lot of pussy-eating time in the long run.

When you're just about ready to do the deed, start practicing on that weird crevice next to the lips. Don't spend too long there or she might start to think that you think that's the actual cunt. By now she should be dying for you to make your move. If you're doing it right, she'll be moaning and trying to force your head between her legs. Stretch this phase out until she looks like she's been holding her breath for three days.

Extra trick: Hover over the bush for about five seconds before the first lick. If you wait longer than that, she might think you're having second thoughts because it smells bad. Of course, we all know that motherfucker smells sweeter than a bowl of steamin' crawdaddies.

Important: Never bite the cunt in any way whatsoever. If this needs more explaining you should probably just stick to jerking off.

Parting the Red Seas

Isolate your playing field. Pubic hairs are to eating pussy what the Cavity Creeps are to dental hygiene. You're never going to be able to identify all the parts if she looks like that PiL album *That What Is Not*. One hot trick is to get her to spread her lips apart so her pussy is all set up for you like a great big buffet.

The Grand Entrance

Do your first lick super slow. It's good to groan and moan too. It shows you're digging it while sending microscopic audiophonic vibrations right up her snapper. Start just above the anus and take it all the way to the fur. Do about a dozen of these St. Bernard licks before moving on (take it really slow, like four seconds per lick).

This is a good time to figure out what kind of clit she has. If it's real sensitive, she'll probably convulse as you pass over it and that means you're in for an easy ride. If there's no reaction when you graze over her clit, she probably has one of those nerveless little pea clits and you're in for a thirty-minute session of tongue tendinitis.

Rock the Boat

Eating pussy is so gentle it can make you feel like a bit of a fag. If you're getting tired of being ballerina boy, take it out on the clit. Figure out how much abuse it can take without making her uncomfortable and show the little bastard who's boss.

After all, Mr. Elusive is precisely what makes muff diving so difficult. He's surrounded by labia and, even after you find him, all the pressure can pop him over to the side. All of a sudden you're giving the pee hole the seeing-to of its life. Think of the clit as a tumor in a pile of earlobes. When you push down on the area, he's the only one that can't be squished. Once one of your tongue troopers finds him, call for reinforcements. Use your lips to get hers out of the way and focus all your attention on getting him alone. Once you find him, give him a bit of a hard time for trying to hide from you. Frisk him and give him a couple of whacks across the head. More on this punk and his bad attitude later.

Extra-important tip: The best way to stimulate the clit is to run your entire tongue over it after you isolate it from the lips. The man in the boat should feel the texture of the entire tongue pushing down on his body and his boat.

Identifying the Clit Type

After the slow licks it's time to get this party started. There are essentially two types of clitori: ones that enjoy a serious going-over and ones that don't. The latter suck about as much as a one-inch penis and you should dump her right away.

Extra tip: Clits come in all shapes, sizes, and sensitivities, but that doesn't really tell you much. All of them want to be treated slow and soft at the beginning, but the only way to tell if you can go fast at the end is by reading her reactions. This is impossible to teach, but just do the best you can. All we can tell you is convulsing means take it easy and "Oh my God" means bring it on.

Clits That Need a Serious Going-over

These are the most fun because you can be creative. Pretend your tongue is the bad cop and the clit is the guy who killed your partner. Separate him from his buddies (the lips) and suck him right up into your mouth. Now he's on your turf. Keep him erect by creating an airtight vacuum chamber in your mouth. Slap the little bugger upside the head with one big tongue bonk. He's not going to tell you shit because he's a clit and he has no idea what you're talking about, but kick his ass anyway. After a few teasers and swirling circles, rat-a-tat-tat him senseless like a boxer whacking a speed bag. If she starts freaking out like it's too much, ease up on the interrogation and go back to the St. Bernard licks. The vacuum is a great way to bring her to orgasm, but it's a bit much sometimes, so mix things up with some circles around the clit and some tongue fucking.

As you're closing in for the kill, go back to the vacuum and give the suspect a relentless head smacking. Up-and-downies are usually the most effective, but your tongue will get less tired if you throw in a few side-to-sides. When you feel the inner thighs start to shake, this is it. Be repetitive. Do NOT be creative. You're almost home and this is not the time to start changing tactics.

Extra tip: To keep the rhythm going, try repeating a chant in your head that goes with the movement of your tongue like a Micmac Indian (hi-yi-yi-ya, hi-yi-yi-ya, hi-yi-yi-ya). Any inconsistent action may throw her off, killing the mood or at least setting you back a few minutes, which is bad for morale.

Important: Keep going several seconds after her orgasm. Remember, it isn't over until the hands come down from above and lay you off. If she's multiorgasmic, you'll have to keep going until you've done the whole routine another four or five times. If you're not sure what to do, just keep giving her shit until the magic hands come down.

Clits That Don't

Some clits don't want to be singled out and battered around. These are the boring ones that need to be treated with gentle care. Just do casual St. Bernard licks until she cums, pure and simple. If you're getting bored try going in some different directions for a while. A good way to keep it random is to spell out different letters of the alphabet with the tip of your tongue. You could be looking at half an hour here, pal, and that can be problematic. If you go for that long and she doesn't cum, you're going to be in a foul mood, so if it's too much work, move on. On the bright side, going for thirty minutes is something few people have the patience for, so sticking it out will lead to some payback when period week comes around.

The Conclusion

Once you're done (totally finished), she's going to want you out of there pronto because the whole area is sensitive. Instead of leaving, stick out your tongue and lay it down on her like a thick, soggy carpet. Make sure you don't move it or anything because that can actually hurt her. Just let it sit there like a dead manta ray for about thirty seconds. Then come up and wipe your face like a pirate. You now have a good minute to get the condom on and take her from the quarters of Prince Muhammad Muhammad Saddat to the cockpit of an F-15.

EXTRA BONUS TRACKS

Getting Fired

If two hands suddenly drop from the sky and start pulling you up, you've just been sacked. She'll tell you she never cums from that anyway, but the truth is you suck at sucking. Just give her a jolly good rogering and look at the whole thing as a learning experience. Later you can ask what the problem was so you can get it right next time. If you're really lame, you can ask for a regular play-by-play from the broadcast booth. A bit of the old "slow-down-you're-going-too-fast–yeah-there-like-that-oh-that's-perfect" can turn even the John Wayne Bobbitt of pussy eaters into a Doug Hart.

The Power Lunch

Nothing keeps you in the game and makes her cum harder than a mid-fuck munch. Pulling out in the middle of the race may leave her a bit confused, but it's a great way for all you premature ejaculators to simmer down a bit and it reminds her neglected clitoris that he's a somebody. If after a few seconds she still isn't into it, you can save face by pretending you just couldn't resist. Give it up and get back to the boff.

Extra tip: Unless you like the taste of your own latex-covered dink, keep your mid-fuck snacking to the upper clit region and stay away from the hole.

The Bottom

Fingers: If you are dealing with a particularly saucy vixen she may want something in her bum. A thumb gives you the best leeway, but keep in mind you are doing a raunchy thing and this should be saved until the end. Incidentally, if you're trying to introduce a bum finger as a good thing, try eking it in during orgasm. If it doesn't wreck everything you could have a Pavlovian response on your hands for the rest of the relationship.

Hole: We're not going to get into licking the actual hoop in this section because if you're into that, you're way too advanced for this seminar and should have graduated with a PhD in pussy years ago.

Cheeks: Bum-cheek rubbing is always good. There are over five hundred thousand nerve endings on those cheeks, so giving them a good squeeze or a slap while you lick the pussy will get you instant results.

The Double Whammy

Though some idiots (like us) say it takes away from when you actually put in the dink, simultaneous fingering is a great way to totally blow her mind. Think of it as the crack cocaine of cunnilingus.

Being Knackered

Tongue exhaustion is the number-one cause of abandoned *mange*-ing, but there are many ways to avoid it. Like we said, using your tongue as an inanimate object is a great way to give it a rest. Stick it out as far as it can go and tense it. Then bite into it with your teeth and move it around the cunt using your neck muscles. Another solution is simply to use your fingers on the clit while you give your mouth a rest.

**From Vol. 7, No. 3, April 2000

THE VICE GUIDE TO GIVING HEAD

by Christi Bradnox

After interviewing piles of sluts and exactly one homo, Christi Bradnox brings you this all-encompassing guide that examines every conceivable facet of hog smoking there is.

Giving good head is an art form that I didn't perfect until I was in my mid-twenties. Before that I was constantly bewildered, usually drunk, and often left wondering why I kept getting fired. I had the intent, concentration, and attitude, but I also had an overbite and too many wine coolers. It was high school. What did I know? Then I met Yves, the prototypical older boyfriend. Born and raised in Montreal, he was used to supremo suck from the "filles du roi" and this Ontario girl was going to rank. Since then I have, quote, "rocked," "ruled," "owned," and "paralyzed" some of the best cock this side of the Mississippi. My experience, combined with epic *VICE* research, is available for you now. Here we go!

Don't Spend All Your Chips

Before you even start this discussion you have to look at your budget. You have about twenty minutes of sex chips on any given night. If you spend fifteen chips sucking him off, he's only got five chips left for humping. We suggest saving BJs for mornings and afternoons and period week; you still want to get laid.

The Evil Dr. Tooth

Your teeth don't exist. They might as well be in a glass by the bed. Use the same principle applied when eating a super-cold Popsicle with a mouthful of freshly filled, sensitive molars. You have to make a cave with your mouth and use your tongue and upper and back palate to form a careful vacuum to keep him away from your teeth. Keep this exercise in mind throughout your entire blowjob. It's easy to slip, especially when you're drunk. One trick is to pull your lips over your teeth like they're those boxing mouth guards.

The Right Mindset

The key to cock is focus. You must be fixated for the duration of your down time. Remember the concentration required to kill an ice cream cone without getting any on your blouse? Why do you think they make sex oils in all of your favorite candy/ice cream flavors? It elicits a freaky Pavlovian trance of focus and completion. Think of good head as the Great Pacifier.

Believe

We're not talking about the half-ass, licking-until-hard-then-insertion action here. That's "lovemaking" in the whitest way. If you're not willing to trust him and commit yourself with 100 percent total devotion to his penis, don't bother. You have to worship it like you're Indiana Jones and you've finally made it to the Temple of Doom. (If worshipping his cock makes you feel vulnerable it's probably because he's a macho asshole and you are sucking off the wrong guy.) Remember, there's a psychosexual paradox going on here. You are giving him head and he is getting his cock sucked. You are both a slave to his dick and totally in control of it, like an actress who stars in and directs her own movies.

Heading South

Before you break off from his mouth and head downstairs, prepare the landing pad with your hand. Horse around until it's hard as stone. Assure him there's going to be some heavy mouth action but don't let it start until he's ready to crack.

Rub, rub, rub through the pants like it's a baby animal just about to be born.

Firmly tug at the belt buckle like it's your own. Try not to fumble too much with the belt, but it's OK to ask for his help. Don't get fired before you've even taken on the job. Communication is crucial, because guys have trouble refusing head no matter how bad they think you might be at it. Making sure he's happy with how it's going without seeming insecure is one of the hardest parts of giving head.

Extra tip: Don't fuck up with the zipper. If you hurt his penis here it's all over. Pull the zipper up and out, away from his penis, not straight down. Use two hands if you need to, like if he's huge or not wearing any underwear.

Key: If he seems to be steering this ride (keeping his hands hovering over or on your head), read the road signs and ask some soft questions. Are you going too fast, hard, soft, slow? You're not looking for a detailed map or long discussion. One or two uttered words—a deep moaning "yes" or "oooohmmmokay" or "ohhhh, yeahyeahyeah"—will do fine.

Birthing

Slide your hand into the underwear. The baby animal is a little afraid of being born and has to get to know your hand so it can feel safe and come out. Hover over his groin here for five seconds (not too long or you will seem like a spectre and that will make him feel self-conscious).

Extra tip: If he starts mashing your head down, don't smack his hand away. Gently grab his wrist and place it down by his side again. Hold it there for a second as if to say, "Relax, guy. I've got it." Incidentally, where did you meet this guy?

Getting the Balls Rolling

Now, somebody hasn't received much attention up until now. Here's where our face and hands have a bit of prep work to do. Cup and caress his balls in the hand you don't use for writing. They can take a bit of abuse, but only with your heavy wet tongue. Find his balls first with your mouth by burying your face in the space between his thighs and crotch and take one of them in your mouth and wet and spit it up. Don't be afraid to make things wet as hell.

You'll need your dexterous hand to complete the lock and seal around the shaft. It's wet from your spit, too, and remember, you don't have any teeth. This is a game you play with yourself: No teeth, I have no teeth, I only have gums and lips and tongue. No teeth. At the base, your mouth finally meets your hand and your tongue slicks up the shaft with more hot spit. Wet hand goes down around the shaft with forefinger and thumb acting as the extension of mouth. Moan on it, because everybody's just met. Here's the freeze-frame: mouth puffed out, lips like an anus, down around the top few inches, tongue pressing the cock into an oral groove, good hand around the shaft and bad hand rotating around the balls with slightly firm yet gentle rubs. Teeth not invited to the party.

Now that you've made the lock, never take your hand and mouth off or away from his cock. You're not gobbing on it, and you're barely hitting a rhythm. You are wetting down the penis with spitty, rhythmic foreplay to achieve the correct balance of slickness and traction. No baby kisses here; you're all mouth and tongue and hand. The whole area should begin to feel like a wet, well-greased-down, slow-moving internal combustion engine that is just gearing up.

Extra tip: At some point while your mouth is first introduced to his cock, lock eyes with him. Remember, he's filming this with his brain and may use it as masturbation fodder for years to come. You can even jerk him off for a bit. It's a nice break for everyone and the variety keeps things interesting.

Rhythm and Motion

He will instinctively begin to rock slightly. Never stop moving along with him, but be a bit off so you're undulating over his weenie slightly offbeat. It's important at this point to make sure you avoid getting skull-fucked. Control the tempo yourself.

Your hand should form a tube like a skirt around your mouth, with your thumb and forefinger like a belt that meets your lips. Keep it well lubricated and don't stay static. Your other fingers can fan and fold and tickle and tug as your mouth and tongue circle and bob up and down the top part. Most of the feeling is in the head of the penis, so don't waste too much time on the shaft. You're looking for a tempo akin to "Pop Goes the Weasel" played at half speed. Never lose the rhythm or the concentration of your mouth up and down around the tip of the penis.

By now you're gripping the shaft gently and firmly with both good and bad hands in a tizzy of fingers and spit. Fan down and grip up, grip up and fan down. Mouth stays on over the top, deep then shallow, all the way out, all the way down. Hands have to help out the mouth. Mouth can't do all the work.

Don't make the goal here an orgasm. Have no expectations. This is the slick middle of giving head that gets you familiar with his rhythm and lets your mouth be the most talented pussy since your own.

Extra tip: Again, it helps to lock eyes. It reminds you of what you're doing and who you're doing it to. It's an intense moment and it breaks a trance if you've found yourself in one. A guy can tell if you're sucking to get it over with instead of getting him off, and it hurts their feelings. A little.

The Final Countdown

Something happens between giving the blowjob and the point of no return. His balls get hard and begin to disappear. Cute. You will know this because bad hand is on the job. He stiffens and arches his body toward your mouth and his moaning may get a bit more whimpery and ardent. Now everything gets a lot harder but a lot easier at the same time. Good hand is pumping a bit more penis into the mouth.

Both work together, making the tempo a bit stormier but still controlled. Moaning should be almost frantic here. A vacuum begins to form between the hand and mouth, working up and down as you slightly suck in your cheeks.

There's an important distinction between sucking the shit out of it and simply making a vacuum seal out of your mouth. Vacuum is better. Sucking hard can make him convulse. He's so hard now that it might be difficult to take it all in, but try relaxing your throat muscles. Make a deep "ahhh" sound. Move your mouth and hand up and down with more ardor and purpose. Vary your mouth movements, but don't lose the gentle vacuum. Use good hand to control the pumping, and keep your mouth firmly wrapped and sealed in spit around the wet cock.

The Finish Line
This is it. Increase the speed of your mouth and good hand. Let him feel you pulling his orgasm right out of him. Guys, it's OK to tell her you're about to blow, but don't be a rock star. Say it nice and soothing like you're going to cry and you don't know why. (Who's the subordinate little puppy now?) Your hands are slickly wrapped, and your mouth is sucking his cock faster but with subtle undertones of a gentle coaxing. Start to make swallowing motions, press your tongue on the shaft and slightly relax your lips. Moan hard and low in anticipation of the best orgasm you've ever created.
Extra tip: If it's so good you start losing him in some surreal never-ending ending, stop and let him have a wank while you lick his balls. That's always a surefire way to get things back on track.

The Blowing of the Load
Spitting it out means like. Swallowing means love. And gargling with cum makes you look like a crazy slut that probably has STDs. Most guys don't care about where it goes eventually, but there are some ways to keep it sexy and fun. If he's into it, he may want to cum on your face. It's just cum and you trust him. It has to go somewhere and it's good for your skin. Wherever it goes, wipe it up soon. No one can relax and fall asleep when paste is hardening around them.
Extra tip: Push on his t'aint while he's cumming.

Swallowing
Swallowing is important. It shows a kind of love and acceptance that has big pay-offs during pussy-eating time, morning sex, and menstruation. The easiest way is to be upright and kneeling between his legs because gravity cuts down on the gag factor and if it's far enough in the back of your mouth, it slides down like a slutty oyster. Swear to God.
Important: You are not going to get AIDS from swallowing. It's safest to make sure you don't brush your teeth right before or right after, but relax. We say it's fine.

The Aftermath

Once he's spent, he's pretty exhausted and probably in another land. You're not going to get him back. Keep a warm hand on top of it for a bit, like a shock blanket used by paramedics. Just lie there while he mumbles "holy shit" to himself for a few hours while you fall asleep. It's your lullaby.

EXTRA BONUS TRACKS

Booze

Sucking sucks if he's soused. Nobody wants to be singing cock karaoke for 45 minutes so forget about it. Mount it and ride that sucker for all it's worth. Oh yeah, and don't you have more than three beers yourself. It kills your concentration.

The Bone Moan

Moaning or humming creates a subtle vibration that both shakes his dink and keeps you in the vibe. That makes a superhero out of you, girl. Half woman-half machine. Oarrrrr mmmmmmmmmooommm mmm!

Bumming Him Out

This is dangerous, but gently slide bad hand below and under towards his anus. If your boy doesn't flinch, you may want to rim him with a wet finger. Guys act like they don't like anything in their bums but most are dirty little bitches that need a good seeing to. Make sure to time it right. As his balls hide away, his back arches up and he's just about to blow, slide it in and gently wriggle it. Be prepared to stop an avalanche of cum with your face.

The Danger Scrape

Here's a shocker. Break the rhythm off mid-tempo, stop and gently take the whole thing in your mouth. Softly scrape your teeth up along the shaft. This move should be reserved for the kind of guys who wear leather pants and don't call their moms.

Foreskins

Circumsized guys are easier to suck off, but they're less sensitive. Uncircumcised guys are better because you can do all kinds of tricks with the foreskin. Roll it up over the head and put it in your mouth like a sausage roll. The tricky part is the hand job. If you grip it too high up the shaft, your downstroke is going to rip it. Gripping it too low means your upstroke will feel redundant. Get him to show you exactly where to grab. A steady hold about a quarter inch below the head usually does the trick. Use your writing hand to avoid mistakes.

**From Vol. 8, No. 7, September 2001

THE VICE GUIDE TO FEMALE EJACULATION

by Amy Kellner

Until recently, female squirting has mostly been considered a somewhat dubious fetish, even comprising its own subgenre of straight porn with such unappealing titles as *Gushing Orgasms* and (I'm not even kidding) *Stinky Stained Perverse Squirting Party*. If you watch these videos you'd probably think it's all a big sham, like these chicks either just stuck a hose up there and are squirting out water, or perhaps they're simply peeing. It's not a sham. It's fun, and you know more about it than you think.

Chances are if you've ever felt like you were gonna pee during sex, what you were really feeling were the beginnings of an ejaculation, which is precisely why squirting for the first time can be so alarming. You're all like, "Holy shit, did I just pee myself? Am I some kind of big perv?" Well yeah, you are a perv, but not because you're a golden showers queen. You're a perv because you're a squirter.

Congratulations! You will now be able to impress family and friends with your new-found ability to shoot like a dude. It's even better than boring old male ejaculation, because if you stick your nose in the stuff, you'll notice that it is pretty much odor-less and watery-clear. I don't know where it got this "don't be grossed out" reputa-tion. A lot of the material on the subject, for example, suggests placing absorbent bed pads or wee-wee pads (for house-training puppies) underneath you to soak up the splooge. That sounds like one whopping mood-killer to me. The stuff is so non-staining that you can basically marinate your entire mattress in it and no one will be the wiser.

So what exactly is this substance? Basically it's like semen, minus the sperm. It's not entirely clear what it's made of (doctors are too busy inventing Viagra and curing prostate cancer, instead of just cutting the damn things off like infected breasts), but I hear there's some protein and glucose in it. It's an ejaculate fluid created by ducts in the paraurethral gland located within the urethral sponge, otherwise known as the G-spot. The G-spot is neither a myth nor a mysterious, magical locale that only men wearing velour sweatsuits and gold chains can find. It's kind of like the equivalent of the prostate gland, and it's easy to locate. If you stick your finger in your vagina and make a "come here" gesture, you'll notice a spongy, bumpy area on the upper wall an inch or two in from the opening. That's it. If you or your partner rub that area in a motion like you're gently trying to squeeze out the fluid (most often combined with your regular clitoral stimulation), you can totally female ejaculate. You just have to relax and if it feels like you're gonna pee, don't hold it in. Use your muscles to push it out. You'll probably feel a watery rush or release of some kind that's different from a solely clitoral orgasm. It's different for everyone, but if you pay attention, you'll soon learn to recognize the signs for yourself.

Oh yeah, it also helps to tone your PC (or Kegel) muscles. You see, it turns out that the clitoris is actually much larger than the little nub that we all know and love. The erectile tissue of the clit extends all around the urethra, and by exercising your PC muscles (the muscles that cut off the flow of urine), you can learn to control your squirting. Even if your PC muscles have been hitherto ignored, you can still female ejaculate, except you probably won't shoot very far. It'll be more like a trickling or a subtle seepage, which is fine too. Did you ever notice that occasionally after some hard fucking there'll be a wet spot under you? That ain't butt sweat. You've probably female ejaculated a little bit and didn't even know it.

Don't be discouraged by all this talk of fountain-like spurts. It's mostly the seasoned pros who are the ones you read about having squirting contests to see who can shoot the farthest or the highest (read lezzie sexpert Tristan Taormino's account of such an event in *Pucker Up*). The pros suggest doing 100 flexes daily, which sounds like a lot, but since it's invisible to others, you can do them anywhere—while driving, waiting in line at the grocery store, talking to your mom on the phone, etc. Personally though, I can't do more than twenty without starting to get all horny.

Does this all sound confusing? It might help to rent this instructional video called *How to Female Ejaculate*. Your local woman-run sex shop should have a copy of this definitive female ejaculation primer. Plus, the video is hilarious. It's narrated by this crazy lady named Fanny Fatale, who is the publisher of lezzie sex rag *On Our Backs* and a director for Fatale Videos, makers of quality lezzie porn. She wears aviator glasses and a purple blazer as she soothingly intones advice like, "Dancing exercises the PC muscles, especially African, striptease, and belly dancing!" She talks like a spaced-out sex-ed teacher who's really happy with her job, and we get to see a close-up of her vagina, spread open with a speculum, as she calmly points out the G-spot for us and demonstrates flexing it. I should emphasize that this video is hardly erotic, unless your idea of erotic is four older women who look like your mom lying around on towels discussing the sociopolitical aspects of squirting while a scary-looking, skinny S&M lady sticks out her tongue all pointy and shoots all the way across the room. (My favorite part is when this one woman describes the taste of female ejaculate as a mixture of buttery popcorn and seaweed. The other women are all like, "Uh, not really.")

With just a bit of research and effort, you will be giving out pearl necklaces like a rich Italian. Be a pioneer! Grab some videos. Get your fingers in there and embrace the exciting future of sex.

**From Vol. 8, No. 2, March 2001

THE VICE GUIDE
TO ANAL SEX

by Gavin McInnes

Back in university, while having sex with my thirty-two-year-old militant feminist girlfriend, a phrase slipped out of my mouth. We were in that primal mode on autopilot when weird sounds come out like "goood" and "do it, fucker." This time, however, out of nowhere I go, "I love hurting you." Instead of getting angry or disturbed, her eyes lit up and she said, "I love it when you hurt me."

That was the first time I totally understood what it's all about. Love hurts and sex is hostile. As Robert J. Stoller writes in *Sexual Excitement*: "The absence of hostility leads to sexual indifference and boredom. Humans are not a very loving species, especially when they make love." In a time when everything is about egalitarianism and feeling good, we are forgetting the merits of pain. What about the joy of dirty smells and helplessness? The joy of taking over someone's body like a snake with a frog in its mouth? I love that shit.

So without further ado, here is the *VICE* guide to the cruelest of lovemaking. The only sexual taboo left: getting reamed up the cake.

Fags Go Home

Before we get started, we have to zero in on who we are talking about. This article is not for fags. Telling fags how to have anal sex is like telling Puerto Ricans how to have babies. Fags are so over it they could wake up in a sea of blood and poo with a hangover and say, "That didn't work out so well. Let's go get some amyl nitrate and try it again." They are the masters of the sport and have all kinds of great tips on how to use crack and other drugs but, I don't know, that's just not the hetero way.

This instructional guide is for heterosexual couples who want to put the boy's dink in the girl's bum. See "Turning Him Over" at the end of this piece on how to nail hetero guys, which is so easy it only deserves a few words.

Girls Not Down with the Brown

Not all ladies are potential sodomites. Maybe she was raped in the bum at fourteen. Maybe she grew up with a lot of homophobic brothers and believes that "anuses are for fags." Or maybe she's just not built for it—you know, the same way middle-aged men can't do gymnastics and thirteen-year-old girls are notoriously bad lieutenants.

The "no way in hell" girls have two distinct characteristics. One, they hate bands with female singers and two, they shake their heads when you ask them if they liked the first try and then go, "It felt like I had to go poo." If your girl is like this, stop reading now and try to get over it.

Girls Down with the Brown

There are several types of ladies that are perfect for sodomy. First-generation immigrants are great because, after being bombarded with all kinds of new experiences (baseball, MTV, spaceship cars), they are ready to try anything. Virgins are good too. They just figured out how to work their vagina, so adding another one next to it isn't so absurd. It's like someone coming over with an extra cup when you're doing the dishes. You're just like, "Oh that too? Oh, okay, let's get it soaped up." The ultimate catch as far as willingness goes would have to be Catholic schoolgirls. Thanks to oppressive fathers insisting their hymen stays intact, every other orifice gets a rigorous workout before graduation. In fact, nine times out of ten it's the Catholic schoolgirl that introduces it to the boy. "You don't need a condom," she'll say. "We can bungi" (that's their special word for it), and then that spoiled little boy is ruined forever.

Odds are you're in a relationship with someone in between. She's not totally against or totally into it. If so, you should be reading this, which you are, so, good.

Good Pain vs. Bad Pain

Oh wait, there's more shit we have to clear up. Before you start hurting someone, let's make it clear what kind of pain we are talking about. There is good pain and bad pain. Good pain is dull and all-consuming and bad pain is sharp and very localized. If you've ever put a girl's legs behind her head and had your boner ram her cervix during sex that's what bad pain is like. You can tell because she gets up fast like your dink's an electric eel and it makes her so mad the lay is usually over. A well-lubed, slow, and careful intrusion is a good pain, like being sat on by a fat person you love. The bad pain of an unlubed and rushed anal intrusion cuts her ass, pisses her off, and kills the whole thing forever.

Getting in the Door

She won't like anal sex until her seventeenth time. It's an acquired taste. But you have to get her to want to go through that good pain, seventeen times. To get that response, you must employ the "Pavlov's dog" technique. When you're eating her out, occasionally touch around the asshole. Give it small and swirling "hellos," as if you were trying to pet a newborn squirrel without scaring it too much. It's best to try this when she's totally horned up out of her mind and plastered. If you take it slow and easy and smart you're looking at a total time of five months. Don't be afraid to lick it sometimes. Salad tossing is not gross with women because they shit roses. Put your finger in there and smell your finger. See? Roses.

After you've got through the taboo front gate you can start being more and more friendly with the baby squirrel.

Emergency Rescue

If things are going too slow you should skip to "Turning Him Over" and have her try it on you. Once you've gone through it her curiosity will be awoken. She'll be like, "Didn't it feel like you had to go poo?" and you can be like, "No, I loved it." Then she'll be like, "Really?" Nice save.

The Brown Cave

After massaging becomes totally commonplace you can occasionally inject a well-lubed pinkie in there when she's cumming. This is called the Trojan Pinkie Pavlov Horse, or "TPPH" for short (pronounced by making a fart sound with your mouth).

You are going to notice some weird things in there. First of all there's a lot more room than you expected. Once you get past the bouncers, it's a roomy club. That's why butt plugs are cinched where the anus goes but are all big where the rectum is. You may also notice a very prominent pulsating vein. I have no idea what the fuck that is. It's a vein. Probably a good way to check someone's pulse if they have fat wrists because the thing is like, "bong, bong, bong, bong." Don't worry about the vein.

The third thing you may or may not notice is a little soft finger poking back at you like a squishy little Turkish E.T. That is a piece of poo. Don't tell her you felt that or she'll be all grossed out. Just treat it like a pussy fart and pretend it never happened. Incidentally, the poo finger means you are going to get some shit on your cock. You're probably wearing a condom anyway but if you aren't, get to the bathroom the second you are done. DO NOT PASS OUT! Waking up hungover with a shit-encrusted foreskin is a dangerous way to hit the showers. The hot water reactivates the stench and your already delicate stomach will kick food out of your body like a shovel throwing dirt.

The Second Dink

Once she's kind of into finger cameos, start incorporating the lubed finger during fucking. Then you can start going from pinkies to index to a thumb. Then maybe even two fingers. You are at the point now where the anus has become a baby vagina.

Now she actually looks forward to her daily anal penetration. Don't underestimate how far you've come. This is as exciting as the first time you got a girl's pants off and were able to finger her properly. If things keep going this well she may eventually learn to cum from it. Just kidding—only God gets that.

Toytown

Before moving on to Dinktown you can put butt plugs and other fun toys into the equation. Your basic dildo is a good way to stretch out a rookie ringpiece, because it has no ridges or things to trigger a cut.

Prom Night

Don't get too excited, you fuckers. You're not there yet. Lube the shit out of her ass and your dink, and place your dink's face right at the anus. Then go, "It's going to go in your ass." Make doubly sure it's lined up and say, "Push back." Unless you're a fourteen-year-old on Viagra, things may get a bit bendy here. Hold your dick solid by grabbing it just behind the head the way you would a deadly snake.

It's important that she relaxes and doesn't freak out, or it's going to hurt and then you're back to step one again. One good way to keep it sexual and relaxed is to be rubbing her pussy as she pushes back on it and to even throw in some gentle verbal coaxing.

If she's not into it or it hurts too much, give up and try again in three days. Don't worry, it's not over. If you're really eager to try again you can put it back there just as you cum (assuming you take the condom off like I know you do, you dirty bastard) and all the lube of blowing your load will sloop it in. Not exactly a reaming but it's a good first try.

You're In

Once you get it all the way in and there's no cuts or damage, start going at it at a reasonable pace right away. If you're too slow it's going to hurt her more so get that bad part out of the way ASAP.

The Word

After the "no cutting it" rule the second heaviest piece of information about anal sex is the magical and totally unique sound she makes that tells you you've made it. It's a word that means you have stuck your flagpole at the top of Anal Mountain and, more importantly, will be invited back again.

The word is a magical four-letter word that sounds like "ungh" but is not to be confused with "uh" or "unh." "Ungh" is a deep-throated "uuunnngh" that sounds like the person saying it is not the person saying it. Like a demonic possession made her roll her eyes back into her head and replaced her voice with Barry White getting kicked in the stomach. Seriously, it's almost scary. It's so *Exorcist* guttural you expect her head to rotate 360° and projectile vomit to blast into your face followed by the words "mea culpa lorem ipsum nosferatu."

Surviving the Ungh

Don't get too proud of yourself, partner. You may have made it, but now it's time to run with the ball like Satan would want you to. Keep rubbing that pussy and up the ante with a bit of dirty talk. Getting her to say "You are fucking me in my ass" is really good for some reason and of course "I love your cock in my ass" is great too.

Postcoital

After you cum, take the condom off and throw it far away in case there's poo on it. If you weren't wearing a condom then go "pee" and when you're in the bathroom, wash it off.

Now that it's over let's have a bit of affection. While your red knob throbs down to its original size and jiz seeps out of her ass show her that Dr. Jekyll is back and he still has a huge crunch on her. Try spooning her and singing the following: "Snuggle frog, snuggle frog, I love you. I got a snuggle frog, how about you?"

Now sleep.

TURNING HIM OVER: HOW TO GET REVENGE

Max Headroom & Christi Bradnox

Guess who's a dirty little bitch. Guess who's going to get it like a dirty little whore. He is. That's who. He's going to get it for a change. Here's what you do girls.

No Nicks

I know this is starting to sound repetitive but the "no nicking" thing applies to women, especially. If you have any kind of fingernails put a condom over your poo finger. I mean it.

Bottoms

Guys who wear overalls, like R&B, and plea feminist causes at the MTV Music Awards just because their girlfriend was in a bad mood, are pretty simple to lay in the ass. Just reread the main article and change every "she" to a "he." Replace the "rubbing the clit" part with a reach-around while you're at it.

Tops

Like most hetero men, even cool hetero men, he probably has a weird thing about ass sex being too "faggy" (I'm writing that on the board). The best time to kill this stereotype is when he's most vulnerable: during the blowjob. The next time you're down there give his ass the grazing we mentioned during the baby squirrel metaphor. What's he going to do -move? He can't even talk.

If you've got Wet Wipes around you could even do a little salad tossing but if you're down with that you probably don't need to be reading this. After a while you can get it to the point where a finger in his rear during a blowjob is "de rigeur." Men's asses are nine times more disgusting than women's, though, so take Margaret Cho's advice and don't let that finger touch your steering wheel on the drive home. Keep it up like you're saying "hey" to a fellow driver.

But Wait There's More

Once you've gotten even a finger in there, the sky's the limit. Now you can move up to butt plugs, strap-on butt plugs and even strap-on real dongs (good luck). We highly recommend you start with the jelly butt plugs because they have a little more play and will hurt less. It's funnest to sodomize girls while they're on all fours. If you're reaming a man with a strap-on, butt plug however it's actually better to have him on his back with his legs up. Now he can wank while you do your thing and it's more freaky.

Oh yeah, don't let him look at you with a strap-on. That is going to freak the shit out of him and it may blow everything. Lights out and heads averted above the waist is best.

The Aftermath

There is a weird thing that happens to men after the strap-on thing. They behave differently the next day. They seem to come to a kind of realization that being a bottom isn't as subservient as it sounds. They finally understand that you have to be kind of brave to let someone put a bit of their body inside yours. The next day you're going to hear him say things like, "yeah, that's a good idea. I should put that picture there." That's because, instead of hearing "meow meow meow, blah, blah blah meow" everytime you talk he's hearing "hey that's the guy that served as Scientific Director of the DOD Navigation Satellite Program Executive Director of the Four Service Group which initiated the Navstar GPS program in the early 70s."

The Big Guns

Unlike fucking women's bums, where you have to keep going until you get to the "ungh" stage, sodomizing heterosexual men is far less ambitious. You can stop at each level, indefinitely, and not go any further. Many women are satisfied simply putting a finger in his bum during blowjobs. Some stop at the odd butt plug in there. Don't feel bad if you stop at an early stage.

You're not going to get an "ungh" out of him from the butt plug (even though, for a guy it feels like you just put an Encyclopedia in there). The only way you are going to get the "ungh" out of a him is to get something penis sized in there.

For information on that you are going to have to consult the gays because you have now gone into some Jedi knight shit that is way over our heads.

**From Vol. 5, No. 5, June 1998

There it is again!

The original article featured Aliza's X-Ray.

LOST IN URANUS

After Hearing a Hundred Nurses Tell Us Horror Stories from the Emergency Ward, We Tracked Down One of the Patients and Got Her Side

by Suroosh Y. Alvi

Hospital emergency rooms attract the bizarre and grotesque on a daily basis. Bloody, maimed folk sit in waiting rooms while tired doctors run to and fro, and jaded receptionists file their nails. Any doctor will relay standard tales of gangsters getting shot in the ass and gory car accident victims. But here at VICE, it's the emergency-room situations of a sexual nature that we find truly entertaining; those urban myths of bananas in bums and hockey pucks in pussies and surgical extractions performed by teams of highly trained professionals. That's why we forced a good friend of ours, who we'll call "Aliza," to tell us about the clear latex dildo called Luther that got lost deep inside her ass.

VICE: So, how big was Luther?
Aliza: I would say, uhh, eight inches.

Were you trying to spice up your sex lives and decided to venture into dildo terrain?
I would say this sort of thing was common play with us. This is what happened: We were playing around and suddenly, in the heat of the moment, my boyfriend tells me, "Luther's gone." I didn't quite understand what he meant, so I looked under the bed and looked under the mattress. He was just standing there looking very pale.

Did he know where it disappeared to?
Yeah, but he couldn't say it. He was just kind of in shock and then he said, "No, Luther's inside of you." This is when I broke into a panic. We tried to figure out the best way to get Luther out of me. We called the sex shop where he was purchased and asked the transvestite working there, who had never encountered anything like that ever before and who suggested eating ice to get rid of it.

Eating ice?
That's exactly what he said. He said, "I don't know what you should do. Why don't you try eating ice or something?" Anyway, my boyfriend suggested eating a lot of fibrous goods, such as crackers and bread, to try to make myself take a shit so we could get him out that way.

But when you were walking around, didn't things feel kind of awkward having an eight-inch dildo in your ass?
No.

You're telling me it felt perfectly normal?
Yes.

Did you try to force the issue on the toilet?
I went and sat on the toilet, and he brought me a bunch of crackers and bread. (laughs) I tried that. And then suddenly I had a flash of getting constipated because I ate all that stuff. Then I would definitely not be able to get Luther out. So I stopped that and phoned a friend who's sexually adventurous and asked her if she'd ever run into anything like this before. She just laughed at me.
I tried to use a flashlight to see where it was and that didn't work either. Then we phoned the hospital, and my boyfriend pretended it was his boyfriend who had the problem because I was so self-conscious about being a female with this thing up my butt. The hospital told the boyfriend to get down there immediately. If the item came in contact with my bladder, which is very sensitive, I could have ended up with a colostomy bag . . . for life.

Why?
Because your bladder is in the same region and is easily punctured. It was an emergency situation, and we had to get to the hospital right away. We headed out of the house and stopped off at my friend's bar first to have a few drinks because I couldn't handle this sober any longer.

How were you feeling at this point?
It was a combination of panic-stricken fear and just laughing at myself. Laughing to the point of crying and then crying out of fear.

What were you afraid of, a colostomy bag for life?
That's exactly what I was afraid of. So over at the bar, I had a few drinks. I was talking to the bartender and then my boyfriend leaned over and whispered to me, "Just imagine if he knew that you have a dildo in your ass right now." I dropped my drink. I couldn't stay any longer. We hopped in a cab and went straight to the emergency ward. We got there and the woman at the reception desk asked me what I was there for, and I couldn't bring myself to say it.

So what did you say?
I said, "I'm having a problem with the lower region of my body." (laughs) She asked me to be more specific, so I said, "I have an item lodged in my anal cavity." (laughs) My boyfriend is laughing on the floor at this point. The receptionist was very calm and said to me, "Is it a vibrator?" And I said, "Yes, it is," just to get out of the reception area. Then they put me in this room and three doctors came in and one of them put his finger up there, trying to feel for it.

He did an anal probe?
Yeah, but he couldn't locate it.

They were all male doctors?
Yeah, but very nice guys. It was as bad as it could have been. I kept saying to them, "Is this the first time you've had a woman up here with this problem?" And of course it was. They told me that about a year prior a guy came in who had a glass vase up his butt and it shattered and they had to take out all the little pieces.

You must have been trippin' by now.
I was just freaking out but I couldn't feel anything. Then the doctors said that the reason you can't feel anything is because the entrance to your anus is just like a small passageway and it takes a lot of work to get through that, but once you're through it's just floating around.

So Luther was home free?

Yeah. This nurse brought in a big silver box full of lights and stuff, and the doctor made equipment out of it on the spot. He put together something to try and grab Luther. He was turning to the other doctors and saying, "This should fit in with this and we'll put a light on the end that'll help us out and blah, blah, blah." It was obvious they rarely ran into this sort of thing.

Were they sure there was something there? Could they feel it?

The doctor could feel something, just the very bottom of it. The reason the anal probe was so problematic was that they couldn't get a good grip on the latex. They put me in for an X-ray, and I was panicking because they said if they couldn't get it out, I'd be in surgery in the morning. At about 2 AM, I'm talking to the X-ray guys and they're saying, "Look at her face. You'd never think she'd be into this kind of thing." (laughs)

Were they messing with you a bit, like you were depraved or something?

No, not at all. They were being really supportive and saying, "Look, don't worry. We had to deal with this guy a year ago who had this shattered vase in his ass. Don't freak out." They did the X-ray and nothing showed up at all. I came storming out of the room and grabbed my boyfriend—who was patiently sitting outside—and took him inside all mad and said, "Look at this, look at the X-ray! There's nothing there! It's not there!" He looked at it and then he says, "No, no, it's definitely there." He swears up and down it's there. The X-ray guys say to him, "But if it was there, the batteries would have shown up in the X-ray." And then we both clue in and say, "But there are no batteries because it was a dildo, not a vibrator," which I had reported at the reception.

So they were searching for a vibrator?

Yeah, they asked me what color it was, and I said clear, which is why it didn't show up. So then they pumped this white liquid up my ass—it's called a barium enema. They got an outline of it in the next X-ray. Then I go back to the same three doctors who are trying to grab at it. This is like half an hour and I'm getting so uncomfortable. So they said, "We're sorry, but it's not going to come out this way. You'll have to go in for surgery in the morning." They hooked me up to an IV, the boyfriend goes home, and I spend the night in the hospital.

This must have all been rather embarrassing, no?

Yeah, embarrassed in front of the nurses, humiliated in front of the doctors. And then, to top it off, I'm lying there and the nurse comes in to change my IV bag. I'm sort of half asleep at that point, and she comes in and says, "Hi, my name's Claire. I'm your nurse for the next hour." I recognized her voice and name and opened up my eyes. She's very distinct-looking, with red hair, and sure enough it's Claire, my tennis instructor from about ten years ago.

Your tennis coach? That's totally insane! Didn't she recognize you or your name on the chart?
My name on the chart was my full name and she knew me from my middle name. I just pretended to be asleep, kind of pulled the blanket over my face, and changed my voice, praying to God she didn't figure out who I was. Finally, in the morning, a team of seven male doctors all came in to look at me and said, "We're going to prep you for surgery. We're just checking to see how you're doing, and we'll be back in thirty minutes." Once they left I had to go to the bathroom to pee and Luther just slipped out! I don't know how it happened.

You didn't even try and poo?
No, it just happened. I ran back to my bed, phoned my boyfriend, and said, "Luther's out! I can come home now. How do I get this IV thing off?" I called the nurse and said, "The problem I'm here for is no longer a problem. I can go home now." So the chief nurse figured I was lying and sent a young nurse down to check on me. She came in and tried to calm me down and said they'd give me something to relax my muscles and it wouldn't be major surgery. All this time I'm just looking at her in disgust, and then I just said, "It's not about that. Just look in the garbage. It's there." She didn't know what to do. She was all embarrassed and went back to the chief nurse, who sent her back again and said she had to fetch Luther and bring it back to her. So she comes back and is fishing through the garbage can and paper towels . . .

Fishing through the garbage for a dildo that's been in your ass for the last eight hours!
(laughs) I know! I just looked in the bathroom as I was getting dressed and saw this little girl washing Luther off in the sink, then wrapping it up in a paper towel and walking down the hall with it back to the head nurse, while I packed up my little belongings. When the doctors came back for the surgery, I explained to them what happened, and after they conferred, they made me stay for breakfast just to make sure I was all right and then I left. It was quite a night.

Wow.

**From Vol. 9, No. 4, May 2002

From left to right: a hostess poses in the machine, the thing you put your dick in, a sign at the bottom of the stairs, necking with the tit part.

SEX MACHINE

Intercourse Has Been Replaced

by Robbie Dillon

Be honest. How many painful hours have you and your erection spent pretending to listen to the inane prattle of some excruciatingly self-absorbed twit while wondering whether or not she's ever going to shut up and let you stick your hands in her pants? How many times have you found yourself thinking: "Is this really worth the trouble? Isn't there some way—aside from wanking—that I could milk the mongoose without actually having to interact with yet another annoying, vapid (not to mention smelly) human being?"

Well, if you're like me (and you are, whether you care to admit it or not) the answer is "far too many." But unless you live in close proximity to a large flock of sheep, there was never really much that you could do about it.

Until now, that is. Yes, after only a few millennia, science has finally pulled its gene-splicing, space-shuttling, nuclear-missile-building head out of its ass and invented something that will actually improve the lives of human beings.

Ladies and gentlemen, I give you the SEX MACHINE.

Following in the inspired footsteps of Einstein and Edison, Montrealer Patrick More came up with the idea for his creation while polishing his car with an industrial-strength buffer. After noting that the machine sent waves of pleasant vibrations through his crotch, he set out in search of a way to share this sensual revelation with the world.

The final product is an eight-foot-tall sheet of Plexiglas, molded into the shape of a voluptuous woman as if, say, Pamela Anderson had run into a wall of molten plastic and had her every curve and bump preserved unto eternity. Between the legs of said indentation is a metal tube that has been lined with an inflatable  blood-pressure cuff. The client slides a specially designed latex sleeve (with French ticklers on the inside) over his enthrobbed magnificence, inserts it into the tube, and pumps up the cuff to the desired tightness. A nearby rotary dimmer switch allows him to control the degree of vibration that surges through his genitalia, all the way from a delicate brushing of butterfly wings to an oo-ooh m-mm-my g-g-g-god I-I'm f-f-fucking a d-d-um-p-t-t-ruck effect.

Meanwhile, on the other side of the wall, a very naked young lady presses her body into the indentations in the Plexiglas and wordlessly urges the client towards an orgasm that could be described as a religious experience if going to church ever made you feel like cum was shooting out of your eyeballs. For those who care about such things, the whole deal is completely legal, according to the Supreme Court of Canada, because there is never any physical contact between the hostess and her client.

"So where do I sign up?" you're asking. Sadly, this world-shattering technology is currently accessible only to those who dare to journey into the heart of Montreal's red-light district. But it seems only a matter of time before the sex machine replaces television as the primary source of home entertainment.

The implications are stupendous. Men, no longer forced to waste innumerable hours nodding and smiling in the hopes of swabbing the honey pot, will use their newfound time to move our civilization forward, create magnificent works of art, and invent an even better sex machine, something Patrick says is already in the works. Women, so used to fending off unwanted propositions, will suddenly find themselves liberated from their role as sexual objects and do whatever it is that women do when drunks are not harassing them in bars.

Frankly, the future never looked so bright.

**Vol. 4, No. 7, August-September 1997

GRANDMA BLOWJOB

VICE Gets Down With the World's Oldest Professional

by Robbie Dillon

Angela has just given me an incredible blowjob. She stands near the doorway of my bedroom, stuffing herself back into her black merry-widow corset, and tells me that she had a lot of fun. I'm inclined to believe her, if only because my $150 is already stashed in her purse. Even so, as I watch her slip into a loose-fitting, floral sundress and adjust her sensible blonde perm, I can't help but wonder, "What's a nice, fifty-eight-year-old lady like you doing in a job like this?"

No sooner do the words spill out of my mouth than I realize that this is a really stupid question. Considering that Angela's work involves having sex and getting paid, two things that most people enjoy, I should probably ask why everybody isn't doing it. Even a humble idiot like myself can see that ageism and outdated moral ideas about sex work are all that's keeping the elderly from making a few bucks on the side. But in the last few days, I've discovered that just hearing the words "fifty-eight-year-old prostitute" can make people grimace. I'm still not sure why this hap-

pens, but I recognize the pained expression on their faces. In the mostly white, working-class neighborhood where I grew up, it's a standard reaction to the news that a local girl is dating a black man or someone's high school buddy turned out to be gay.

But let's get back to Angela. Two months ago, she was a "respectable" woman involved in a long-term relationship. Unfortunately, her companion, who was also her business partner, wasn't exactly respectful. "The guy I was living with was a jerk," she recalls. "He used to sit around the house, telling me to 'Do the laundry' and 'Get my fucking supper.' Then, after I finished the dishes, he expected me to top it all off by giving him a blowjob. Whenever I did something he didn't like, he'd threaten to throw me out of the house."

For some reason Angela decided to leave this haven of domestic bliss and found herself on the street. Although she is an experienced office worker, she quickly realized that her vocational choices were limited to barmaid or sex worker. "I didn't want to work in a bar," she says, "because the bar scene is full of drugs and other bullshit. This [escort] business is a lot more honest. I go to a client's hotel room, we spend an hour together, and then it's thanks and bye-bye. For me, right now, it's great."

Nevertheless, the decision to work as an escort didn't come easily. In Angela's case, it was complicated by the fact that she had done it before. Forty years earlier, as a teenage runaway, she had supported herself by working the streets of downtown Montreal. "Back then, the business was a lot different," she says. "The guys were rougher; they used to squeeze you and throw you around like some kind of inflatable doll. And if you didn't pay off the police with money or information, they'd either arrest you or take it in trade. I couldn't pay them—I was barely making enough to eat—so they kept throwing me back in jail."

After years of shakedowns and bad tricks, Angela decided to quit the business. She spent the next three decades working at various jobs and raising a daughter, who still has no idea about her mother's past and present vocation.

These days, while other fifty-eight-year-old women are baking cookies and spoiling their grandchildren, Angela earns about $1,200 a week providing sexual services to men who are often half her age. "I could make a lot more if I wanted to work all the time," she says. "But I don't push myself. So far, I've met a lot of interesting, kind men who treat me like a lady." But can someone her age really make a living this way? "It's true that this is a young woman's game," she admits. "But even though most of the older, married men want to be with twenty-year-olds, a lot of younger guys ask for mature women because we treat them like human beings. We make them feel like men."

Along with the changes in the sex industry, Angela has noticed a difference in her own attitudes about the business. "When I was in my twenties, it was like, 'Oh! Oh! You're so good!'" she recalls, faking a pretty realistic orgasm. "The whole time all I was thinking was, 'Hurry up and get off me, you pig.' Now that I'm older, it's more sensual, more passionate. It's like, 'Hey, let me enjoy this.'"

Over the years, Angela's clients have come from all sectors and strata of society. She claims to have serviced gangsters, judges, and celebrities.

Angela isn't sure how much longer she'll continue to work as an escort, but doesn't see herself quitting any time soon. "I'd like to find a day job," she admits. "But even if I did I'd still do this on the side because I enjoy the people and the sex is great."

**From Vol. 8, No. 10, December 2001

THE VICE GUIDE
TO SHAGGING MUSLIMS

by Bruce LaBruce

One late, lonely night back in February of this year I found myself, as one some-times does, wandering the dingy halls of a gay S&M bathhouse in the bowels of downtown Toronto. Entering my private cubicle, I caught the eye of a very intense, handsome fellow with a close-cropped beard and brown skin who I figured was Latino, but who actually turned out to be a Shiite Muslim of East Indian extraction born and raised in East Africa. I invited him into my room, and thus began my crash course in the wild world of Islam.

Before I met Akbar, I was inexcusably ignorant (as, I've subsequently discovered, most Westerners are) about a religion practiced by more than a quarter of the world's population. Well before Black Tuesday I'd been warned by both straight women and gay men alike with some experience in the matter to steer clear of Muslim males as potential boyfriend material, regaled by anecdotes of torture and

abuse that made even the Taliban seem like a bunch of Christmas carolers. But as the relationship with my Muslim (who, it must be said, has his own unique set of theosophical beliefs, as most thinking religious people do—no religion is entirely monolithic) began to evolve from a purely sexual one to something deeper and more emotionally complex, I realized that there are a whole slew of misconceptions and stereotypes about Middle Eastern men and practitioners of Islam, many of which have sprung unavoidably from a complicated set of historical and geopolitical realities. Or, as one Islamic scholar puts it, imagery can be reworked to expedite a shifting political economy.

One false notion is that Muslims hate the West because of its sexual and social liberties, which presumes that Islam is predicated on sexual repression and frustration. This is supposed to be the reason the 9/11 hijackers were willing to commit suicide on the promise of a platoon of black-eyed virgins awaiting them in heaven, but doesn't quite explain why they were drinking cocktails, watching porno, and frequenting strip joints before the attack. In fact, just as people who consider themselves Christian will sometimes bend the rules and go on a bender, your average Muslim also knows how to party. From all accounts prostitution is probably more accepted in the Middle East than in North America (the system of concubinage is tacitly sanctioned and the concubines themselves are treated just fine). Brothels proliferate and hash smoking is widespread, and not just among the Sufis, the rock 'n' rollers of Islam. The image propped up for the West by governmental or religious establishments like the Saudis or the Taliban—who, for example, take the Qur'anic entreaty for women to be modest about their sex appeal to an absurd, oppressive extreme—doesn't always reflect the reality of the streets. So if you're dating a Muslim, even one who is so devout that he prays five times a day and blasts the Qur'an from his car stereo system like some crazy mixed-up Islamic James Dean (like mine does), don't expect him to be a shrinking violet, or even someone who is particularly conflicted about his occasional vices.

As As'ad Abu Khalil, a professor of political science at California State University puts it, "Islam has traditionally been much more tolerant of bodily pleasure than Christianity." And from my experience, I can only add, "You can say that again." The Prophet Muhammad himself had several wives, including, when he was twenty-five, an older and very hot-sounding wealthy widow named Khadija who taught him everything he knew. Companions of Muhammad bragged of his sexual prowess, as opposed to the twelve disciples of Jesus, who, the way they tell it, would have you believe that Christ was a sexual geek. In general, Islam promotes sex and other earthly pleasures as something to be fully enjoyed within prescribed moral boundaries (no adultery, rape, or sexual battery, for example). With regard to my Muslim, sensual experience is viewed as the very essence of worship, an extreme appreciation, if you will, of the divine gifts that God has bestowed upon him. That's why it should come as no surprise that not infrequently in bed he breaks into spontaneous recitations of the Qur'an in Arabic. He tells me that Islam is a spare, devotional religion that eschews the worship of idols or even saints in favor of a profound respect for nature (green is the color of Islam), for the rising and setting of the sun (two of the five times for prayer each day), and for the cycles of the moon that govern their calendar. And, as you can imagine, with lines like these, a Muslim can romance the pants off you.

The question of what is "haram" (a.k.a. forbidden) in Islam is open to a certain amount of interpretation. For example, although alcohol consumption is nixed in the Qur'an, some modern-thinking mullahs condone it in moderation (although you still might want to have your beer without pork rinds). But, as in virtually all religions, the question of homosexuality is the mother of all harams. It may interest you to know that unlike the Bible, which in Leviticus 20:13 explicitly states that a man who lies down with another man (let alone fucks him) should be put to death, similar prohibitions in the Qur'an (there are only two references) are more nuanced and open to interpretation. In the Hadith (a collection of sayings attributed to Muhammad), it does state that "When a man mounts another man, the throne of God shakes" (exciting, eh?), but also that you should kill both men. In general, though, Mr. Abu Khalil suggests that historically, "the homosexual/heterosexual categories in Islamic societies have not been as sharply drawn as in the West. People easily move in and out of the two categories with little stigma attached." He points out that many young Middle Eastern men lose their cherry to another man, pedagogically or otherwise, and, most significantly, that effeminate men aren't subject to the same fag bashing on the street as fairies have traditionally suffered in the United States. In Islamic societies in which men are often separated from women, affection between males, even sexual expression, is not so unusual, which might explain, but not justify, why American sailors have been writing, "Hijack this, fags!" on the bombs being dropped on Afghanistan. Faggotry is largely reviled in the Middle East only when people try to organize it politically or make it overt, or even worse, to import Western paradigms of gayness along with McDonald's and Starbucks. To put it bluntly, if you're a guy mincing around Mecca wearing a tight Spandex T-shirt with "Snatch" written on it in gold glitter while singing "Believe," you probably shouldn't be surprised if somebody pushes a wall on top of you.

Like many misguided Western conceptions about Islam, the false notion that Middle Eastern culture forbids homosexual expression amounts to a failure of the imagination, a refusal to accept the profound cultural and social differences of what might well be another world. Just as many in the West (and even in the East) choose to ascribe violent and aggressive meanings to the teachings of Muhammad rather than pay attention to his entreaties for social justice, charity, and rights for women, we similarly ascribe a sinister and dangerous quality to Islamic sexuality. But the bottom line (and it's coming from a devout bottom) is that there's still something extremely sensual and potent about the image of the Islamic male. You only have to compare the stiff, asexual frigidity of Bush and his schoolmarmish wife with the moist-eyed, sensitive, and soft-spoken quality of the bearded bin Laden, feminine yet virile, with his multiple wives and vast progeny, to grasp the difference.

Like I said, I can only speak from personal experience. But if my Muslim is any indication, the sexual boundaries that many of us know in the West—top vs. bottom, oral vs. anal, masculine vs. feminine, heterosexual vs. homosexual, missionary vs. doggy-style—are all false dualities under Islam. In other words, he's a real Bedouin in bed. And if we occasionally act out a certain true-believer-vs.-the-infidel scenario in the bedroom, whether consciously or unconsciously, despite its political incorrectness, it's no one's goddamn business but our own. After all, raping and pillaging are two of the most common sexual fantasies I can think of.

**From Vol. 8, No. 2, March 2001

DARTH VADER ÜBER ALLES

Kellogg's Corn Flakes and the History of Genital Mutilation

by Absinthe NYC

Foreskin and severed glands ago, a Calvinist morality permeated everything and everyone. In the early 1900s, for example, grain food hucksters like Samuel Graham invented his namesake cracker in the belief that its ingredients tempered one's libido. Sexual promiscuity, and especially masturbation, were feared to drain one's life. Every orgasm ushered one closer to blindness, dwarfism, epilepsy, and tuberculosis.

Having been rendered impotent by a childhood bout with mumps, Dr. John Harvey Kellogg also took up the anti-sex cause with gusto. One need only cast a casual glance at his ludicrous manual on clean living to see how totally insane he was. Check out this extract where he describes a very early stab at what would eventually became circumcision: "The prepuce, or foreskin, is drawn forward over the gland, and the needle to which the wire is attached is passed through from one side to the other. After drawing the wire through, the ends are twisted together, and cut off close. It is now impossible for an erection to occur."

In the case of female mutilation, the labia are lacerated and then stitched together, leaving only a small opening for discharge (eventually the groom uses a box cutter to get in there). Both male and female circumcision are considered a cultural tradition. Sanely, the latter is implicitly outlawed by the Fourteenth Amendment to the Constitution. Why is the male organ not given the same sympathy?

Intent on eradicating masturbation and not satisfied with the twist-tie technique, Kellogg turned his genius to permanently snipping the evil foreskin that was making everyone's palms so hairy. The conclusion he had reached was that contact between the foreskin and the head of the dick illuminates boys to "the terrible secret." Once he figured out you could just chop off the whole thing he was ecstatic: "A remedy which is almost always successful in small boys is circumcision. . . . The operation should be performed by a surgeon without administering an anesthetic, as the brief pain attending the operation will have a salutary effect upon the mind, especially if it be connected with the idea of punishment." He deduced that any knowledge of masturbation will "be forgotten and not resumed."

This was such a smashing success that Kellogg decided to let young girls in on it. After all, this is the patriarch who "would far prefer to place his daughter in the grave than to see her grow up a wretched victim of this vice." His idea was to Agent Orange any secret-garden goings-on. Kellogg stated: "The author has found the application of pure carbolic acid to the clitoris an excellent means of allaying the abnormal excitement." Masterfully adding the double whammy of enormous five-gallon douches of scalding hot water to this vaginal assault, his treatment had girls immediately testifying to being cured.

After conquering masturbation, Kellogg became totally obsessed with keeping his bowels moving, often shitting four times a day. To keep up, he trained like an Olympic athlete with a strict diet and regimen. His belief that the bowels were the key to good health led to giant evacuations comparable to the fall of Saigon. He invented granola just to shit bigger. Rumors speak of defecation so huge he put a sombrero on it and called it "El Grande."

Kellogg was now at the point where he could combine his obsession with bums and his obsession with young boys' penises. Childhood erections, he found, were caused by "the irritation of worms in the rectum," common constipation, and (my personal favorite) something called "fissure of the anus." To cure these anal demons, Kellogg made gut-wrenching superenemas as standard a hygienic practice as brushing your teeth. Forget all you know of rectal irrigation. What we're talking about here are fifteen-gallon überenemas capped off with a serving of yogurt blasted up the ass with a G-force that not even an astronaut could tolerate.

The Battle Creek Sanitarium, a posh health spa for the affluent, was the anal marauder's laboratory for cleansing the system. After inventing the electric blanket, Kellogg made Mengelesque progress in developing vibrating chairs, electroshock baths, more violent enemas, and a glowing electrostatic vacuum tube used as a dildo (ages before amateur proctology terrorism hit hardcore shelves). His orificial probes showed a Victorian obsession with everything rude, and he even added his own "turn of the screw" by using a newfangled thing known as "electricity." To effect a woman's sexual interest, he noticed, "the application of faradic electricity to the vagina by means of a proper electrode is of very great advantage. One electrode should be placed in the vagina, while the other, connected with the sponge, is passed over the lower portion of the spine."

One can draw one's own H conclusions O about a man who M remained celibate O with his wife whilst driving furious instrumentation up his ass. But what about us? In the '50s we had advanced way past Kellogg's "no pain, no gain" philosophy. Clinical finger-fucking was used to treat hysterical women, and Dr. Wilhelm Reich was drafting cumfest theories on orgonomy, yet our circumcision rate climbed to 90 percent. People were sold on it being cleaner. Even today, fear of locker-room teasing forces more than half of North America's parents to remove their children's foreskins. That means laying them in a baby-shaped tray called a circumstraint and attaching leather straps on each limb. Hey, while you're at it, why don't you ash out that cigarette on his face? Why bother with powder-blue walls and a plush menagerie? Welcome your newborn with two weeks spent in blinding pain, just as his perceptions are forming.

Modern prejudice against the foreskin as being dirty and unstylin' stems from a sadistic deep-seated hatred of sexuality. The dreaded smegma (which only shows up on crusty punks who haven't had a shower in a week) is actually chock full of minerals and is nature's way of *cleaning* the penis. Even if it gets a bit dirty, the inner side of the foreskin is an erogenous zone with more nerve endings than the head itself. It serves as erection slack, lubricates the cock, and maintains sensitivity by shielding the knob from constant abrasion. The head of a circumcised penis is dry, with dull, thicker skin that is rendered less sensitive from the constant chafing.

Despite what well-educated British skinheads want you to think, the sadism of circumcision has nothing to do with the prominence of Jewish doctors in North America. The man behind your cock is the same man behind that green cock you stare at over breakfast every day. So unless you are a sadistic retard like your parents, try out this revolutionary idea—don't genitally mutilate your babies.

**From Vol. 9, No. 9, March 2001

THE VICE GUIDE TO FINDING YOURSELF

A Dozen Tried and Not-So-True Methods

by Lesley Arfin & Christi Bradnox

When you become more than twenty years old, you have to find yourself. By "find yourself" we mean everything from figuring out why you're here on this planet to becoming a man/woman to coming out of the closet to being ready for a real relationship.

Technically you're supposed to do it by going to Europe, but for most people it's more innocuous things like using a vibrator and moshing (not at the same time, just, in general). It's not what you'd expect. Seeing a therapist, for example, doesn't do shit, and all acid does is make you go "whoa." Some people don't figure it out until they're 50 years old. Have you ever seen how fucked up parents get after a divorce? That's because they never read something like this:

1. BACKPACKING THROUGH EUROPE

This has become the Disneyland of finding yourself. I'm not saying it's not fun to blow tons of your parents' money riding around the continent on a Eurorail pass and getting w-a-s-t-e-d, but all it does is help you understand the news more when they show maps. Sorry.

PS Make sure you don't fuck any American guys on tour. They are in date-rape-spring-break mode and will eat you alive.

FINDING-YOURSELF FACTOR: 4

2. TELLING YOUR DAD TO FUCK OFF AND BEING PREPARED TO FIGHT HIM

You have to have already moved out of the house for this one. Obviously your Dad could pulverize you if shit did go down—this isn't about that. It's about cutting the cord by burning a bridge. After all the dust settles from this fight the next step (and this takes years) is to become his pal. This involves getting drunk with him and realizing he is as shitty as all your other friends.

FINDING-YOURSELF FACTOR: 7

3. ACID AND MUSHROOMS

Supposedly, the reason we experiment with these drugs is a self-exploration via some sort of magical mystery tour that will change the way we think about the world forever. Maybe it helped Timothy Leary realize he was a boring and pretentious fag, but all it ever taught me was that my feet are crying. You can do all the acid and shrooms you want, but you're fucking totaled when you are high so all you're learning when you trip out is what this fucked up person is like when she's really stoned and guess what—she is toasted.

My boyfriend once said that when he looked at himself on acid, he realized what he looked like to other people and he still believes that: "girls don't like me because I'm handsome. I'm not. They like me like a messy rat guy like Shaggy from Scooby Doo. I wouldn't have known that if it wasn't for acid."

Big whup, Allan.

FINDING-YOURSELF FACTOR: 4, no, 3

4. ECSTASY

Before I went to my first rave, I was an angry punk rocker who hated the whole world and everyone in it. Then I swallowed an E "stamp" (they don't make those anymore), and an hour later I was kissing strangers and realizing that everything was "all good." It didn't matter how stupid everyone looked in their baggy jeans dancing to happy hardcore, they were having fun and "being themselves" and that was all that mattered. I don't do the drug anymore, but I can still tap into that optimism whenever I'm feeling shitty. That's a crucial finding-yourself tool.

FINDING-YOURSELF FACTOR: 7.5

5. DYING YOUR HAIR

Dying your hair is a total rite of passage. At age thirteen, when you realize that the only part of your body you have any control over is your hair, you do as much as you can to fuck it up. This is the first time you feel "different" and maybe even the first time you can rebel against your parents and there's nothing they can actually do about it. This hair-control realization is huge. If your mom yells at you, all you have to say is, "It's my body and I can do whatever I want with it!" She won't say shit after that because she's scared of you not getting an abortion when you get pregnant.

FINDING-YOURSELF FACTOR: 7

6. GETTING SLUTTY WITH IT

This is the biggie for girls. That's why your Mom was so fucked up after the divorce. Shit, that's why she got the divorce. If you don't have your slut phase, you are perpetually high school.

Not every dude you sleep with is going to want to be your boyfriend, and once you figure that out and ride with it, sex gets a whole lot better. Next thing you know you're indulging yourself and telling guys how to make you happy and even doing shit like making them wear tighty whities. You know when you start telling guys what to do you are majorly finding yourself. Once you up the ante to buying a few dildos and having a few threesomes and not feeling weird about it you are basically there.

FINDING-YOURSELF FACTOR: 9.8 (We didn't give it a 10 because people can sue you if you make it a 100% guarantee, but it's basically 10.)

7. SNEAKING OUT OF THE HOUSE

I used to love sneaking out of my house. It was fun and liberating and risky. Once you get to that age where making out with cute guys is worth the risk of seeing a ghost or getting kidnapped, you have reached a milestone. You have found the beginning of your preteen self, the era when your parents start to become more and more of an embarrassment. You even close your door now when before you needed a drink of water and a kiss goodnight. Your parents are all dumbfounded and resentful but you're like, "Later, suckers!" Sneak out as much as you can. I don't know why exactly, but to this day I believe it made me a better person.

FINDING-YOURSELF FACTOR: 8

8. THE MAGIC FOUR

This one is only for guys. In order to become a man you have to: 1) break someone's heart; 2) have your heart broken; 3) get the shit beaten out of you; and 4) beat the shit out of someone. That means: 1) she has to be so fucked up she almost kills herself. Like, doesn't eat for three days and falls down the stairs drunk; 2) you are so fucked up you have to punch yourself in the head to stop thinking about her;

3) you end up in the hospital with a severely broken nose and some sort of permanent facial scar; and 4) he's not really moving at the end. You're kind of just kicking a blob.

FINDING-YOURSELF FACTOR: 9

19. HAVING A BREAKDOWN

OK you have to have two, actually. When you're 16 you have to have a complete breakdown in front of your parents where you're convulsing and crying for no reason. THEN, when you're about 23 you have to hit an existential brick wall where you realize you're going to die and not go to heaven or anything. After about three days of going, "Why am I here?" you will figure out if you're here to fight for justice or worship Allah or entertain people or just totally indulge yourself with as much sex, drugs and attention as humanly possible.

FINDING-YOURSELF FACTOR: 9

10. WATCHING *A CLOCKWORK ORANGE*

At first maybe you didn't really like it, but you said you did because you were supposed to and everyone else said they did too but then you finally did get it. Next thing you know you're renting *The Wall* and dressing up as Alex for Halloween.

FINDING-YOURSELF FACTOR: 4.5

11. MOSHING

It can be scary to mosh for the first time. Especially when you're a fourteen-year-old girl who weighs 100 pounds soaking wet. But fuck it, get hurt. There's nothing better than a war story from the pit. Moshing is great because it's so utterly ridiculous, but at the same time so liberating, to just throw your body into a mass of people. It's like, the music is so good it turns us all into mental patients and retards and we run around in circles and that is AWESOME. It was a very new way for me to let myself go, to not be self-conscious when I dance and fully embrace the music. It sounds so corny and it should, because if you think you are too cool to mosh, you are wrong! Moshing is too cool for you!

FINDING-YOURSELF FACTOR: 9

12. THERAPY

You won't find yourself through therapy, but it is really fun sometimes to talk about yourself for an hour. You can talk shit about all your friends and cry about your ex-boyfriend. It will make you feel better, no doubt. Therapy may also help you understand yourself on a level that may make you not hate your parents so much, or at least realize why you started cutting yourself when you were twelve. But you can give or take therapy. It's more of a relaxing thing to give yourself, like a massage or a cup of snugglepuss tea. It is good for you, like medicine, but it's no moshing.

FINDING-YOURSELF FACTOR: 4

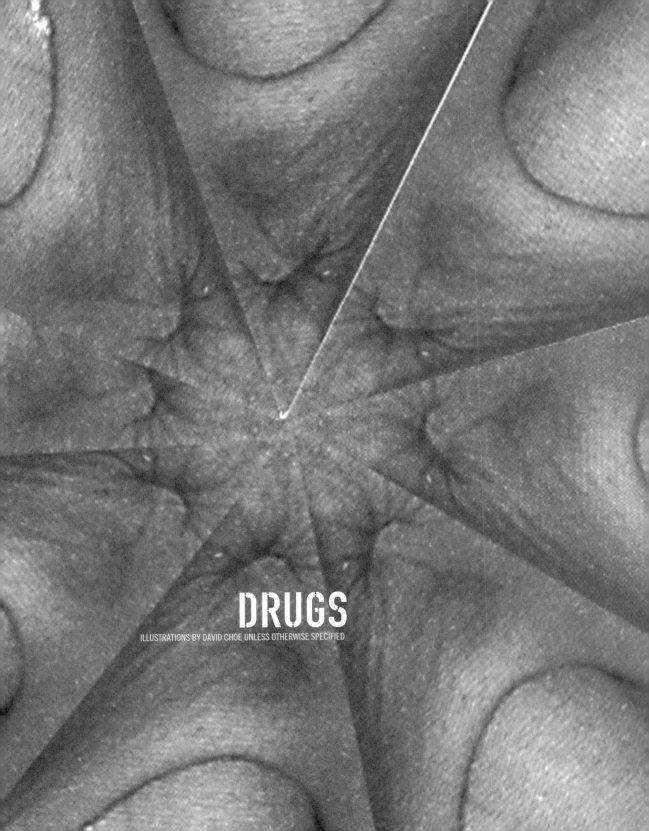

DRUGS

ILLUSTRATIONS BY DAVID CHOE UNLESS OTHERWISE SPECIFIED

**From Vol. 8, No. 3 April 2000

THE WAR ON DRUGS

by Amy Archers. Photos by Sahihi

Ashkan Sahihi (above) is an Iranian/German photographer who is infuriated by the war on drugs. "I find it despicable," he says. "If the American government was really concerned about stopping drug abuse, things like legalization and free needle programs would at least enter the discussion. In the absence of that, all we have is a silly political tool to please the Christian Right."

It is this hypocrisy that inspired Sahihi to take eleven people out of their daily environments and get them high. He chose eleven different drugs and fed them to subjects who were relatively foreign to the drug they were doing. "It was difficult finding people that hadn't done a lot of drugs. No matter what the race, class, and background, everyone seemed to have tried E and coke and other drugs. Only crack was untouched by most."

When you go to see Sahihi's work in a gallery the reaction is almost always the same. A guy drifts by all the portraits in a matter of seconds until his girlfriend grabs him and says, "Don't you get it? All these people are high." Then he stops and goes over each shot incredibly slowly. They both laugh and share stories about what they did when they were on that drug and then they stop the next couple and say, "Hey, these people are all high." And so on.

Here are his comments on the eleven people he photographed and the drugs they did.

CRACK
Side effects: This was a scary one. She showed up to the shoot a bit nervous, but the more she smoked the more normal she got. Then she kept smoking more. I had to stop her at one point because I was getting worried.
Fucked up for: Twenty minutes, off and on.

SPEED

Side effects: She was frantically trying to grab at things. She kept saying, "Nothing is different, I feel fine," and then talking really fast for a long time about nothing.

Fucked up for: Two hours. She did it twice.

MESCALINE

Side effects: He had a blast. He was singing and doing impersonations. Out of everyone he got the most high and seemed to have the most fun. He was way out there.

Fucked up for: Three and a half to four hours.

COCAINE

Side effects: She was tense and not fun to be around. She did five or six lines and then just stood there saying, "What do you want me to do?" It made me nervous. I was concerned about her.

Fucked up for: Three hours.

PSILOCYBIN

Side effects: He seemed to get slightly paranoid. He really wanted to sit down on the couch, but one of the rules was you had to sit in the chair for the whole high.

Fucked up for: A full eight hours.

KETAMIN

Side effects: This guy puked ferociously. Three times he got up off his chair and puked his guts out. For about forty-five minutes he was doing really bad. He was in a K-hole, a K-grave. I would say 50 percent of the people's reactions were bad and about 50 percent were good, but he was one of the worst.

Fucked up for: Three or four hours.

HASH

Side effects: Nothing at all. That's what makes all these pictures such bad portraits. A good picture shows a good dynamic between the photographer and the subject, but the drugs took that context away.

Fucked up for: Impossible to tell.

ECSTASY

Side effects: It hit her really quickly and she started bouncing all over the room. I couldn't get her to sit still.

Fucked up for: Four to five hours.

LSD

Side effects: She was really, really high. She kept apologizing and then giggling to the point of absurdity.

Fucked up for: Eight or nine hours. After her session ended she had some friends over and they stuck around.

MARIJUANA

Side effects: Like a lot of these it was exactly what you see. She was off in her own little world, totally oblivious to me and my assistant and the nurse (I had a nurse check everyone's blood pressure before and after the shoot). Totally happy by herself. Fucked up for: Forty-five minutes.

HEROIN

Side effects: This session scared me completely. She never barfed and just sat there for a really long time scratching her face. This shoot changed my opinion of drugs quite a bit. I became very turned off by them, especially heroin. She seemed incredibly bored, uncreative, unemotional, and numb.

Fucked up for: One and a half to two hours.

**From Vol. 7, No. 10, December 2000

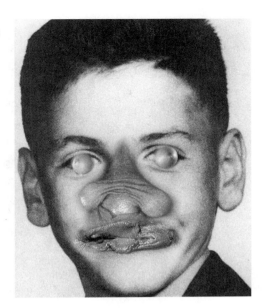

BAKED AS TOAST

An Interview with the Most Stoned People in the World

by Christi Bradnox

You probably don't know this, but the pot in Amsterdam has about 600 times the THC of your average North American joint. After noticing that everyone in the city is either lying on the floor with their eyes wide open or giggling hysterically while pointing at a bird, we set out with our trusty Fisher-Price tape recorder and found the most stoned people in the city of Amsterdam (who are probably the most stoned people in the world).

There were a lot of eligible contestants. We met a Michael Cox from Calgary whose peripheral vision had become smaller and smaller until all he could see was a pinhole in front of him and then he passed out. Then there was a California girl named Jill who was so high she hallucinated a man frantically trying to deal with gale-force winds and an inside-out umbrella. She almost pissed herself and was gasping for air holding her stomach, but the guy was just standing at the bus stop holding his umbrella. It wasn't even windy outside.

The winners by far, however, were these two brothers we met named Dan and Phil Langford. They were Middle-American boys who we met with their pants down. They were screaming with their hands in the air, and then they collapsed like they were shot.

VICE: What happened here?
Dan: I just got some really good news.
Phil: We've been smoking since early this morning and my head feels like cheese. Like floaty cheese. (hysterical laughing)

What was with the nude victory thing?
Dan: Oh, yeah. We were totally high out of our minds. It got to be a bit too much. I almost bad-tripped.
Phil: I couldn't feel my body. It was a huge body buzz.
Dan: Yeah, your nerves feel weird. My hair felt like cobwebs. Anyway, we were in a taxi and I felt shit trickling down my ass. I didn't even fart but I guess I lost bowel control.

How did you deal with that?
Dan (laughing his head off): I told Phil and he agreed.
Phil: What?
Dan: You shit your pants too.

Phil: Oh yeah (laughing), I was like, "I think I shit my pants too." Because I felt it. I felt it spreading all over my ass. Then I was like, "What are we going to do?"

Dan: Yeah, the more we talked about it the worse it got. We could smell it, too. I had to try to tell the driver that we had to go to a park because of an emergency, but I was laughing too hard. He must have thought we were totally fucked.

Phil: He must have totally known we were stoned.

So you ended up in the park.

Dan: Phil just stood there because he didn't want it to go anywhere. I ran behind this bush (points to a large shrub behind us) and I yanked down my pants. I was almost looking forward to seeing how bad it was. But when I looked down there was no shit at all. Not even a skid mark. I was filled with so much joy (laughing) I put up my arms and cheered. I go, "I didn't shit my pants!"

Phil (laughing): Then I checked my pants and I hadn't shit either and I go, "Me nei-ther!" Then I think we realized how we were being like *The Sound of Music* about not shitting our pants. That's when the laughs really hit me.

Dan: I collapsed face first with my pants down and I laughed so fucking hard. Holy shit. (shakes head back and forth)

Phil: That's when you guys showed up with your tape recorder. We must have looked so fucking funny.

At this point both of the Langfords fell into each other laughing like girls and we had to go.

**From Vol. 7, No. 10, December 2000

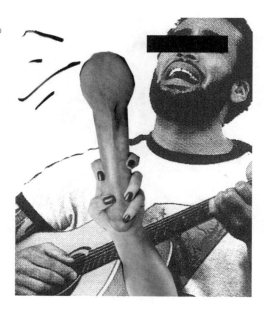

COKE JAMS 2002

Two CDs of Pumped Intensity to Nurture Your Up

by Absinthe NYC and VICE Staff

All these compilation CDs are for shit. How many times have you found yourself high as fuck and having to deal with swiping out album after album, DJing the succession of music to nurture your state? What we really need on the record shelves are *Opium Grooves Vol. 1*, *Coke Jams 2002*, and *Music to Trip By*. Mix tapes suck because no matter how cool your friends are, none of them have the Journey or Night Ranger album you need, cuz these fucking albums are impossible to find (outside of used bins in Jersey). Now, thanks to CD burners and the Internet we no longer have to wait until the next Metal Karaoke Night at Arlene Grocery to kick it into overdrive. The following list is tested, approved, and totally ready to max out your coke high.

Volume 1

"Don't Stop Believing"—Journey
Penultimate. One doesn't even need a line of cocaine to feel the buzz. Ideally, the ultimate coke album would just be twelve tracks of "Don't Stop Believing," constantly building. It's the most complete use of every single second of recorded music and it's impossible to fight off the urge to do some double-fisted pumps at every chorus. If everyone listened to "Don't Stop Believing," it would be a drug-free, bad-attitude-free world.

"Sister Christian"—Night Ranger
I never got what the term "you're motoring" means and I have yet to figure out what the fuck it's all about, but the earnest pleading at the end of this power-chord maelstrom brings a tear to my eye every time. Just like every other piece of '80s music, it's stigmatized by kitsch until you actually listen to it high and appreciate the epic nature of this emotional cyclone.

"Starship Trooper"—Yes
Fuck Verhoeven's film, this is even more coked out. The trick is to forward it to the 5:40 mark, where it just builds and builds into a spiral staircase jam that goes up and up. I mean, it's on the cusp of this orgasmic climax but never gives in, for like, four minutes. No one else, to my knowledge, has done a riff that just goes on like this, getting better all the time.

"Here I Go Again on My Own"—Whitesnake
This Zeppelin-lite ballad is a hollow masterpiece of falsetto vocals and arena-rawk guitar riffs. Kinda like how Gregory Peck is more fun to watch than Cary Grant. Not having the hair to whip about, you'll think about how work and life have stripped you of this feeling.

"Centerfold"—J. Geils Band
This is a bigger air-guitar jam than "Jesse's Girl." The peeping toms next door will think you're doing step aerobics. Incidentally, one thing you'll notice about coke songs like this and the Whitesnake one is they are all perfect choices for karaoke. In both genres of music appreciation, you are The Shit and all slow jams are going to do is kill the party vibe—*au bout*.

"Electronic"—Belle and Sebastian
Teases you a little, before dropping the pacemaker beat. Totally new wave and indie-rock cool at the same time. Pump your high while showing the neighborhood that your record collection isn't stuck in the '80s.

"Ladytron"—Roxy Music

At this point, your high needs some regal bagpipes to laurel your ego and then take you higher than the clouds of Avalon before Eno's space-synth goes apeshit and has you flailing around in ecstasy.

"Pride"—U2 (*Rattle and Hum* version only)

It's the sonic equivalent of Leni Riefenstahl's *Triumph of the Will*. Everyone joins in step and why not, for something that's this alive and earnest? Remember how bug-eyed Bono was in the film? Now go look in the mirror.

"I Wanna Be Your Dog"—The Stooges

Relentless building of tension that forces you to hump the end table in a fevered sweat while shouting along with the "Come on" parts.

"Magic"—The Cars

The most perfect use of power chords ever. They drop right in, precisely when you're totally worked up to a peak by the first ten secs of this track. When I can't score coke, I put on sunglasses and this song.

"Suspicious Minds"—Elvis

Fucking backup singers, epic arrangements, and the King. I've always known this song was totally about blow. The title's also a great reminder of why you don't want to come down. That means it's time to put *Volume 2* in the box.

Volume 2

"Bittersweet Symphony"—The Verve

Mild synth twiddling provides the perfect time-out to do extra booster lines. Then the wicked drum loop hits and the strings make it all dense and layered, just like how the details drop out of life with clarity when your mind is at 200 percent. Not to mention the total fuck-you attitude of what this song is about. Yeah, that's right, he knocked over old ladies in the video. Fuck everyone, I'm king!

"Firestarter"—Prodigy

It's an extension of your ego: "I am the fire starter." Music used to be alluringly dangerous, like this gem that feeds your need to be fucking shit up right now.

"Run to the Hills"—Iron Maiden

Just for the rush of the galloping beat alone, this song makes the list. As a bonus you got some heavy metal guitar licks on top of it all to drive your shit crazy.

"Live Forever"—Oasis

Even drunk dads sing along to "Maybe I just wanna fly / Wanna live, don't wanna die." An empowering working-class anthem that recognizes that getting fucked up and doing shit on your own terms can lead to selling out Wembley and knocking up supermodels. "We see things they'll never see / You and I are going to live forever." Brother, you are a fucking coked-up immortal genius. Now go do your thing.

"Bombs over Baghdad"—OutKast

This jam is strong enough for Stevie Nicks' asshole. After rappers pull off a hit album, the record company gets them set up with enough cash for a mountain of blow (check the Beatnuts' *Stone Crazy*) and the result is so expeditiously BANG! you need a straw to hear it. Your mind is overloaded trying to take it all in, so you just accept it as your own thoughts (thoughts usually reserved for the minds of syphilitic geniuses, homeless lunatics, and berserk androids). If only you could live life this much to the max all the time.

"That thirteen-minute song where everyone's partying in the background"—Marvin Gaye

VICE talks about this song way too much so just burn it and move on. BTW, you may have noticed that most of these jams are white people music. That's because cocaine is predominately a white drug. And that is why Ronald Reagan gave fifteen years to anyone who did crack (black) and a slap on the wrist to anyone who did coke (white).

"125"—Lupine Howl

The Intercity 125 is the fastest train in the UK, and thus a euphemism for Charlie. Lupine Howl are former members of Spiritualized. You are high.

"Ring the Alarm (Pimp Juice's Magic Mix)"—Fu-Schnickens vs. Pimp Juice

Fu-Schnickens sucks the shit right out of Shaq's ass, but this song from Jive Electro's *Old School vs. New School Vol. 2* is so pure cocaine that if you rubbed it between your thumb and forefinger they would get all oily and numb.

"Whatever Happened to Thames Beat"—The Gents

This is from the killer coke album *The Countdown Compilation*, featuring the most esoteric post-punk pop bands of all time. All mod songs are hot as hell when you're high because they're made for sweaty soul dancing with svelte chicks in go-go boots. You can trip out about how mods were all working-class yobs that pissed everyone off by wearing suits and listening to darkie music. That's when you do a line and go, "That's it! I'm going to become a mod."

"Panama"—Van Halen
Flat-out, balls-to-the-wall embracing of everything indulgent. Supreme air-guitar material, replete with back-bending noodling solos. How much blow must they have been doing for this album? They must have had fucking feed bags on.

"Pills"—Primal Scream
Continually climactic, it deconstructs lyrically to just repeat, "Fuck you, fuck you, fuck you," just like those thoughts in your head.

"Ring of Fire"—Johnny Cash
"Wait, what the fuck is country music doing here?" Fuck you. The man's done more blow than everyone else on this list. After washing down some Quaaludes with a fifth of Jack Daniel's backstage, he'd go on talk shows and discuss salvation. Layering of instruments with a stroke-inducing chorus is the cornerstone of what we're talking about here.

"Risingson"—Massive Attack
"Why you have to take me to this party and breathe? / I'm dying to leave." Here's another album that was made on Snow Mountain. This doesn't necessarily convert the jaw grinding to a good trip, but it makes you feel so dark and evil you can enjoy your "too high" bad trip.

Now that the second CD is over, you can try to come down or can "not stop believing." I suggest you get that Metrocard out and arrange three more lines, cuz Journey is coming up just around the corner.

The Comedown EP
"Leb Wohl"—Neu!
"West Palm Beach"—Palace
"Sea of Love"—Catpower
"Immune"—Low
"A Man Called Sun"—The Verve

**From Vol. 8, No. 5, June 2001

Judd Nelson in *Shattered*.

JUST SAY, "OH, NO WAY!"

Antidrug Propaganda Tests Your TV Trivia

by Derrick Beckles

The Government of the United States of Hollywood is possibly one of the greatest inventions of all time. Trading arms for coke and then combating cokeheads with everything from life in prison to public service announcements is a switcheroo not even Crockett and Tubbs could pull off. 1980s antidrug movies are a perfect example of the Hollywood flimflam. They smell like a judge telling a rich Hollywood has-been he can either do time or use his celebrity to discourage other people from taking the same path. The stars want to help the kids, but when you look at their pasty faces and odd medical tics (profuse sweating), all you can think about is them screaming, "I said an 8-ball!" So to the prosecution's dismay, it's impossible to take them seriously. They are, however, a great set of flash cards to play "Name That Celebrity Loser" and test what our own drug abuse has done to our TV and movie knowledge.

Drug Free Kids—1987

Starring: Everyone.

This treat features more stars than there are in heaven. A veritable roast beef submarine of acting that is beyond digestion: Elliott Gould, Ned Beatty, Bonnie Franklin, Marla Gibbs, Melissa Gilbert, Adam Rich, and the list goes on. Hosted by Ken Howard, this video cleverly combines community-theater minimalism (mismatched furniture) with German impressionism (black backgrounds with windowpanes defying gravity). A magical place that allows Ken Howard, who has the power to lumber into any living room anywhere, to immediately influence family relations with a "Whoa" or a "That's more like it." A place where Ned Beatty's anger-management problems can be featured, alongside Adam Rich, in a skit about not being able to drink like a man.

Most Questionable Advice: Look through your kid's possessions.

Celebrity Superpower: Ken Howard's psychic ability. He uses no guns. No knives. No dynamite . . . only his MIND.

Marketing Hopes: All of these stars will impress someone.

Marketing Reality: Like most of these movies, you spend so much time saying, "Hey, it's that guy from that show!" that you miss all of the riveting information.

Drug Information: Top-notch. Ken Howard ends up having so much information on drugs he comes off like a fifth-generation dealer.

Celebrity Motive: In all cases but one (Ned Beatty) this video felt like an audition tape. With Ned it felt more like a surveillance tape.

Kids Killing Kids—1987

Sixty minutes of cheap video starring: An eyebrow.

Malcolm-Jamal Warner stars in this piece of teen-oriented, antigun/drug propaganda that masquerades as a sci-fi action flick. He plays a mystic warrior from the planet Arturis who has the ability to turn back time. He travels to planet Earth where he encounters a series of shittily acted handgun murders at a high school, brought on by drug abuse. He employs his special time-bending powers to go back and see what would have happened if guns and drugs were not involved in these confrontations. His banal conclusion: Take away the guns and drugs and fewer people will get shot.

Most Questionable Advice: Confront the kid who has bragged about having a gun. Then talk him out of killing you. It's bad advice, but very entertaining.

Hidden Face: MJW wrote an autobiography at age eighteen with a slipcover that explodes into a poster of . . . him.

Marketing Hopes: By using Malcolm, Arturis will not wage war against Earth.

Marketing Reality: It's too late.

Drug Information: All children are arms dealers.

Celebrity Motive: To find out how many acting gigs he can get away with.

Desire to Clean VCR Heads: Constant. Haunting, in fact.

Crackdown on Drugs—1988
Starring: Scott Valentine.

"Nick" from *Family Ties* uses this antidrug video to try to get laid. It starts off as gay porn, then slowly morphs into a headline torn off the front page of a 1988 newspaper: "Desperate Star Visits Local High School." The tape dares to showcase several of Valentine's grueling "rap sessions" about cocaine and crack with a group of twenty-five-year-old high school kids. The session inevitably gets tense and awkward due to Valentine's aggressive and agitated state, which in turn causes his gorgeous Gordon Gartrell shirt to be drenched with sweat. Then the camera cuts back to him, and his shirt has suddenly become a yellow blouse. After his crackdown on sweat, Scott seems to accidentally blurt out his personal crack recipe. Realizing what he's done, he elegantly backpedals by saying, "I don't know if this is the recipe" (thus calling further attention to the fact that he just gave out the recipe). Yikes.

WARNING: Attempting to watch this tape's dizzying combination of true-life testimonials and horrible dramatizations may result in waking up in a graveyard giving a dog a blowjob.

Most Problematic Advice: Always snitch!

Celebrity Superpower: When made nervous, Scott will drown his enemies in sweat.

Drug Information: So much that the viewer will be able to open up a lab.

Malapropism Alert: Scott says that crack has a "crucial" effect.

Musical Number: Pure Faltermeyer-inspired synth-clap electronica.

Be Somebody . . . or Be Somebody's Fool—1984
Sixty minutes of scintillating video starring: Mr. T.

Although this tape isn't exclusively about the pros and cons of drug abuse, it does reserve a portion of its content for smashing the subject over the viewer's head. Monsieur T's method is not unlike Mao's approach to dealing with drug dealers: Kill them. Although the Chinese use the efficient but predictable method of death by firing squad, Mr. T opts for the more urban and dramatic use of the elevator shaft.

Don't get caught up wondering what that elevator shaft would smell like after a few days. Mr. T just kept rapping along so we just kept clapping along.

Most Questionable Moment: Mr. T describes a teen model like this: "With her mustard socks and ketchup sash, she's a real hot dog." Later, he says of a twelve-year-old: "Here's Janine, cool as a peppermint ice cream in her pink ensemble with frosty white pumps. Stir up a breeze, Janine. It's getting hot in here."

Marketing Hopes: This would launch a career as a European telethon host.

Marketing Reality: TNT.

Drug Information: Kill dealers.

Musical Numbers: T busts out an old-school funk jam in a style reminiscent of the Gap Band, where his mantra "Treat your mother right" is drilled into the listener's dome.

Shattered—1988

Starring: Burt Reynolds, Judd Nelson.

Burt and Judd, together for the first time in an action-packed, antidrug journey through teen desire, ignorance, and escapism. Watching from the safety of cars, trees, and suburban park benches, Burt 'n' Judd seem like two cops on a stakeout who can't stop talking about drugs and teens and teens and drugs. The kids in this film start with weed and soon find themselves addicted to powdered cocaine and solid cocaine (a thing called crack). The parents (often hypocrites themselves) drink their way into argumentative stupors with the young and old alike until, with the help of counseling, they realize how much fun getting your kids off drugs can be. Watching the unrehearsed Burt and Judd talk about abstaining from drugs is like watching the Metzgers talk about the importance of the United Negro College Fund. If you watch this movie without reaching for drugs then you are a big fat nun.

Most Questionable Advice: Telling the director to start the movie with a close-up on teen toes.

Celebrity Superpowers: Judd Nelson's hair is constantly accompanied by a breeze that can be used to make him look sexier than any of his enemies.

Marketing Hopes: No one, absolutely no one, can get through to teens like Burt 'n' Judd.

Marketing Reality: No one, absolutely no one, can get through to teens.

Drug Information: So much that you want to start partying.

Desire to Do Drugs While Viewing Tape: When you hear the lyrics "Get wasted, just taste it, let's party right now!" how can you resist?

Musical Numbers: Metal song "The Snake Is Back," used whenever someone looks at drugs. I found myself singing it while calling my dealer.

Tough Love—1985

Starring: Bruce Dern.

The movie that put more kids on the streets than pimps did. This is the film that started America's most notorious catchphrase of the '80s; within a year of its release mothers and fathers around North America were poking their kids in the chest and frothing, "It's time for some tough love, Buster!" The ultimate message behind tough love is that sometimes you just have to freak out and kick your kids out of the house and let them die before they'll learn a lesson.

Most Questionable Advice: Beat a confession out of your kids right now.

Marketing Hopes: The government will make it illegal to be a teenager.

Marketing Reality: It worked.

Drug Information: So much that parents acted like Starsky and Hutch.

Celebrity Motive: To get free drinks from parents who love saying "tough love."

**From Vol. 6, No. 7, Sept 1999

ROYAL TRUX'S JENNIFER HERREMA DEFENDS PSYCHOTROPIC DRUGS AND THE LIKE MOST AWESOME

by Jennifer Herrema

Psychotropic drugs are among the safest legal and regulated mind- and mood-altering substances available today. This is precisely why I have such a hard time understanding the almost puritanical resistance to these drugs. I have heard the argument against them in many forms. The egotist believes that these substances are somehow different from nonprescription narcotics in that they would impair his or her unique "vision" to a fault, rendering it subpar, due to the drug's capitalist conformist nature. Illegal, "dangerous" drugs are really so much more romantic

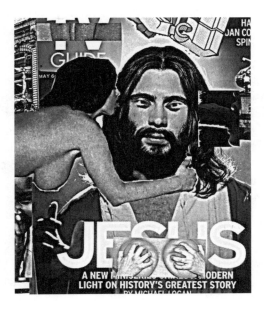

and antiestablishment. The feminists believe that psychotropics are female pacifiers controlled by the male-dominated drug industry. Let us not forget the Mafia, who injected heroin into the black community so many years past, and the CIA, who did the same with crack, all in the name of keeping undesirables in their place. Yet those drugs supposedly provide road marks along the distance between shallow and deep, and that is bad-ass. There are also those who believe that taking anything that might make life more livable is weak, cheap, and cheating; a decidedly bourgeois idea—just tell that to the person who can't leave their bed for fear of flying objects and bad vibrations.

All right, all arguments are arguable, but some seem to generate cognitive dissonance and all the above arguments would have me ringing totally out of tune. A lot of people have talked to me with deaf speech and wonder why they feel so uncomfortable; you know, like the ones who eat organic lamb burgers at an anti-fur rally. No matter what the rationalization, it's all dissonant, and I know very well how dissonance affects a lot of people cuz lots of people have hated and feared Royal Trux.

So, with all of that I give you this, my very own story of the psychotropic discovery; because they are most awesome. Six years ago at the too-young-to-quit age of twenty-two, I checked myself into the hospital for troubles with my heroin addiction. The whole idea of this was to give myself a much-needed rest. Well, it would suffice to say that this vacation from the daily chores of an addict became pretty appealing, so I followed a strict itinerary, touring all the area hospitals over the course of a year and a half. Each time I left, I came up with a new and more responsible way to abuse drugs. It did not occur to me at the time that reconciling was responsible and abuse was more trouble than it was worth, so my situation quickly became all or nothing. I went for all and hit the wall. I called my doctor for advice and it was then that I learned about endorphins, dopamine, and seratonin, all naturally occurring chemicals in the brain that can be amplified by drug use. She decided that one way of explaining my drug abuse was that I need more of all these pleasure-inducing chemicals. I was very happy with this diagnosis. I was to be prescribed drugs that gave me the same elevated chemical levels that heroin and the like had previously given me at great cost. I immediately set out to find all the best antidepressant, anti-anxiety, and mood-stabilizing drugs that I could find.

The following is an annotated description of some of the psychotropic drugs I tried and their subsequent drug action. Remember that one person's side effect is another's desired effect. These pills can't cure all your ills, but they can sure cure mine.

Prozac (green-and-white SSRI antidepressant). In high doses, this drug produced a hallucinogenic-type action along with a feeling of speed, totally dilated pupils, lack of appetite, and serious energy.

Paxil (pink or blue SSRI antidepressant). In high doses, this drug had a strong sedative effect and made me really spaced out and hungry.

Wellbutrin (purple or blue, prescribed for depression and attention deficit disorder). This drug in high doses gave me lots of energy and the ability to concentrate on one thing for a really long time—aggressively.

Elavil (hot-pink tricyclic antidepressant). In low doses, this drug totally calmed me and made me hungry and more prone to waking dreams.

Neurontin (caramel-colored mood stabilizer). Neurontin has a second purpose as a painkiller and it does this quite well, along with providing a sedated sense of watching oneself on TV and losing all track of time.

Thorazine (bright orange or white for manic depression and tranquilizing animals). Thorazine definitely gave me an otherworldly feeling, totally calm and always in the zone.

Ativan (white or baby-blue sedative hypnotic). In large doses, everything started looking silver and shiny and I felt like I was walking on air—no aggro, just mellow.

**From Vol. 6, No. 2, March 1999

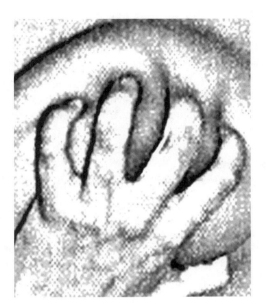

PEOPLE WHO HAD BAD TRIPS IN HIGH SCHOOL

Maybe you were trying to understand the radio and it kept saying, "You are a coward." Maybe your parents' heads came out of the sky and asked you what you were doing with your life. Everyone had at least one really bad trip in high school. Here are nine doozies:

Doug Poirer: Cocaine, Grade 13

I was in London visiting some old friends, and after going to a few pubs, one of them said he didn't understand why I had come there. He said he had read some of the letters I had written my friend Dominic and he said I was mad. At that moment I realized not only were these people not my friends, but my letters had been the laughingstock of everyone there.

Dave Hicks: Acid, Grade 10

You know how you're not supposed to look at your penis? I didn't know that. I started asking everyone if I should go to the bathroom. You don't know if you're cold or if you have to go to the bathroom or anything. Eventually, I just decided I should be going pee by figuring out how long it had been, so I went to the bathroom and I could barely stand. When I looked down, it looked like a 500-year-old wrinkly worm. I was ashamed of it. It sort of had a face. I wasn't really hallucinating a face on it, I was more imagining it. But when you're that high there's a fine line between seeing and imagining. For the rest of the night, I wasn't totally sure if my penis wasn't a 500-year-old man. I could almost feel its face there in my pants and it wrecked my trip.

Michael Chang: Acid, Grade 11
I once had a bad trip because I thought I smelled really bad all night. I didn't at all. I've never done any kind of drug since.

Kim Fraser: Acid, Adult Education
My friend and I were at a bar in Vancouver and an ex-con sat down to talk to me while my friend went to the bathroom. It was a good atmosphere because all the tree planters were in between contracts and everyone had money. The convict and I were getting along fine and we were talking French because he was from Quebec. Everything was great until I overheard him speak German to a friend. I spoke German too, so I said something to him and he asked me if I was a smart-ass and started getting really mad. When my friend got back, the convict said he was sorry about taking his chair and when my friend said, "No problem," the convict punched him in the face. There was blood everywhere. We had to go to the hospital, but we didn't tell any of the doctors about being on acid.

Peter Gibson: Acid, Grade 13
I took three hits on a bus ride from Calgary to Ottawa and started bad-tripping right away. The person next to me smelled so much like piss, I was sure he was pissing his pants right there and I kept checking to see if he was getting any on me. A perfectly happy baby looked at me and started crying hysterically after looking into my crazy eyes. It was so loud I went over to the lady and asked what was the matter. You just don't do that.

Brenda Pagotto: Acid, Grade 10
It was when my twin brother started pretending he was a paraplegic. He sat in our dad's chair for hours like he was Stephen Hawking or something and wouldn't answer me. I was positive the drugs had paralyzed him for life, but when we came down, he apologized and said he couldn't help it. He had started it as a joke and then got lost in it. He's not even sure if it was bad or not.

Craig Gibson: Acid, Grade 10

I dropped with my friend Sean and two other people that we met on vacation. Things were going all right until one of the guys burned Sean by pretending he was really into Elton John. After that, Sean thought everything was a burn and was really awkward and cruel. They got into this passive/aggressive battle where everything they said was a subtle diss at the other guy. At one point I broke down and yelled, "Will you guys just leave each other alone? Jesus Christ!" I found out the next day the whole thing was in my head. They were getting along great.

Tim Wilkinson: Mushrooms, Grade 9

After doing way too many mushrooms, I took off on my friends and went home to bed. I heard my parents come in and didn't move, but I was getting higher and higher. There were hundreds of tons of maggots behind every wall and they seemed to be moving really close to me, then really far away. I knew all the hallucinations were the drugs but they were getting so intense I could barely breathe. It got so intense I was sure I was ODing, so I went into my parents' room and insisted they take me to the hospital. They're British and don't understand drugs, so they panicked. At the hospital everyone was very calm. They gave me some muscle relaxants and I passed out.

Bruce Pilsworth: Mushrooms, Grade 12

I did mushrooms with my friend who had a birth defect. I became obsessed with his bad trip, which I could tell he was hiding from everyone. He would let things slip like, "Don't look at your driver's license, guys. It's a bad trip," or "Who cares who sees us?" He always wanted the lights dimmed. At the beginning of the trip, we were lying on our backs looking up at the clouds. I thought it would be good to stick to basic hallucinations and not get too philosophical. I said, "Are you seeing these slowly rotating hexagons?" And he said, "I see Play-Doh where you push your head in and it makes a face on the other side." Then he sits up and looks at me and goes, "It's like God gives you a face and that's the face you have for the rest of your life. Do you know what I mean?" I said yes, because I really wanted him to stop. Then he lies back down on his back and goes, "I really hope you know what I mean. I'm going to ask you tomorrow morning if you know what I mean." It was all downhill from there.

**From Vol. 8, No. 9, November 2001

ENGLAND IS DREAMING

As Liquid Acid Replaces the Pint

by Jack Steel

Coke is boring. Look at the bad music, bad movies, and bad art that are made on it. It kills ideas. Dealers may as well cut their shit with oatmeal and charge a week's wages for it. Yeah, let's talk shit all night, try vainly to have sex with anyone who has eyes, and make big plans with big cunts who, in normal circumstances, you would move house to avoid. What else is there to do?

OK, MDMA powder and Ecstasy are all right, but can you really live with yourself the day after, when you've been hugging that slightly attractive person that you work with but actually wish you'd never swapped numbers with or, Jesus, tongue-kissed?

Thankfully, a lot of rave children (read: rich hardcore psychedelic drug fiends) have started families, moved to the country, and started to dole out their best drugs to pay for their kids' day care. They call it the new liquid acid and, to proles

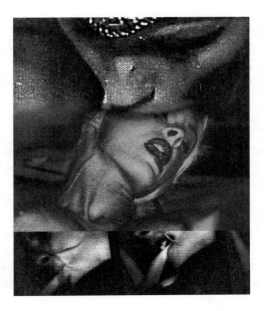

like me, it's the best drug in the world. If you're in the know, there's a network of people all over the world who sell cute little bottles of this stuff. It costs from £150 to £200 a bottle, which contains around 150 micrograms of pure drug magic. Depending on how hardcore you are, and how much you give away to people at parties, it can easily last you six months. The Leftfield electronic crowd is getting into it (the promo stickers for the new Aphex album say, "Come on you cunt let's have some Aphex acid") and there's always two or three people at the party with some.

This may be the first time in Britain's history that the country has drugs made by people who care—perfectionists who want to provide the best possible high. The result is essentially the stuff Albert Hofmann was originally working with when he invented acid by accident back in 1938. Not the 1960s blotter, mass-manufactured acid that beardy weirdys like Ginsberg and the like popularized. This is the stuff that, before it was passionately banned, was used in the '50s to cure alcoholism (nice try), and to encourage soldiers to fight better in the '60s.

After soldiers started staring at their hands for three hours at a time, the dream turned sour. The authorities were shit-scared and clamped down on acid, which made the kids think it was even better than it actually was. It was suits versus college kids with flowers on their faces, and everybody thought they were fighting for freedom or something. Again, it was just drugs. As all this stuff happened, everybody wanted a piece of the pie and acid became mass-produced. The criminal element got involved more heavily and we were left with awful, life-wrecking, strychnine-flavored acid that you can only do four times in your life without going completely fucking wrong.

But this stuff is ridiculous. You dab two square centimeters of it onto your hand, lick it off, and get a nice peppermint taste. The guy we got our most recent batch from told me, "The stuff that's in those bottles, that's from California. The Dead just bought into a huge fucking batch of it. There was a huge amount made (in the '60s) which was never accounted for. The cops raided places and took so much in and people said, 'That's how much we produced,' but there was other stuff stored in other places and this is it, man." He continued like the drug expert guy from the movie *Withnail and I*: "You know you're fucked, you know you're having a great time and you're fucked but you can still go, 'All right, I've got to go and deal with something now,' and you can go and deal with it. You can go to the bar and you can walk around and not get your head kicked in by some scally in an alleyway, because you can still keep a hold of what's going on instead of being some gibbering wreck in a corner." Like regular acid, this stuff takes twenty minutes to affect you, but it does so in such a sly way that you're tempted to take another drop for good measure just before it kicks in. And then you're on fire. The person who first gave it to me described it as sheer "digital bliss" and that sums it up perfectly.

If you do a normal dose (one sizeable drop), you come up for about four hours. The rest is pretty cool and intense as well. I cannot stress enough, however, how much the coming-up process is sheer, hilarious bliss. You feel like you're the star of every single Coca-Cola advert ever made, you feel drenched in sunshine, and you cannot help but laugh your leg off at even the grimmest of subjects. Most importantly, though, you can maintain control of your faculties, even when your skin feels like it's glowing under a Hollywood halogen lamp in a Steven Spielberg movie (of which you are the star).

The main production center for this fantastic invention is on the west coast of the United States, but there's leagues of acid freaks who operate underground acid labs in England, Amsterdam, Israel, and South Africa, and, crucially, make shit-loads of money selling it. A drug dealer is a drug dealer, after all. As our lad said, "If you think about it, one gram of powder (crystal LSD 25) will make up, errmm, 100 bottles at 150 micrograms, so if you've got a kilo you've got an income for life. A gram of LSD 25 crystals is worth thousands. It makes gold and coke seem like nothing. If they've been running a lab for six months, they might have produced a couple of kilos of LSD, which is enough to retire on."

**From Vol. 4, No. 7,
August-September 1997

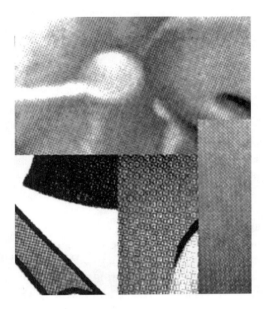

CONFESSIONS
OF A SERIAL KILLER

by the Minority

I killed two people.

The second died in New York recently from a heroin overdose. The three days that followed were painful, not so much over her death (we weren't that close) but over my role in her death. I introduced her to the needle. I taught her how to use a syringe, and repeatedly injected her with smack (at her request, mind you) until she learned how to do it herself. Years later, she died alone with a needle in her arm.

In November 1994 (about three months after I got clean), the closest homeboy I've ever had, P., overdosed and died. He was the first person I killed. He, too, had been introduced to heroin and taught how to use the needle by me. His death made me cry like a baby and the only thing that gave me solace was my mom's embrace. I was devastated, pure and simple. Overcome by anguish, dumped by my girlfriend, and filled with chemical imbalances from years of hardcore addiction, I went into a depression of such unparalleled lows that suicide seemed like my only friend. I later found out most drug addicts go into deep depressions long after they're clean because two-thirds of the drugs, like Valium (which I also consumed in mass quantities), are stored in your fatty cells and slowly released into your bloodstream for years after you stop ingesting.

My soul was like an open sore that without smack took in all emotions full-on. With time, however, my strength returned. I managed to get over his death, and I reached my present, somewhat retarded form of normalcy. In a space of about two and a half years, five other people I knew died from junk-related deals. With each individual case, I grew stronger in resisting the pain.

Junkies die; it's what they're best at, and it's an inevitable end because heroin addiction is merely a slow form of suicide. Clean junkies would best be described as an endangered species.

Every time another friend died, I became more and more brutalized. You numb yourself, repress emotions, and your attitude is, "They died. It's inevitable. Too bad for their families, but me, I got lucky." During the last couple of years, I had this callous "they were goin' down anyhow" attitude that helped me get through successive downs.

I've fallen into about six heroin comas/overdoses during my time of active using and shared-needle use. But whether it was the medics shooting adrenaline into me or divine intervention, I survived (HIV-less, no less). After the grim New York incident, the ramifications of my past hit me. I sat in my house alone, filled with a feeling of impending doom, with all of my past actions and their results to keep me company. The issues of responsibility and guilt ran through my mind. Am I a murderer? Was it manslaughter, or am I innocent in all of this? For the first time since I got clean, a hard, inward investigation ensued on this topic of murder.

I went back in time six years and transplanted myself into my ghetto apartment above that needle exchange, which was like an oasis in the desert. A place where the harsh, blunt needles that couldn't even break the remembrance of a being could be traded in for shiny, beautiful new spikes. An efficient tool employed by technicians around the world that kills or gives life, depending on who's wielding it.

It was summer, it was hot, and there was a lot of heroin. Surrounded by my "friends," all of us were fiending the deadly powder. They were smoking it; we were shooting it. "You really oughta try shooting it," I remember saying. "It's way more economical, and the high is about fifty times more intense." She said she was afraid because she had never shot before and needles scare her. After that I did it for her. When I look back on that time, I see myself saying, "It's time to die; let me show you how." I cooked an ample amount of dope up in a spoon and then took off my leather belt and strapped it around her arm. When the vein was bulging, I inserted the spike with surgical precision, pulled back on the plunger, saw a stream of thin, highly pressured blood fill the syringe, and then gently pushed the plunger as far as it could go. Her eyes started closing, and the words "that's nice" stumbled out of her mouth. She felt the gloriously deceptive, satanic rush like a sledgehammer to her head and she converted to the needle then and there.

That is the link between introduction to and eventual death from—two cases where an irrefutable causal connection was made that ultimately killed. Unfortunately, I'll have to deal with this situation again in the future. I need resolution, something conclusive, an answer to the dilemma that's messing with my mind. I need to know how to feel the next time this happens, because I'm afraid. The repression of responsibility is the path of least resistance, yet righteousness lies in the acceptance of guilt. In the future, do I suffer my emotions or play the tough guy?

The callous attitude is championed by many a recovering addict. The "not your fault" mentality is accepted in recovery programs, and it is definitely the easiest way to deal with the problem. Much to the dismay of my recovering peers, I'm starting to doubt this solution to blame. "You can't take responsibility for this," they would tell me. "They were destined to die, and if you hadn't introduced them to the smack and syringe, someone else would have." Neil Young summed it up in "The Needle and The Damage Done" with the words "every junkie's like a setting sun."

The gentleman who coined the term "brutalized" said that guilt can be seen in two ways. When you *feel* guilt, remorse comes into play. You know you did wrong and wish you could repair it. On the other hand, you can *be* guilty without *feeling* guilty: "I did it, but I had my reasons. And, really, I'm not guilty."

Now that I'm admitting the connection, the responsibility makes me suicidal. I am responsible for their deaths, and I'm starting to feel like a serial killer. All I can do now is hope to stay clean, never introduce anyone to a syringe again, and help other addicts recover the best I know how.

In order to continue my days with some kind of sanity, I know I will act like a Social Darwinist and keep repeating to myself that only the strong will survive, while the weak will perish. But this is a façade of necessity: Deep down I know what I've done. I've admitted it here. But the truth is more than hard to take; it's impossible to take. Feeling like a serial killer has been the result of my actions, and the message here is simple: Turn people on to hard drugs, and they'll eventually die. And if you get clean and face up to yourself, their deaths will haunt you till the day you die.

**From Vol. 3, No. 10, October 1996

for a walk and knew better breathe it in and out.
interfere with them.
Pros: Punk.
OXIDE
Cons: Zits, brain damage, lung cancer,
ughing gas.
blindness, serious liver and kidney
utiously inhale it. Comes in
nk.
kes you laugh your

ur stomach
hurt the
Good
ting
of

from underneath and inhale it v
tube. Some shoot it.
Pros: Perfect for slamming all
at a No Means No show and
returning to the bar to beat eve
up.
Cons: You can feel your b
total exhaustion at te
the next morning
you still can't s
Going for
without
Too
C r y
M
a y

At
enty
kinds.
used as
alzheimers
ployed in mar-
nseling, this drug
d in Texas and soon

brain s
out your m
forever.
Jim's comment
watched a friend
his nice old Volvo w
under the influence of C

The illustration Jim did for the original article.

THE VICE GUIDE TO DRUGS

by Jim Woodring and VICE staff

We don't know if it's because he's been hallucinating since age six or because he can see thirty-four more colors that anyone else, but the art of cartoonist Jim Woodring perfectly depicts that strange dimension only drug users can understand. If you're not satisfied with his hallucinatory comic art and want to experience that world firsthand, please use this guide with moderation or you'll became a bug-eyed junkie who spends all afternoon trying to get up off the ground to mug old ladies. Here we go . . .

Marijuana
What: Ganja, dope, wacky-tabacky, Bob Hope, kaya, weed, sensi, Mary Jane, grass, bud, etc. We'll also include hash and oil in this category, since they're just more intense versions.
How: Roll up the Buddha.
Pros: The world is funny, and if you smoke enough, you become infertile.

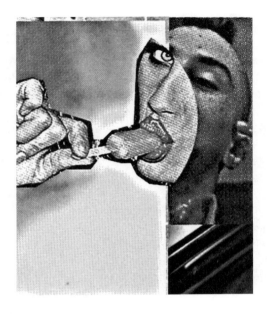

Cons: Potheads sleep all day, their short-term memory is shot, and they never get anything done. A gram costing $15 only makes three quality joints.

Jim's comment: $15 for a gram of pot?! That's an outrage.

Alcohol

What: Made from rotten things.

How: Drink booze.

Cons: Hangovers and inability to socialize or function sober. Addiction to it is brutally common and means severe liver damage with no life.

Jim's comment: Alcohol was the bane of my existence for ten years. I cannot bear to remember the things I did in those days. I repent again and again, and proffer my heartfelt apologies to everyone who ever had the misfortune to cross paths with the arrogant, loud-mouthed fuckhead, the drunk me. I could write a book. Alcohol is the worst monster I ever had in my life. I would have no family, no life, no nothing today if I hadn't been able to give it up.

Magic Mushrooms

What: Psilocybin, shrooms. Tough to legislate against because they grow out of the ground and are really easy to come by in places like the suburbs of Washington State (all that fertilizer in the housing complex lawns paid off).

How: Eat them in pizza or in peanut butter because they taste gross. Should only be taken at your friend's cottage.

Pros: The insight of acid without the urban edge.

Cons: They make your tummy feel funny (so rub it) and you may bad-trip, but the chances are way lower than with acid. They look exactly like the poisonous ones.

Jim's comment: In 1978 I was able to observe the town of Palenque, Mexico, where the mushrooms grew in the fields surrounding the ruins. And the police would literally turn their back on the tourists crawling up Main Street at high noon, painted in mud like Mayan warriors and gasping out incantations. Elsewhere in Mexico those cops would have whisked them off to the malodoro before you could say "Pedro Guggenheim." It was as if the police felt the mushrooms were taking the people for a walk and knew better than to interfere with them.

Nitrous Oxide

What: Laughing gas.

How: Cautiously inhale it. Comes in a big tank.

Pros: Makes you laugh your head off.

Cons: Your stomach muscles hurt the next day. Good luck getting hold of some.

Ecstasy

What: E. At least twenty different kinds. Once used as a cure for Alzheimer's and employed in marriage counseling, this drug originated in Texas and soon took over the UK rave scene. Contains speed, which prevents the annoying "hippie factor" of most other hallucinogens, and has a granular strain similar to MDS from the '80s. The best ones are Spectra and Snowball, and (like all varieties) should never be taken with beer or cocaine. You can't really get good stuff anymore.

How: Pill.

Pros: A euphoric sexy feeling enhanced by inhaling Vicks VapoRub and dancing. Makes you feel really horny.

Cons: Can cost up to $40. Can drain your spinal fluid until you snap in the wind like a twig. Stay away from the herbal stuff; it made two people we know go completely insane forever.

Jim's comment: I like to talk with people who are high on it because they say the most unintentionally revealing things about themselves, and I come away feeling better.

Glue

What: Used for putting model planes together.

How: Put some into a paper bag and breathe it in and out.

Pros: Punk.

Cons: Zits, brain damage, lung cancer, blindness, serious liver and kidney damage, and severe headaches.

Jim's comment: For a few weeks in my late teens, I was acquainted with a small band of pathetic glue and spray-paint sniffers who lived in an abandoned trailer and who would literally cry early in the morning because they were so sad and ashamed that their lives had become so wretched. They knew the glue was injuring their minds; they could feel their brains dying, and it frightened them. They were just little boys, sixteen and seventeen, desperate to stop, but they couldn't. Finally one of them, Kenny, hanged himself in a coffee-shop rest room, and I terminated my association with the others forthwith.

Speed

What: Amphetamine sulphate, billywhizz. Crack version is called crystal meth, which is originally from Hawaii and took over the west coast in the 1970s.
How: Put it on aluminum foil, light it from underneath, and inhale it with a tube. Some shoot it.
Pros: Perfect for slamming all night at a NoMeansNo show and then returning to the bar to beat everyone up.
Cons: You can feel your body's total exhaustion at 10 the next morning, but you still can't sleep. Going for a few days without sleep. Too much crystal meth and your brain spills out of your mouth forever.
Jim's comment: I watched a friend ruin his nice old Volvo, while under the influence of crystal meth, by writing poetry on the doors and hood in whiteout. It was terrible poetry too, poetry so bad that he had to sell the car.

Mescaline

What: Well, ideally it's peyote from the cactus plant and gets you nailed off your trolley for three days like Don Quixote, but by the time you get it, it's horse tranquilizer. We're lumping this in with PCP and angel dust because it's all the same now.
How: Pour a third of a cap ($3 worth).
Pros: It's like being a highly coordinated, drunk rocket scientist. No bad trips.
Cons: Too much means lying in your puke all night. Long-term brain damage is uncertain, but you wouldn't believe the kinds of things I forget.
Jim's comment: Mescaline is personality plus.

Ketamine (a.k.a. Special K)

What: Cat tranquilizer. Used almost exclusively by gay men.
How: Pour the powder into your beer.
Pros: See mescaline description and take it down a notch.
Cons: Dizziness. As with mescaline, it makes you feel stupid after a while.
Jim's comment: The people I know who use it skin-pop it and describe incredible

carnival ride–like experiences. Observed effects include psychic abilities, loud affirmative bleating, and immobility.

GHB
What: Gamma hydroxybutyrate. Nobody knows yet. Related to Rohypnol, the date-rape drug.
How: Drink it. Takes about five minutes to hit you. Be sure to have no more than half a vial for your first time.
Pros: Easy to synthesize and very available. It's like your blood is replaced with honey, and unlike E, every facet of intercourse is improved 1000 percent.
Cons: Like most drugs (exceptions include acid and shrooms), this is dangerous when mixed with booze. If you take too much, you will pass out (as most people end up doing) and forget everything you did, which is why jocks like it so much. My friend broke a vial in his pocket while dancing, and it melted his pager.

Amyl Nitrate
What: Poppers. Originally used to stop heart attacks. Hunter S. Thompson's favorite.
How: Snort it or take the pills. For the best orgasm of your life, snort a little as you cum. But time it well because the rush only lasts one minute.
Pros: So dangerous it's cool.
Cons: Can induce spasm and seizures, which look really uncool. Can dry out your contact lenses and contract your eyes so bad they fall out of your head.
Jim's comment: I once had this offered to me on a train by a terrifying cross-eyed muscle man. He actually propositioned me in front of a pair of nuns! Me! What kind of drug appeals to someone who would do that? Brrr!

Downers
What: Include Mandrax, Mogadon, Librium, Valium, Largactil, Quaaludes, Scooby snacks. Huge with suburban housewives in the 1950s.
How: Take the pills.
Pros: Makes coming down off speed and crack a little less depressing. Heaviest with booze. A good one is the heroin substitute, DF118.
Cons: They bum you out. Your friends are goth.
Jim's comment: My experiences with downers consist of the bemused observation that they appeal primarily to women, and a single incident of recreational ingestion at the beach which resulted in my nearly drowning and having to be rescued by a lifeguard, whereupon I insulted him until he slugged me in the face. And I didn't mind a bit.

Pam
What: Cooking spray.

How: Spray it into one of those big milk bags and inhale it when the bag is full. The gases play with your heart rate, thereby restricting the amount of oxygen that gets to your brain.

Pros: You feel like an excited retard and say, "ANGANGANGANGANGANG!" for about thirty seconds while drool pours down your face. Sometimes you even hallucinate.

Cons: So little oxygen in your brain that you die.

Jim's comment: I was once forced to do this by a bunch of hillbillies. It was a real nightmare all the way around. Fortunately, my hosts loved the hideous stuff so much that they sucked up huge blasts of it, which rendered them completely inert. As soon as they were too poisoned to move, I rolled away as fast as I could. Anyone who could get to like that shit deserves it.

Cocaine

What: Blow, snow, Snow White, Charlie, charge. Crack, the harshest form of blow, is actually a shitty version of freebase (coke and baking soda cooked into rock form). Speedballs (coke and heroin) feel great but tend to kill cool people.

How: Most snort, some smoke, and a few shoot.

Pros: You are in a great mood, which is perfect for people who hate themselves. Freebasing (smoking it) is the heaviest and deadliest.

Cons: Incredibly expensive ($100 a gram) and highly addictive. Long-term abuse can blow your nasal cavities so bad that you need steel reinforcements. It also makes your face fat and gives you glassy eyes. The comedown from crack is suicidal.

Jim's comment: I was horrified to discover at a teen blast that the girl whom I regarded as the smartest, most personable, and beautiful girl in my high school, would do the most debased and sickening things for cocaine. Ugh. Memory, stop.

Acid

What: LSD, doses, trips, hits. Includes almost extinct species like microdot. Created during Vietnam and used to replicate insanity. Incredibly powerful stimulator of all five senses.

How: Small pill or a square of paper for your tongue. With liquid acid, place one drop on a sugar cube or directly into eye for immediate hallucination. Hendrix used to put it in his headband and let the drug soak into his skin.

Pros: Hyperawareness and insight into who you are and exactly how the universe works.

Cons: Relinquishes the suspension-of-disbelief powers that make life manageable. If you're older than fifteen and know the world is not a beautiful place, bad-tripping is highly possible (see *Jacob's Ladder*). Some people snap and stay like that forever.

Jim's comment: LSD was the first drug I ever took. I was eighteen, virginal, psychotically wound up, and repressed. A total stranger to myself and the rolling mess inside of me. I had never smoked a cigarette, never broken a law, never had a beer. On a whim I took an eight-way red barrel stuffed with strychnine and speed and whatever other harshifiers it took to create "sunshine." Then I walked out into the street and into the single worst experience of my life to date, hands down, by a country mile. It changed my life for the better, though.

Heroin
What: Smack, H, horse, jazz, dope. A derivative of opium (the drug that destroyed China), it is the big-daddy king of drugs. Killed more young aspiring rock stars this year than in any previous decade.
How: Smoke it (chase the dragon), snort it, skin-pop (shooting it into your flesh but not your veins). Mainline (inject directly into your veins) for the best results.
Pros: Temporarily live life anxiety- and stress-free, focus clearly and directly on your work. Great rush. Gives you a feeling of immortality until you find yourself pissing and shitting your pants and committing crimes to support your habit. Prevents aging.
Cons: Death. After a while, your dosage only keeps you from being junk sick. Nearly impossible to quit. Withdrawal symptoms include the feeling of having third-degree burns all over your body.
Jim's comment: It never ceases to amaze me that people will buy dope of completely unknown origin and composition from some street stranger and jam it right into their blood.

Cigarettes
What: Smokes, cancer sticks, fags, butts. Nicotine, made from tobacco plant.
How: You know.
Pros: ?
Cons: Kills more people than all the other drugs combined. The most addictive drug and the hardest to quit. You have to live with the fact that you're killing yourself so some executive can make the payments on his Saturn. Cigarette companies are hired by the devil to commit evil acts like recruiting Third-World kids—very tacky.
Jim's comment: Goats love to eat cigarettes so much that they ask for them by name.

THE BEST HIGH
IS A GOVERNMENT HIGH

How 68 Percent of the Population Circumvents the Drug War

by Jessica Kinfinboogler

After being prescribed pills for everything from a bad mood to the simplest of common colds, the entire globe is now under the shadow of drug-resistant bacteria strains that make the black plague look like a bucket of cheesecake. Add to this happy pills replacing psychiatry and you've got preteen Liza Minnellis passing out on the shitter after a bad hair day.

Patients today see all the paraphernalia at the clinic as elaborate menus for synthetic heroin, chill pills, and renamed Quaaludes. And with ads that have phrases like, "Ask your doctor what's right for you," there can be no doubt we live in a society where you decide how high you're going to get and when.

The fact that the shittiest actors (Judy, Liza, the King) become the biggest pill-

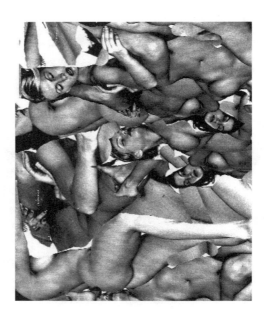

poppers shows how easy it is for Americans to break the law and abuse drugs (something we would never condone—ever). All they need is the right sob story and a health plan. Considering that clinics make their profit based on how many people they can shuffle through in one hour, Americans don't need to go into much detail.

NO PAIN, NO GAIN (Faking Doctors)

To get a groovy prescription, Joe Schmoe needs a groovy doctor. Outside the city centers, your average American finds small clinics that are unaffiliated with hospitals and consequently hurting for patients. Most likely the clinic has foreign-trained doctors who will go out of their way to keep patients coming back and will not have a problem prescribing narcotics. A no-lose way to score a prescription, however, is to visit a pharmacologist. These pill administrators will often give people a month's supply of Benzos within two minutes of arriving at their "session," with a note attached reminding them of their follow-up (mo' patients/hr = mo' money/hr).

The prescription is then commonly padded out and shopped around until a needy pharmacy cashes it in. The classic move with a prescription for ten Percocets or whatever is to add on a zero, changing it to 100. That's called "Perc-ing right along." Again, the only pharmacies that are going to go along with this are a bit out of the city and in need of regular customers. Plus in some cities, prescriptions are in triplicate, forcing Americans on day trips to places where pharmacists can't check records with the clinic/doctor before filling up a pillowcase. Of course, any Narcotics Anonymous meeting will prove this is just greasy kids' stuff.

CRUSH GROOVE

"If they snort something they get, like, 55 percent of it. Smoke it they get 65 percent. Shoot it they get 85 percent . . . but they have someone blow it up their ass, that's an easy 95 percent. Right now, I'm working on a device to blow drugs up my own ass."

—Nick, a prescription drug dealer.

When getting a prescription filled, most Yankees ask for capsules, but taking a pill orally is the least effective way for drugs to hit their system. Until Nick refines his method, kids will keep working the old standby. First, they take a McDonald's straw (they're oversized and exceptionally rigid) and, spreading their ass cheeks wide, have someone slowly drive this well-lubed puppy about a couple inches in. Then they scoop a hit into a normal-sized straw and slide that baby inside.

Most of this shit burns, so these poor kids are doing coke first to numb their asses. Then who knows what kind of perverted sex acts they're getting into?

AMPHETAMINES

Speed pills are terrible for you. They don't make them much anymore because all those diet-pill users brought speed manufacturers a ton of lawsuits. Ephedrine (one of the few left) and over-the-counter stuff so ineffective that users keep popping them until they lose track, and this can really get them into trouble. What makes pharmaceutical-grade speed pills different is that they fucking last forever—the hang time is insane. This also makes them easy to detect weeks later, in a drug test.

Ritalin (Methylphenidate)

Before prescribing meth to four million brats became a gazillion dollar industry, ADD/ADHD was medically referred to as "mild brain damage." Thanks to these little fuckers, though, your mom and dad got the best speed since fat people ruined Dexies for everyone. Kids with ADD are given speed to throw them into overdrive, thus burning them out. Now everyone is giving it a try.

Taken orally, Ritalin hits in about a half hour, peaks at two hours, and is gone in four, but nobody has time for that so they crush it. Because it wears off quickly, many doctors are into giving out Concerta, a long-lasting/higher-mg version of Ritalin with a time-release coating that vanishes when crushed.

All they need to hear: "I have a problem paying attention, and specifically with focusing on learning my lines which, as an actor, is detrimental."

Adderall (Dextroamphetamine and Amphetamine)

Four amphetamines combine together in this mighty pill. It's known as "add-er-all-up," because Dexie and everyone in her drug family comes over to fuck your system at once. It's intense. Being wired on Adderall, users can get, like, three days of work done in an hour whilst also figuring out the 4,000th digit of pi.

The pill hits hard enough that users don't need to snort it. After popping it, the next eight hours are in focused energy. If they get all worried about this electricity coursing through their system, most Americans chill out by remembering it's intended for six-year-olds. They have to keep in mind, however, that with amphetamines you are totally out there, which wears out the mind.

A day passes and they start seeing something out of the corner of their eye. Two days go by and they're full-on hallucinating. ER doctors can't tell the difference between amphetamine users and schizophrenics.

All they need to hear: Simple. "Ritalin/Concerta isn't working for me." This is the next notch up.

BENZODIAZAPINES

These are happy pill tranquilizers. They cut through anxiety to make people all groovy and relaxed. This sorta gives them that post-orgasm sense of everything being allllll-right. Additionally, nothing can faze them or make them too upset because they are totally at ease and open. Benzos are also said to be fantastic for coming down off a coke bender or any other gear-grinding activity that would normally keep them up all night.

Valium vs. Xanax (Benzodiazepine)

Valium and Xanax are two opposite types of the same drug, differentiated by how gradually they chill you out. With Valium, your aunt and uncle get it all right away in one big hit. The problem is, Valium doesn't last too long and just when they're getting into it, the buzz fades away. This is why people end up popping this again and again and that's just plain bad. Conversely, Xanax has a really long duration and doesn't hit as hard as Valium. Right between the above bookends is Serax. It hits pretty hard and lasts about four hours. Physicians are less cautious when writing it up than Valium or Xanax because it's rather low profile. Granted it takes a little while to kick in, but with pills there's a placebo effect so Uncle Ian is already kind of rocking when the high arrives.

All they need to hear: "I'm going through a very difficult breakup and, in addition to canceling the wedding, my novel's getting harshly edited, and it's all building up to the point where my work is suffering. I just need to get through this phase and my mother said Serax worked really well for her."

Klonopin (Benzodiazepine)

This is the pharmacologist's drug of choice and it's pretty much the same as Valium, so if your mum's friend Fran can't pull off the above routine she'll probably end up with this. Klonopin is also great because she can get 150 of them generic for five bucks on her insurance. Most pharmacologists would rather you take a daily dose than as needed, so Fran can expect a jackpot of low-mg pills. Klonopin scores high marks with the ladies for being so easy to sink in the hole.

All they need to hear: Klonopin is commonly prescribed for panic attacks. "Sometimes I'm on the subway and get these tremors which uncontrollably trigger these gigantic, deep breaths to the point I nearly black out. Shit, I even totally went blind from the panic, even though my eyes were wide open." Whoa.

Ambien (Not Benzodiazepine, but it still goes here because it's made to act like one)
Frank Pard, a thirty-four-year-old straight bartender, says of Ambien, "Sometimes I just want to get down on my knees and roll my tongue endlessly around the fleshy anus of the scientist that invented this winner." It's that popular. Ambien is a sleeping pill that acts like a Benzo, with a little extra wizardry sprinkled on top. Most drugs have a trail-off that leaves residual feelings. This one doesn't. The next day the user gets up free and clear, like nothing happened.

On top of that nice comes the spice, in that people can also trip on Ambien by fighting off the urge to sleep. Most people who take Ambien indulge in the crazy dreams that come along with it, but if they snort a couple of the ten-mg pills and decide to stay awake it's a hallucinogenic experience. Flipping Ambien with caffeine is, to quote Charlton Heston, "A madhouse! A MADHOUSE!"

All they need to hear: This is prescribed for short-term use. "I'm self-employed, needing a proper, regimented sleeping cycle that is being screwed up by my room-mates having guests over for the week. I've tried this before and it worked well."

NARCOTICS (a.k.a. The Good Shit)
Most doctors are extremely reluctant to give narcotics out and that's why they usually underdiagnose pain. The first thing they will give your neighbor is Tylenol 3, which is way more Tylenol than codeine. Pain is subjective, however, so it's really up to her.

Narcotics are evil as shit, because basically they're all synthetic heroin and the stronger they are, the better it feels. Percocet is the entry level into the serious narcotics, and from then on we're talking about a warm energy inside that feels better than an orgasm. That entire bad junkie shit follows suit. For example, it's near impossible to stop taking OxyContin and many people are just switching to H because it's cheaper and easier to obtain.

All they need to hear: The girl next door can avoid the Tylenol 3 trap by saying that she's allergic to codeine. If the doctor says, "Allergic?" then she says, "Yeah, I start getting hoarse and have trouble breathing. My throat swells up." That's guaranteed Percocet. The fear of malpractice gets the old pen out more than the fear of losing his license. All the latter means is waiting a few weeks while he petitions to get it back.

Percocet (Oxycodone)

If your average American citizen is in a shitty mood, has a hangover, doesn't feel like going out, or feels like going to bed; he takes a Percocet and everything's on. With Percocet it's three to four hours of a soft fuzzy feeling, the kind you feel through your fingertips. Pop a Perc and have a beer and that's it, sweetness all evening.

All they need to hear: Back pain, accident, intractable tooth pain, anything. Ideally something short-term and simple like they missed a step and fell, temporarily aggravating an old sports injury that has them in pain sitting down at the job.

Vicodin (Hydrocodone)

Junkies getting off heroin like Vike because it's the same thing. Vicodin is a serious-deal painkiller that is the next, stronger step up from Percs. Hence to score Vike, they have to be fronting that they are in some serious pain, the king of all serious pains being a tailbone injury. The thing with a broken tailbone is there's nothing you can do. They won't even bother with an x-ray because the diagnosis won't change. When Dr. Prescribeaway flips out the pad, junkies and anyone else that wants to write good songs fake the pain really hard until the Vicodin arrives.

All they need to hear: It doesn't matter if the tailbone is broken or not because there is no cast for your ass. Being carried in by friends helps, as does moaning.

OxyContin (Oxycodone)

Percocet has four to five mg of oxycodone, whereas OxyContin starts at ten mg and goes to 160. On average, one pill of Oxycontin is equivalent to sixteen Percocets. Hence, Oxy has a time-release coating that gradually releases the drug over time. Of course, as the *New York Times Magazine* pointed out, people have figured out that crushing the pill kills the time release and makes it just like smack. Like with Ritalin.

Doctors get away with overprescribing Oxy to dealers because it pays well, and what's the worst that can happen? They have to petition to get their license back? If Americans can't get a prescription, they don't worry about it. There are so many pharmacies getting ripped off that it's now on the street for a buck a mg.

All they need to hear: Oxycontin is getting prescribed huge for this weird, very iffy twentieth-century disease called fibromyalgia. Basically, it's a lot like chronic fatigue syndrome and often comes with the same ambiguous causes and symptoms. The condition means constant pain around the pressure points that has them immobilized to the point where they can't get out of bed. People who take Fibromyalgia seriously think it stems from diet—Whatever. *VICE* knows this "illness" was invented by housewives and computer programmers out to cop better painkillers. The doctor has no lab test or exam to prove or refute their story so they'll often just follow the trend.

Fentanyl (synthetic codeine)

The real holy grail of pharmaceuticals is a Fentanyl patch. Your old high school principal slaps that on and he is golden in a 2001 Star Baby way. It is thirty-six hours of a low-level, absolutely blissful existence that is life made painless. Nothing else can touch this.

Corrupt radiologists and anesthesiologists all over the country are dropping like flies because they don't realize one drop of Fentanyl is worth, like, a couple vials of anything else. That's why they get a patch. But even cut into thirds, a patch will fuck you to the point of puking. "Puking out of the biggest shit-eating grin the world has ever seen," insists an anonymous source.

All they need to hear: "I want to volunteer to work around cancer patients."

OTHER PILLS EVERYONE POPS . . .

Flexeril

Soma was the classic muscle relaxant, but we've moved on since those days and now the real deal is Flexeril. People tend to accumulate stress in their muscles and Flexeril just melts it away like a warm bubble bath. It has a mild addictive quality, but anything this good is going to be mildly addictive. Tracy, a fact-checker and researcher for a New York film company, told us, "On two Flexerils, I remember crawling up to the edge of my futon, looking down like half a foot and thinking, 'I can't make it—it's too much of a leap.' So I just sat there all day. It was fantastic."

All they need to hear: "A sports injury to my back gets really bad when I'm stressed out, to the point I just lie awake in bed, unable to sleep."

Quaaludes (Methaqualone)

This shit turns everyone you knew at college into trashed hookers. Dude, I'm serious. Americans do so much of it they end up rolling on the floor of some kid's loft, laughing their asses off because no one has the ability to change the channel. In order to stay semi-human they mix it with coke. This cuts through it a bit and allows them to walk around without bumping into walls. They lose all their motor skills until they can't feed themselves unless they coke up. The fact that no doctor will hook it up doesn't seem to be slowing things down. The pharmaceutical companies just unload this shit off to places like Russia for a profit. So it's available on the street and looks like a big Sweet Tart with a perforation down the center and can cost about $25.

Of course, there are much more popular downers out there. If your college buddies really want no coordination, Dilaudid (hydromorphone) is a motherfucker. If they do enough Dilaudid they get the exact same effect but stronger. With Quaaludes they're just a bit out of their mind, but without that fuzzy warm feeling, or that total-sense-of-loving feeling they get with the other stuff. Quaaludes just make them sloppy.

Failing the above, they might also get some Seconal, the old-school barbiturate from back in the '70s. These little red capsules look like candy and act like horse tranquilizers. Again, no motor skills, but this time there's a higher chance of passing out.

All they need to hear: "I have this pain, I want Dilaudid." And the doctor will be like, "yeah right." Instead they say, "I wouldn't mind Tylenol 3 but I really have a hard time breathing when I take that." His mind will automatically go to Percocet. Then they try the Percocet and they go back to the doctor and say, "It just doesn't cut it, is there anything else?"

Viagra

There is a full-on conspiracy to convince people that this pill doesn't work on girls. For real, half a hit of Viagra and their clitoris is poking out like ETs trying to phone home. Plus it doesn't react with too much and is just that little extra something on top that Americans adore.

A prescription's not necessary. Users can't do it too much or they'll get depressed over how weak their sex-style is normally. To save money most get the free samples every time they're out shopping for the other shit. Doctors are the puppets of the pharmaceutical companies, so people consider it trick or treat.
NOTE: Since AIDS kinda backfired, the government's been having a hard time reining in the homos. Hence, Viagra is engineered to be fatal when taken with amyl/butyl nitrate poppers.

All they need to hear: "My depression stems from the fact that I can't sustain a decent erection, which in turn fuels my depression, which makes it hard for me to get an erection."

From sea to shining sea. The people of the land of the free know what's going on. They are getting pill-trading groups together to cut down the visits and pump up the stockpile. They are laughing their heads off for no reason. Most importantly, they are completely fucking high.

Disclaimer: This article is intended as an exposé of the shocking complacency surrounding the ease with which an indeterminable number of people habitually abuse health care systems. It should not be seen as a guide to getting prescription drugs. VICE and the writer believe drug abuse hurts everyone, especially those who genuinely need prescription drugs, and do not condone any of these highly illegal scams.

**Vol. 5, No. 4, May 1998

A GUY WHO WAS ON ACID FOR A WHOLE YEAR

The Ups and Downs of Putting Your Brain in a Frying Pan

by Christi Bradnox

Lysergic acid diethylamide is at the very least a heavy trip. What started out as an accidental discovery by a Swiss research scientist way back in 1938 became the spearhead of the psychedelic age and gave everyone with five bucks the ability to visit the world of total and utter insanity for a day, guilt-free. For those of you who don't know, when we say insanity, we mean real crazy insanity. Not kooky mood insanity where you laugh a little longer at things and maybe put on a pair of orange pants. We're talking full-on arguing-with-plants-and-watching-people's-sweaters-do-animated-lessons-on-why-Canada-has-so-many-provinces crazy.

Acid takes you to the core of your very being and completely distorts your senses

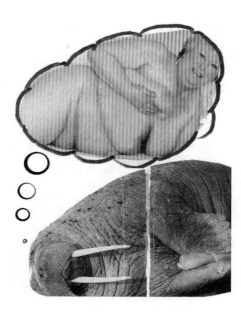

while you're down there. A bad trip can be as bad as watching your whole family die in a car crash, while a good trip can be a euphoric learning experience that changes you forever. The only problem with this drug is that by the time you're twenty years old, your brain has too much information in it and tripping becomes more like doing your taxes. You need ignorance and a lack of respect for society as a whole to enjoy that kind of self-annihilation, something us post-teens just no longer have.

The final time I ever did acid, I bad-tripped hard because a bunch of drunk jocks were teasing a Tim Horton's worker who I could tell came from Lebanon and was just trying to save up enough money to bring his kids over before they got drafted. A few years before that I could have been peaking right there next to them, asking the donut man how his nose got so big and then collapsing into hysteria. The other drawback is that if you do acid more than, say, thirteen times, your DNA will get restructured and you will be chemically unbalanced forever. Apparently, there is a price for that kind of profound introspection. Just go to any mental institution and ask the guy with the long hair how he got there. He'll go off on a tirade about how LSD was the size of a Life Saver back in the 1970s and how the acid today is shit because you only trip for a few days at the most.

One Ottawa, Canada, resident did so much acid that he didn't come down for a year. I don't care how many yuppies put on Gore-Tex and climb Mount Everest for the Discovery Channel. That's not adventure. Exploring the inside of your mind for one year straight with the intensity of an avalanche, now that's adventure. With this unsung hero about to disappear into hairstyling obscurity forever, *VICE* rented a Dodge Stratus and drove down to our nation's capital to meet the man behind the legend. What we found was a surprisingly sane goth hairstylist with black fingernails and a shy, yet confident, demeanor well beyond his twenty-five years. Though Darren Jessup (that's his name) still sees tracers if he moves his hands too fast, hates large crowds, and can only sleep in two-hour intervals, he is at peace with the world.

VICE: How much acid did you have to do for your trip to last a whole year?
Darren: On October 10, 1993, I took a thousand of crystal, liquefied it, and put it on a sheet of 100. I took three and a half, so I was on about fifty hits. I was feeling okay at first; it was intense. But then I started having sex and lost my erection. I went impotent and realized how high I was and then started freaking out. I went over to my neighbor's room yelling, "I'm too high! I'm too high!"

What was that like?
The only way I can describe it is that I *became* LSD—mentally, physically, everything. After the trip started and I realized I was way too high, I went to get some air. I walked about twenty feet from my house and was completely lost so I just kept going. It was in Victoria and there's this place called the Dead Zone. It's this park with all these tombstones in it. I stayed there for about eight hours trying to come down a bit, but I was just getting more and more anxious. Even after I got home, I was still feeling way too intense, way too high, so I decided I'd better get to the hospital. I asked them to give me something to bring me down. This lady checked my pulse and then she called in the other doctors and turned me face-down in a bed and strapped me in.

Did you tell them you were on acid?
Yeah. Then they put me on this heart machine and it was going, "beep-beep-beep," really fast and then I could hear, "beeeeep." There was a really intense pain in my chest and I started praying to God. I'm not religious and all, but right then I was all like, "Jesus, I'm sorry for all my sins and whatever," because I was truly afraid. They kept me there for about twelve hours after that until I came down a little. Then I went home and tried to sleep for about three days. It was the ultimate high. You can't be any higher than I was without being dead.

You did die.
I died again about three weeks after that in this tiny little hotel room in Toronto. It was like twelve feet by six feet and all I had was a mattress, and I stayed there for around ten months of my trip.

Anyways, there was this night where I smoked three joints with some of the people on my floor and died for almost two minutes. No pulse, no heartbeat, no nothing. I fell flat on my face and woke up bleeding. I had ripped the skin under my eyebrow open to the bone, and I had ripped part of my nose back. I didn't know I had had a fit. I felt fine. I just started having pains in my chest and I went to the washroom and I walked back to the living room and blacked out. When I came to, I felt like I'd just taken a nap. I thought I had just lay down, but everyone was like, "You're bleeding! You're bleeding!"

A few days after that, things went really wrong. I went into psychosis. I started thinking about killing people all the time. I'm totally passive and I can't fight. I'm not violent at all. I'm not that type of person, but I started having violent thoughts. I'd look at people and imagine pulling out their throats and watching the blood pour down their chests. It turned me on.

It would be like a sexual pleasure to murder them?
Oh, yeah. Really intense urges. After I left Victoria and came to Toronto, I'd get on the subway or streetcar and watch people's heads and faces melt and I could see what their skulls looked like underneath. Sometimes I still enjoy it. I saw this book two Christmases ago. It was a book on all these different murder scenes from around the world, and I got a total erection. It was stimulating.

So would you say that acid has put you in a situation where you could be a killer?
Maybe. I understand the mentality now. How they feel, why they do it. I'm a good person and I know that it's wrong to do something like that to someone, but my urges were so strong. I thought about it all the time. And I actually did get into one violent situation after that. I got into this guy's car in Victoria with my ex, who was my best friend. The guy was really drunk and he drove into a wall doing about seventy, and my head went through the windshield. I had a hold of the door with my arm, and I kicked the door open. I had a baseball hat on and it protected me from the glass. My friend's nose was bleeding. Anyway, I kicked through this guy's window and kicked him in the face and dragged him out by the face and pounded him a few times. I robbed him of like $400. Then the cops came and I asked them if I'd get in trouble for the broken window, but they were like, "What window?" That was the only time when I went completely ballistic for no reason, and I kind of impressed myself. I kept thinking about it because I was always bugged as a kid and was seen as king of the wimps at school.

Were all your acid trips this violent?
Not in the beginning. All my trips were beautiful. I've had amazing acid experiences. If I could still do it, I probably would, but there's no way now. I'm too fried.

Now, your father was an alcoholic asshole who made you and your mother's lives a living hell. You grew up shy with low self-esteem, and today, though your brain is a bit

frazzled, you seem to have a fairly confident composure. Do you think all this psychotic violence was the LSD forcing you to deal with your anger toward your father?

Yep. I started doing acid when I was fifteen, and I think it was to get away from the reality of my family. By the time I was seventeen, I was doing it every day. The irony is I first did acid to get away from that stuff, but with that yearlong trip I ended up having to confront every fear in my life head-on.

Do you think acid is good?

I did it too much in extremes, but I think it's mind-expanding for sure, definitely. Because I had no self-confidence at that point in my life, before I had this experience, everyone talked *at* me. They didn't talk *to* me, so I had totally different personalities for everybody. I had no mind of my own. Since that experience I can deal with my childhood and I can articulate myself to just about anybody, you know what I mean? I could sit down and talk to just about anybody without being intimidated.

Was that year you spent in the hotel room purely evil psychosis or were there flashes of sanity here and there?

There was never any sanity. But if things were good, I wouldn't feel too stoned. Other times I would have flashes where I was back in the second hour, you know what I mean? I would be sitting there and just rush so hard. I would be hallucinating so hard, like I was before the psychosis, and I would be getting the feeling that I had that night in the hospital all over again.

Was that kind of exciting?

No, I was scared. I just wanted it to go away and end.

So you just sat on a mattress for a year, watching patterns on the wall and occasionally eating a small plate of pasta. Did you ever get laid?

I don't know why—and I'm not being egotistical—but at that time because I was still crazy, all these women were coming on to me all the time. Like when I'd get on the subway or in a hotel. I couldn't even go on the street without women coming up to me and being like, "You wanna go for a beer?" I don't know why. I have no idea why. I'm not the greatest-looking guy in the world, but I was just crazy, and I think that women are sort of attracted to that. Or some women, anyway.

It's probably just that Toronto goth thing.

I don't know what it was, because I would try to talk to people and I wouldn't make any sense at all. Like, I felt like I had lost a part of me that was really important. I don't know if that makes sense.

How do you feel right now?

I'm always a tiny bit high, but it's nothing close to that year in Toronto. I don't have the taste in my mouth and I don't have the mental anguish—just some constant visuals. It's sort of printed itself permanently into my vision. When I haven't slept for twenty-four hours, it gets more intense, and when I smoke pot it gets really intense. I get really, really big hallucinations. I once hallucinated that Spiderman was in my living room.

Have you done acid since the yearlong trip?
No, I've been clean—off acid—for almost two years. After seven years your body cleans out everything. I can't smoke more than two puffs off a joint without getting really, really high. I can't drink more than half a beer without being drunk. I overdid it. I tried Ecstasy recently because I thought I was better, but I overdosed. I wasn't used to rushing and it freaked me out. I puked a lot and I was hallucinating and it took like a month to come down. That's when I realized my system was still screwed. A few days after that, this kid sold me PCP that was cut 1-5. He sold me a gram and told me it was E and I took the whole gram. I was drinking, and I couldn't see. I couldn't walk, and I told him to call me an ambulance, and they didn't and they just left me there.

I understand you're on some kind of weird welfare?
I'm on mental disability. I have what they call severe post-traumatic stress disorder. It's still hard to do stuff. Like some days I feel really good, and I could go to work and be totally normal. But then other days if I went to work there's no way I could be around the people I have to deal with.

Why did you go public with your one-year-long acid trip?
I don't tell too many people that I was psychotic. It's not the kind of thing when you're sitting next to someone that you'd ramble on about, you know? "Yeah, I thought about mutilating people." You don't really want to hear about that if you're the guy sitting there.

I think a lot of people want to hear about that.
Well, that's why I told you.

ROCK AND ROLL

ILLUSTRATIONS BY BRIAN DEGRAW UNLESS OTHERWISE SPECIFIED

**Vol 7, No. 5, June 2000
Updated June 11, 2003

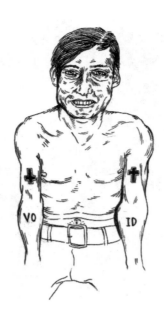

LORDS OF THE DANCE

VICE and the Mayor Fight to Keep Dancing Illegal in New York

by Gavin McInnes

Dancing is getting out of hand. Last year almost three people in America died from moshing (one died and two hurt themselves badly) and, in the movie *Footloose*, the mayor's daughter or something like that died in a car crash while listening to grunge. Even besides the deaths there are tons of other shitty things about the dancing movement. A lot of people do drugs who listen to dance music, and drugs equal death. Within the past few months lots of people have been taking GHB and alcohol and dying, and sometimes girls take it at dance bars and get all blobby and then they even get raped. The list goes on. People who go to dance clubs can have a bad trip if they mix E and coke.

What else? Sometimes a girl that wants her boyfriend to dance will, like, pull his arms and try to get him to the dance floor and he ends up looking like a total fag retard getting his arm away. That or he does the stupid shame dance where he's like, "Oh well, you got me." And what can people do to stop it? There are cases of

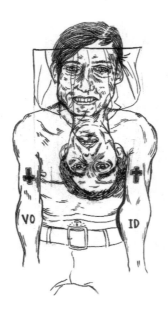

drunk drivers in Quebec smashing into people's legs, and there's always a few stoned guys laughing at the dance floor and making people feel self-conscious, but until the mayor of New York stepped up, nobody had the balls to really tackle the problem.

The point is that dancing is escalating to the point where it's starting to affect people's rights and freedoms and we are here to stop it. In 1997, Mayor Rudy Giuliani revived the Cabaret License Law, a zoning by-law which states that any for-profit establishment that sells alcohol and features music and dancing requires a cabaret license. Bloomberg, the present mayor, liked it so much he made this license even tougher to get, and without it dancing (more than three people moving to music) is completely illegal.

Some young upstarts have been ignoring this law and walking around pubs with their asses shaking from side to side like it's no big deal, but the mayor's crack team of dance enforcers is doing its best to snuff this out. "It makes for an embarrassing courtroom display," says the owner of a New York club called Brownies. "I've attended trials where you literally have this spoiled rich-kid lawyer shaking his ass from side to side saying, 'Yes, Your Honor. The accused was moving his posterior in this manner while Ms. Blah Blah and Mr. Blah Blah were next to him going like this.' It's ridiculous." Ridiculous maybe, but they laughed at Noah, too, pal!

Another group opposing the fight to not dance is the DLF (Dance Liberation Front), who are currently trying to raise popular consciousness through events like the recent Times Square "Twist-a-thon." Unfortunately, the list goes on. There are street parties called "Reclaim the Streets" that are constantly going on without proper permits and even the fucking New York Civil Liberties Union is threatening to interfere. Like the pro-lifers, we've been putting up with rebellions like this since forever, but we will always overcome. Back in 1926, the Cabaret License Law was created to control Harlem clubs that had white girls going up there to party and dance all night. This has led to the cabaret law being called "racist" in origin. How is that racist? Wouldn't you be concerned if a Negro was touching your daughter in her vagina all night? They could be from Africa and have AIDS for all you know.

In the salad days, even the performer had to have a license to play in the cabarets. This was designed to keep dancing and drug-promoting sluts like Billie Holiday out of the clubs. She had hers revoked when she was caught with heroin (thank God). A lot of people were really mad after Billie got banned, and the law received its most notorious blow soon after when hippie anarchist Frank Sinatra said it was "bullshit" and decided to have his own multiracial gatherings no matter what the police said.

The law was put on the back burner and bad shit like what we said in the opening paragraph continued for almost forty-five years . . . until now. The Antidance Movement is still threatened by potential mavericks like Kevin Bacon, but the mayor has a team above all teams to make sure there won't be no smart-ass superstars trying to "shut it down," as Chuck D would say.

The mayor's Social Club Task Force is a group of large menopausal women who randomly go from club to club putting potential dancing places on a blacklist called "The March Program." After that, all the police have to do is send an underage cadet in to get a beer. No matter what happens with the cadet, they can now bust the bar and, at the very least, fuck those dancing bastards out of a good $5,000 worth of Friday night income by clearing everyone out. Some, like Bob Bookman of the NY Nightlife Association, are quick to point out that bars bring in more revenue for the city than Yankee Stadium and Broadway and a bunch of other things combined but, like Steven Seagal, the Antidance Movement isn't concerned with bullshit like money. Nor are we hindered by red tape.

"There is no due process whatsoever," says the owner of Baby Jupiter, a bar we have had to close down several times for dancing. "The NYC liquor law is a 500-page book and it says whatever they want it to say. There's nothing you can do."

This attitude is not surprising. No matter how hard you fight for what is right, there will always be perverts like this to stand in your way. The secret is to get out there, to show the world that you care about the right to not have people dancing. Don't do it for yourself—do it for all the dead moshers, embarrassed boyfriends, and jealous people in wheelchairs out there. As long as the Cabaret License Law continues to flourish, we will eventually be able to wipe out the dance monsters that are making being alive a fucking joke.

Footloose Invades New York!

Kevin Bacon on New York's Antidance Crusade

VICE: One of the best things about New York now is the mayor. He has put a cap on all those dancing motherfuckers and made bars safe again. What do you think of the Cabaret License Law?
Kevin Bacon: I think it's absolutely insane. You know, when it comes to Giuliani, I like some of what he has done for New York, but this is just going too far.

There are no more dangerous types and drag queens. All the bums have been killed. It's like an urban paradise now. How can you deny that?
The city has never been cleaner and safer, but of course there's always gonna be some problems. This is just crazy. You know, I remember when I first came to New York, there was this bar called The Tap-A-Keg, which had a great jukebox. There wasn't really a dance floor, but you could just dance. You could just . . . *dance*. And then you could stop. It was great.

One of the things we here at the Antidance Movement are most concerned about is you coming to New York like you did in *Footloose* and getting everyone dancing again. You have to understand that this isn't some hick town with a power-hungry mayor who lost his daughter or whatever to a car crash. This is a place where people have been dying from dancing. Dying.
Yeah! Ren MacCormack will come running back and go head-to-head with Giuliani.

You can't do that.
Now that I've taken care of the preacher, I'll have a new dance-off. That's quite a concept.

**Vol. 6, No. 4, May 1999

PUNK MAGAZINE'S NOT DEAD

The Damned's Rat Scabies on Who Started It

by Rat Scabies

The Damned released "New Rose" in 1976. It was the first punk rock single ever, and every Pom from Tony Blackburn to Billy Connolly swears blind it was the beginning of the whole movement. Rat Scabies sees things differently. For him, Sid, and everyone else on welfare and glue, punk rock began with New York's Punk *magazine.*

When the Damned formed in late '75, we had little to listen to and even less to read. We didn't mix with the commercial music scene, and I'm afraid to say that being the first of a few can be a lonely place. We did have a local record store, though, where we hung out after we had been to sign on at the dole office and killed time before the pub opened.

The store was owned by a burly Frenchman who wore knee-high platform boots and had hair like a thatched roof. He carried one of the few decent traits of the French (as a race), which is a love of revolutionary thought and the willingness to throw a mischievous spanner into the works of whatever they can. This anarchistic "head" would import copies of *Punk* and rare Iggy Pop bootlegs into his shop while doing his best to subvert the staid Bob Dylan fans who made up the bulk of his customers. His assistants, meanwhile, were sniffing amyl nitrate and listening to Blue Öyster Cult way too loud (when isn't it?).

We, in turn, would collect our dole and go to his store to pore over *Punk*. We drooled at Deborah Harry's image as she, Tom Verlaine, and usually some Ramones, surrounded by scantily clad lovelies, wore cheap sunglasses, carried guns, and took part in what can only be described as post-hippie mondo photo stories seemingly written by one of the Chumbawamba monkeys. There were no records available from the NY scene at that time, so we had to try and guess what each band sounded like by the photos we saw and the song titles we read. Imagine the landslide of preconceptions when stepping between the bondage-induced, gunshot, bloodstained images of "Mutant Monster Beach Party" and eventually hearing the musical dignity of "Little Johnny Jewel."

We used to read *Punk* mostly for band gossip and the occasional erection-inducing pictures of Niagara. You see, the printed words on the page were mostly an irrelevant 3,500 miles away, but the subtext, the attitude, the state of mind, that was a very real connect—that, and the fact that it also had a lot of very cool cartoons. But more importantly, it brought to light the searing sociological criticisms that only comic book culture can achieve. We could see the artsy commercialism at work in the background—a desperate bid for intelligent sanctioning if you ask me, but what do I know? (Fuck art, let's fight.) But *Punk* did understand how to convey important (?) information so that the average glue-sniffer could understand it.

The Damned read *Punk* magazine and then wanted to go and scour Bleecker Bob's bootleg racks for hallowed recordings of the MC5. We looked at the ads and wanted to buy clothes at Trash and Vaudeville. We wanted to hang out in St. Mark's Place. But only because we saw it in *Punk*. We had found a kindred spirit in print, and more importantly we knew that the people at *Punk* would and could vilify, nauseate, and provide taste for the tasteless. A service which, coupled with an unhealthy hatred of disco, finally cemented our full literary respect.

**Vol. 5, No. 6, July-August 1998

THE TIME IS RIGHT TO FIGHT!

A Black Sid Vicious Is Destroying the System with His Music and Then with His Bare Hands

by Christi Bradnox

Punk rock's rebellion has come to mean everything from buying Manic Panic and cleaning people's windshields to singing power ballads with a bunch of jocks.

Or it had until Carl Crack came along and saved it. Instead of playing some old Eddie Cochran riffs really badly while singing about destroying the system, Carl Crack is making ambient-dub-noise-ruff-'n'-fast-Berlin-jungle-death-metal-mixes at 1/100,000th of a beat per minute and then going out and ripping down traffic signs with his bare hands. Carl Crack is more than just the screaming genius next to Alec Empire in the most punk rock band of all time, Atari Teenage Riot (ATR). Carl Crack is a black Sid Vicious.

At the airport in Germany when ATR were beginning their last tour (which also featured techno-rockers EC8OR and Shizuo), Empire noticed Carl wasn't around. He decided the best thing to do was to call Carl and tell him to come down to the airport. Carl replied, "All right." He showed up within minutes of the plane's departure with the clothes he was wearing (including a pair of karate pants) and nothing else. As if that wasn't punk rock enough, the man filled out his landing card by drawing a Rastafarian smoking a joint, and spent the rest of the time doing airplane food sculptures. Sure, this scared the shit out of everyone because they thought he had finally completely lost it, but they were just being wimps.

Alec Empire once told *VICE*, "I am an anarchist and I believe the system must be destroyed." That's all fine and great and everything, but destroying the system by making really fast techno music can take hundreds of years. Carl Crack is literally destroying the system. Not only does his debut solo album *Black Arc* smash the state by taking dub to unheard-of levels of noise pollution, the man is also physically dismantling the system. Before ATR played Montreal, I saw Carl ripping down a stop sign all by himself outside the club. I should have told some of the band members he was so close by, because they were starting to panic after not seeing him all day. He showed at the last minute, of course, pulling a cameo on stage with Shizuo (possibly the person the most scared of Carl in the world) which involved screaming "fuck" and punching Shizuo in the face (enabling Shizuo to keep repeating, "You zee? I told you he vaz after me. I told you I vasn't paranoid," for the rest of the tour).

When ATR came on, Carl grabbed a mic stand and sent it into the audience. You don't go see Atari Teenage Riot to check out their moves or see how "The Time Has Come to Fight" sounds live. You go to see the band to have your mind blown and if that means getting a mic stand right through it, then so be it. If you want safety, go see John Tesh.

After the show, Carl disappeared again and was discovered several hours later drinking whiskey in the security guard's office and typing on a computer. Carl was so ballsy and calm that the security guard assumed this drunken German black guy was coming in to replace him for the next shift. When the tour people showed up to take Carl back downstairs, the security guard was still asking Carl where he should put the keys.

Later at their Toronto show, the rest of the band was so inspired by Carl's dedication to punk rock they took off all their clothes and yelled, "Toronto sucks!" about a thousand times before walking off stage. Carl, of course, inadvertently outdid them all the next day by standing in the shower wearing everything he owned for several hours. Nobody knew where he was, but they were able to eventually locate him by following the caved-in ceilings and dripping walls of almost every room in the hotel.

Other Crackisms on the tour include: annihilating an entire hotel room in Boston right down to the ashtray (ooh, the Rolling Stones painted a door black? I'm so scared); kicking in every single monitor—cone by cone—at a Washington show; losing all his clothes every night during their stay in New York; smoking toilet paper spliffs regularly; thanking Alec Empire for a pair of new shoes and then flushing them down the toilet; throwing a full bottle of beer at Shizuo's head; and (my personal favorite) challenging Mike D to a dance competition at a chic New York party that included fancy names like the guys in REM (Carl goes, "Hey look, Michael Stipe is here"). Mike D was totally petrified as Carl stopped the music, put on one of his famous German jungle mix tapes and screamed, "Show me the new style, Mike D. Right now!" while gyrating his hips in a retarded, fish-like manner. After they were kicked out, the host noticed that someone had written, "To all the dumb shit bands—we write this in blood and piss in your veins," all over the bathroom in German.

Unlike the laid-back Malcolm McLaren dancing Sid around like a skinny marionette, the people behind the Digital Hardcore Recordings tour were petrified of Carl Crack. But they were too scared to put him on a plane alone. He could not be left unattended. They wanted him on medication, which was laughable. The system has tried to institutionalize Carl many times, and he's always like, "Fuck you." Just when his antics were on the verge of becoming predictable, Carl told tour organizers seeing his girlfriend Sarah "would probably make everything better." Within a month they were standing by a pool at a Hollywood hotel being wed. Carl was wearing a karate ensemble.

The only thing that could stop the chaos and destruction was love, man. True love. Sure we want to destroy the system, but at the end of the day it's all about love. I called Carl in Berlin to ask him about this intensely punk rock performance-art metaphor. I asked him about anarchy and how he used the marriage to show people you had to destroy the system to really love it. He said, "I remember it was a really sunny day," and hung up.

**Vol. 6, No. 6, July/August 1999
Updated June 11, 2003

ROCK 'N' ROLL'S MOTHER THERESA

Ronnie Spector Survives the Freak Phil and Shines Like a Little Nugget of Pure Gold

by Adam Gollner

Now dig this: Ronnie Spector has a new single coming out this summer (produced by Joey Ramone), and by all accounts it's hotter than fresh milk. Through an elaborate process of fête and cajolery, VICE managed to score a rare interview with the legendary former Ronettes vocalist and, yeah, we can assure you that the original tomato from Spanish Harlem is back—serious as a heart attack. Ronnie's just the coolest, daddy. She's been up and down, but now, as she puts it, "I wanna go out there and just rock 'n' roll."

"When I first started doing these songs, they were symphonies for the kids. It's been thirty-five years, and the kids are still singing 'Be My Baby.' It kinda blows me away. You know, the other night my son came up to me and said, 'Ma, Ken (this Chinese guy he plays tennis with) wants your autograph.' I said, 'What??!!' I'm always amazed at the age range of my fans—from six- to sixty-year-olds. I'm talking about babies, even. People bring their babies to the shows so I can touch them and give them good luck. I feel like a rock 'n' roll Mother Theresa, ya know? But it's a great feeling when they bring their babies up for me to just touch them and [singing] 'For every kiss you give me, I'll give you three.' It's something. I'm just in awe of my own longevity."

And so is everybody else, Ronnie. The bubbly, pint-sized bundle of energy on the other end of the line who's geysering these off-the-cuff gems is a quotable volcano. She's lived the wild life and she's still going strong. With the imminent release of her new single, it's clear that the velvet-clad tonsils behind chestnuts like "(The Best Part of) Breakin' Up" and "Walking in the Rain" are still the same quivering sticks of dynamite they used to be.

She Talks to Rainbows

"I love the new single," she says. "There's not so much music in it like in all my other stuff, like the wall of sound. I like the recordings because you hear more of my voice than you hear of the production, like with the, um, Phil stuff in the '60s." Ah, yes, the Phil Spector stuff. Back in the pre–British Invasion days, Ronnie and Phil were the quintessential rock 'n' roll couple: He produced and she performed the hot teenage pocket operas that still sound incredible today. Then he became a homicidal recluse and their marriage crumbled under the weight of her depression and his psychoses.

Joey Ramone, a noted Phil Spector acolyte, twiddled the knobs on "She Talks to Rainbows" (interestingly, when Phil produced the Ramones *End of the Century* LP, he forced them—at gunpoint—to put strings on the album). According to diminutive Ronnie, the sessions were a blast, except that "Joey is very tall so when he would direct me on certain things, my neck would hurt 'cause I'd have to look up at him all the time."

She recorded two Ramones tracks, as well as "Don't Worry Baby," the song Brian Wilson wrote for her (which Phil Spector forbade her to record). She also did a version of Johnny Thunders' "You Can't Put Your Arms Around a Memory."

"Johnny Thunders came and saw my shows in the '70s and he would just sit there and cry and then he would come backstage and cry some more. He was doing a little drugs back then, that boy, because I'd be like, 'What are you crying for, Johnny? It's OK, ya know?' But I didn't know about drugs because I was kinda sheltered in the '60s. I was married and living in California and never saw people and stuff."

I Wish I Never Saw the Sunshine

The reason she "never saw people and stuff" is because Phil kept her locked up in a mansion in the Hollywood hills. These days, understandably, Ronnie doesn't like to talk about that period of her life. Although they made beautiful music together (he used to call her his "little nugget of pure gold" and his "precious little music box"), after a couple of years, Phil joined the dark side and became an insanely evil musical genius.

Toward the end of their marriage he threatened to kill her several times, and on one occasion he told her that he'd had a solid gold coffin with a glass top made so that he could keep an eye on her after she was dead. He would confiscate her shoes so that she couldn't run away and banned all books and magazines from their house. For years, the couple's sole form of nightly entertainment consisted of watching *Citizen Kane* over and over again while Phil drew parallels between the film and his self-imposed isolation.

Eventually Phil's insane jealousy led him to have a life-sized inflatable doll made in his likeness. Whenever Ronnie went driving, the doll rode beside her in the passenger seat of her car. Ironically, at one point Phil's teeth turned green—not from jealousy, but from his addiction to crème de menthe. Following his lead, Ronnie also slipped into alcoholism, even though she'd been popping Sominex since the days when she'd stuff her bra with Kleenex and twist the night away at the Peppermint Lounge ("People used to call me Sputnik, because I never stopped orbiting"). After realizing that no pill can cure unhappiness, she turned to grape liqueur, and things continued in their downward spiral.

The consolation prize was that Phil was excellent in bed (she claims that he was able to bring her to orgasm with his voice alone), although there was always the pesky matter of his toupee. When removing it, he'd cover his head with acetone solvent to clean off the toupee glue. "The smell of that acetone could've killed a horse," Ronnie recalls, "but Phil tried to pretend it wasn't there." Adding to the absurdity, he sometimes wore a hat to bed because of his hang-up about being bald.

Thankfully, the tragicomic mishaps that peppered their relationship came to an end when Ronnie's mother finally came and took her away from Phil for good. But, as the saying goes, you gotta get down to get up. Ronnie's low point came the night she accidently spilled cognac all over her head, then lit a cigarette and burned all her hair off. She sees it as the start of her rebirth. "God made me burn my hair off because it was the only way He could make me understand that everything grows back."

She Came, She Saw, She Conquered

These days, Ronnie is happily married to her manager, with whom she has two children. "When I had my first kid, I was like, 'Whoa.' It was awesome. That's why I named him Austin, because it was the most awesome thing that ever happened to me. Of all the years that I've been on this earth, having my kids was the best thing that ever happened to me."

She's still battling away in the longest lawsuit in rock 'n' roll history (against Phil Spector and Allen Klein, the man who also screwed the Beatles and the Stones), but she's also trying to get other performers to stand up for their rights as artists. "I've made so many businessmen rich with my voice. All the former musicians and stars from the '60s are poor now. They're not even carpenters. They work at K-Mart. You get in a car and you hear their voices on the radio, but they have nothing. That's why I love Kill Rock Stars (the label that is releasing the single). That's what they did to the rock stars of the '60s and '70s; they killed those rock stars, man. They squashed them like bugs. For the people that were killed by rock 'n' roll and by being on the wrong label, Kill Rock Stars just says it all for me."

She also made a triumphant return to the stage at a Christmas party in New York where she was joined by Joey Ramone and longtime friend Keith Richards. "Seeing Keith was great. He had his cane, and he was walking towards me on stage, and we just fell into each other's arms after all these years and hugged and hugged for about two minutes—that's a long time if you think about it."

The Rolling Stones opened up for the Ronettes on their UK tour in 1963, and Ronnie returned the favor the following year. "When the Stones first came to New York, they didn't have anywhere to stay, so my mother let them stay at my house. We used to cook them bacon and eggs in the morning and take them to see shows at the Apollo. They slept on our living room floor and we gave them blankets."

As far as beehives, miniskirts, and mascara coming back into style, for Ronnie they never went away. "It blows my mind when girls say, 'Oh, Wonnie, I wear my eyeliner just like you.'"

Ronnie, everything you do blows our minds. Baby, we love you.

Update: Since we ran this article the Ramones album came out to moderate success, Joey died and, as this goes to press, Phil Spector is caught up in some huge imbroglio where a beautiful blond was found dead of a gunshot wound in his house.

**From Vol. 8, No. 1, February 2001

The original article featured Mortiis and his plastic surgeoned gnome face.

BLOOD, GUTS, AND FJORDS

A "Where Are They Now?" on the Bloodiest and Most Violent Music Scene of All Time

by Byron K.

Slathered in a mixture of his own blood and entrails oozing from an impaled cow's head, Mayhem's front man Maniac writhes around the stage wrapped in barbed wire. Dragging a Scandinavian surgical scalpel deep into his arm, he flings his head back as he barfs the lyrics to "Pure Fucking Armageddon." Black metal, the evilest music since Sy Snootles and the Max Rebo Band (Jabba the Hutt's in-house orchestra), may still be as disgusting as ever.

Mayhem's recent North American tour has proven that, while the inherent misanthropy of the genre persists, the new Norwegian sound has more to do with hip hop beats and stark, ambient moodscapes than it does with lightning-fast, inhumanly complex speed metal riffs. In bringing the art form to a new apex of evil, black metal has become a ridiculous parody. The guitar is now frowned upon because it is, according to some of the movement's founders, a "Negro instrument." Founders, by the way, who are now either dead or serving life sentences.

Black metal made its only real ripple in mass consciousness in the mid-'90s, when a series of filthy mcnasty deaths and suicides accompanied the burnings of dozens of churches in Norway, with every single person convicted having an established tie to the black metal scene.

Birth of a Vermin

For those still unfamiliar with the movement, Mayhem invented Norwegian black metal, the musical version of hell on Earth, in the mid-'80s. They were inspired by groups like Venom (a proto-evil band that theatrically embraced Satanic shlock, giving birth to extreme metal) and Bathory (a neo-Viking group who laid the foundations of Wagnerian epic metal and barbarian attire). The Mayhem clique made friends with a few other evil metal men and they started hanging out so much and being so negative and creepy together that it blossomed into a full-fledged musical movement.

Built on a foundation of pagan worship, Nazi ideology, and Norse supremacy, the oft-maligned genre featured Satanists dressed up in baroque, barbaric Viking garb with spiked maces, chain-mail ensembles and theatrical corpse-paint invoking the amoral god of war, Odin. Disdainful of frauds like Venom, they decided that merely singing about evil wasn't enough, and set about backing up their lyrics with deeds. Murder, destruction, rape, and general malaise all followed suit. "It kinda accumulated into extreme bands becoming extreme people and eventually doing extreme things," says *VICE* fave Mortiis, a pivotal member of the black metal scene who currently plays Casio-fueled electronic medieval merry-go-round shanties.

Before going solo, Mortiis played bass in Emperor, the other main force in the early black metal universe alongside Mayhem. After luring a Lillehammer man into the dark woods, Emperor's drummer Faust stabbed him thirty-seven times and left him face-down in the snow. With absolutely no motive to work with, police were unable to solve the crime until Faust's boasting came full circle. Completely without remorse today, Faust sits fuming in his Oslo cell, arguing that the crime was instinctual and not premeditated.

"Ninety percent of the evil black metalers from back in the early '90s were all teenagers, including myself," reflects an older, more mature Mortiis, having undergone plastic surgery to transform himself into the insanely wrinkled and wizened old gnome (complete with leprous witch nose and pointy elf ears) he is today. Why did he go under the knife? "Being generally fascinated by all things dark and dangerous, what else are you going to do?"

Maniacally Happy

While the music has changed markedly, mutilation has always been a constant in the black metal microcosm. "Mutilation is much like being in a very genuine touch with life itself. I feel extremely alive when I do it," explains our old pal Maniac. "Life is the most potent drug in the world actually. I don't ever do drugs at all. I do a lot more natural weird stuff, like self-inflicted pain and stuff like that." Despite barely surviving his latest botched suicide attempt a couple of months ago, Maniac sounds positively upbeat these days. "For me, it's just a question of seeing life from different perspectives. You see it from one view and you don't really enjoy it at all, and then you see it from another view and you really, really enjoy it. Now I hope to live till I'm about 150," he says bouncily.

Former Mayhem vocalist Dead didn't share Maniac's blithe optimism, unfortunately. Another mutilation aficionado, Dead slit both his wrists with a large butcher knife before blowing his brains onto the chesterfield. After finding his vocalist's dead body in the living room, bandmate Euronymous ended up making a stew out of his brain and crafting necklaces out of fragments of his skull.

Due to their utter preoccupation with death, a little murder between friends isn't that big a deal for black metalers. That's why Maniac doesn't resent the fact that Varg "Count Grishnackh" Vikernes (bass player on Mayhem's masterpiece *De Mysteriis Dom Sathanas*) killed Euronymous by stabbing him twenty-three times in the head and body, supposedly for shaming the scene by sporting a white sweater in public. "Varg? I'm not against him at all, even though he killed our guitarist," explains Maniac. "I wasn't very happy when Euronymous died, because he was one of my best friends, but in my eyes, Varg has released some very, very good, very strong albums."

The Future Is So Bright

VICE talked with Varg in his Norwegian prison cell (his mother relays e-mails to him), where he composes synthesizer music for his one-man band Burzum and writes theoretical texts about the future of mankind. According to this excerpt from a piece entitled "Civilisation," the world of tomorrow sounds like fun: "The elite will live like elves far away from the others with their 'magic' (technology), while the rest live like they did in the Middle-Ages, only with cloaks and some other (mostly natural) sciences. Writers like Tolkien actually never 'made up' anything, they just wrote stories based on memories from the past (memories from the blood)! Not necessarily from our world, our planet, but from the last planet we lived on (in the system of Sirius), when we were Gods."

In this utopia several new races will be bred, from dwarves (for mining) to dragons and trolls (to keep the ordinary man in awe of nature and to keep him away from the elves' technological facilities in the forests and mountains). Whenever heroes or heroines from ordinary human society show proof of extraordinary courage and intellect, their children will be kidnapped and raised among the elves, so that the elite of humankind can be concentrated and breed in a few places. With time the elves will return to the stars, build their facilities on the moon and other beings in space, where they do not pollute the planet Earth. From there they will control the masses like gods, prevent humans from destroying nature and from losing their respect for nature.

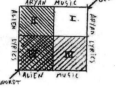

When not writing prophecies, drawing unicorns and composing classical music, Renaissance man Varg makes primitive diagrams like this proving Aryan supremacy. "Varg claims that instruments like guitars and drums are for blacks so he can't use them," explains Maniac. Striving for legitimacy through their ambient synth music, Mortiis and Varg actually want to shed the black metal label. "I know a lot of newer black metal fans, especially younger ones, still expect and sometimes take it for granted that Norwegian metalers or whatever the fuck we're supposed to be called, still kill people, still burn churches and so on, and when they find out it's not really happening anymore they start slagging us off, which I find utterly pathetic," says Mortiis. "I'd like to ask those people, 'When everything went down over here, when the shit hit the fan, where the fuck were you?' A bunch of twelve-year-old kids in blue, baggy jeans listening to God knows what washed-out buttrock band was in at the time."

Although still content to operate under the auspices of black metal, Mayhem (who continue to use guitars) have distanced themselves from their epic past achievements with their new album *A Grand Declaration of War* (Necropolis), a barren tundra of hip hop breakbeats, sterile production, and post-rockish electronic soundscapes. "This is the most clinical and ugly album that Mayhem has ever released," Maniac says in the album's defense. "If you listen to a lot of the old black metal bands, you find that if you strip away the fuzz and its distortion, it's purely rock 'n' roll riffs actually." In place of layers of razor-sharp riffing, they've opted for "disharmonies and stuff like that which are truly ugly." Not to mention downright boring. And where did the falsetto screaming go?

Outside of Scandinavia, black metal imitations are flourishing in Florida and the southern United States, but they aren't criminally insane like the Norwegians were. Hollow, English black metal frauds Cradle of Filth, despite their popularity, are as ersatz as Venom were twenty years ago. The brief window of insanity that existed in the early '90s between these bullshit bookends was absolutely real and totally evil.

Although the music sucks these days, there is still hope for more evil from the kings of metal tabloid insanity. "None of us for the time being have any explosives yet," says Maniac regarding the future of black metal criminal activity. "But we have been getting very much into weapons. There will be a breakdown soon. Mark my words."

From July-August 1998, Page 54

The original article featured photos of the band falling asleep.

A TRIBE CALLED YAWN

Yet Another Boring Rap Interview That Tortures Us All

by Shane Smith

Music interviews are boring. They are boring for musicians to do, boring for music journalists to write, and, by and large, boring to read. There are many reasons for this: Musicians are stupid, journalists are stupid, people are stupid, and the music media is a thinly veiled pretext for organized groupiedom, to name a few. Here is an example of exactly why the majority of music articles are about as interesting to read as your grade-eleven geography textbook.

It begins with a big record label calling up *VICE* and offering to set up interviews in New York with A Tribe Called Quest. Not only is the new record *(The Love Movement)* sweet, but most of us here at *VICE* have knocked boots to *The Low End Theory* or partied to *People's Instinctive Travels and Paths of Rhythm*, and we think that Ali Shaheed Muhammad is a fantastic producer, Phife is a basketball guru, and Q-Tip is the hip hop equivalent of Johnny Depp. So we say yes to the interview and get ready to bring it on.

In the beginning you think that you can really do something new and exciting—dig up a scoop, create a stir, win a Pulitzer, that kind of thing. In your research you find daring questions that will no doubt elicit riveting responses and props from the group. Who wouldn't want to hear if it was Mariah Carey's supposed relationship with Q-Tip that led to her running out and divorcing her fat-rich-Sony-president hubby? What hip hop head doesn't want to hear what one of the most influential producers around has to say about A&R and the direction of music in general? Hell, you were even looking forward to hearing Phife's picks for the finals. You poor naïve sot.

When you get to the Big Apple, a car picks you up at LaGuardia and takes you to the swank offices of the major label. You arrive, you wait. You start to figure something is up. They put you in a conference area with the other "international press," who are: two blond Swedes more familiar with covering Humungluben contests in Stockholm than anything else, a German to whom everything is "supercool," and two Japanese chaps who are obsessed with everyone's shoes. Just before the interview is about to go down you are told that "Q-Tip isn't talking" and that the rest of the band is "very tired" and that certain topics shouldn't be brought up.

The interview room is cramped and hot, the band has been answering the same questions all day, Q-Tip's house has burnt down a few weeks prior with his whole record collection and some irreplaceable samples and new beats, Phife is bored silly, and in you walk—Oh, fuck it, in *I* walk—with a list of now unaskable questions and a special high-profile photographer on loan from Ecko who wants to shoot an elaborate concept piece.

VICE: What do you look for in a group you produce?
Phife: Most people are looking for something mainstream, close to where people are going, you know. Me, I'm looking for more original stuff that'll be around for ten, twenty years—not this short-lived stuff. Just something a little different.

How have you managed to not only stay together but stay relevant over the years in an industry that has a six-month window?
You know, before we were a group, we were always friends. We know how to separate business from pleasure and pleasure from business, you know what I'm sayin'?

I'm now feeling downright rude for keeping them there, and I know my Pulitzer is long gone, so I try and keep the interview short and painless.

The sad thing is, I like Tribe and think their new album is dope; it's just that the standard operating procedures of the music machine weed out any innovation. They are about making tunes that people will listen to and we are about writing articles that people will read, and those two things are fundamentally incompatible.

**From Vol. 7, No. 10, December 2000

REBEL GIRLS

The Time Bratmobile Hurt My Feelings

by Amy Kellner

At 5:30 PM I was told that I was scheduled to interview pioneering riot grrrl punk band Bratmobile at 6:30. I had just gotten home from my unbearable temp job at an investment bank after getting three hours of sleep the night before, but the prospect of interviewing the feisty band excited me and I tore off my embarrassing clothes, threw on a comfy T-shirt, grabbed my tape recorder, and dashed over to the Westbeth Theater. Bratmobile had just reunited after, like, eight years and I was totally psyched about their new album (*Ladies, Women and Girls*, on Lookout! Records). Plus, on a more personal level, I was looking forward to seeing Erin and Allison again, as they had crashed at my house a bunch of times a couple years ago when they were doing a band called the Cold Cold Hearts. I was singing, "Reunited, and it feels so good!" as I walked there and I felt really good.

When I got there I spotted Erin first and snuck up behind her, tapping her shoulder. I hopped around excitedly and then we hugged and she quickly said, "Hold on,

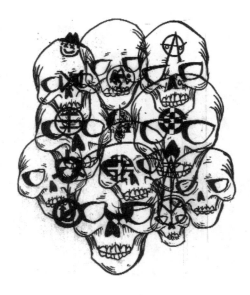

let me go get the girls." I met their drummer Molly and their publicist Tristan, and we were all standing there when I suddenly noticed an uncomfortable kinda vibe. "Listen," Molly said, "we gotta talk to you about this interview, or more specifically, about the magazine you're doing it for—*VICE*." You probably know where this is going. *VICE* is notoriously extreme in its un-PCness, and nothing or nobody is above *VICE*'s policy of "a good joke is a good joke." I'm not even going to bother justifying *VICE*. All I can say is that I don't agree with everything *VICE* prints, but I do write for them and they have never censored me and my oh-so-radical ways. "We just don't know if we want to be in the context of a magazine like that," said Allison, "but when we heard you were the writer, we wanted to talk to you about it and try to decide if we should do it or not."

I chuckled nervously and went on my usual spiel of, "Yeah, people are always getting pissed at *VICE* and I've got my issues with them too, but on the whole I think some of the shit they write is actually pretty subversive and interesting, not to mention hilarious. Their biggest problem is that they're operating in an ideal fantasy world where you can poke fun at every kind of stereotypical 'identity' group and it's just all in good fun, like how you can call your buddies 'faggots' or 'niggas' or 'retards' or 'hos' and you know they mean it as some kind of twisted term of endearment. 'Entitlement' and all that, uh, you know?" The girls each began to list the various affronts they'd either read firsthand or just heard about. Advertisements for skater clothes featuring porn models were mentioned, as well as an article where girls tell of their experiences of being raped. I could come up with defenses or explanations for those things, but I wasn't sure how much I wanted to stand behind them.

I was so put on the spot that I started rambling on about "subverting from within." I'm sure my cheeks were beet-red. I went on and on, my voice getting higher and faster, about how I (a LESBIAN who studied QUEER THEORY, fer chrissakes) have written totally girls-kick-ass articles about bands like Chicks on Speed and Lolita Storm for *VICE*, and how Bratmobile should know that I'm on their side, how there's no way I'd ever write anything not 100 percent from a feminist angle— it's who I am! I was rambling.

The girls were very nice about making sure that I knew it wasn't about me personally. They apologized for dragging me down to the club, and even suggested that I interview them for another magazine, like maybe *Index*. In turn, I offered to have the interview be about issues of sexism or about the very problems they have with *VICE*, in *VICE*. That would have been a kick-ass piece!

Instead I was just like, "Look, I'm not gonna force you to do something you're not comfortable with. I just feel really bad and embarrassed about the whole thing." The band decided that it was cool if I had found a way to resolve my personal conflicts with the offensive material, but they had not. I understood, we hugged amiably, they told me I should stick around and enjoy the show, and they went off to do band stuff.

I left the club in a daze. Halfway down Bank Street I was sobbing hysterically, feeling so humiliated and just plain BAD (bad girl, bad girl) that I seriously considered never writing again (actually, I consider that all the time). I mean, what went wrong? We have the same basic philosophy: Women rule and men drool. So how, all of a sudden, are we divided? Isn't this precisely the divide-and-conquer self-defeatism that tore apart the riot grrrl community in the first place? The pointing fingers and all these new rules? The bottom line is, I know it was their choice to make and I have to respect that. The last thing I wanna do is propagate the retarded "feminazi" stereotype, but I just wish they hadn't handled the situation in such a way as to put me in the awkward position of having to justify the way I make my living, or to doubt my own commitment to feminism. I hate me.

**From Vol. 8, No. 9, November 2001

The original article featured this photo of Didi chilling out by the pool.

SPECIAL REVIEWS (BY SPECIAL KIDS)

by Didi

Every time we check out the Top Five we're like, "Who are these people?" Who the hell is Nickelback, for example? As Puff Daddy would say, "It never seems to amaze us" how out of touch we are with the normal world. That's why we needed a special kid and radio buff like Didi to break it down for us. Originally, "Special Reviews by Special Kids" was penned by brother and sister team Didi and Max. She did this one right after he died (see his obituary at the end of the book) and we don't think she quite understood that he was gone. After she figured out what had happened she did one or two more articles for us and then gave it up. As this book goes to press Didi seems to have lost her enthusiasm for pop music and has gotten heavily into movies. Following are her views on the top five albums according to Billboard on October 26, 2001.

1. Various Artists, *God Bless America*

I like listening to the songs that are on this whole album. Our uncle bought it for us to have. We already have one that has "Tie a Yellow Ribbon" from a long time ago and it's a cassette. The new one is for the tragedy and Celine Dion is in it even though she's still trying to get babies. He looks like Santa.

2. Enya, *A Day Without Rain*

Mum plays this really loud when she's drinking wine . . . Annie Lennox and . . . it hurts the ears, Mom! It doesn't even sound good loud the way 'NSync does. I like the song "Wild Child" because it sounds like she's in heaven with my brother Max [who died].

3. Ja Rule, *Pain Is Love*

He's from near us, in Queens! He sounds all tough but you know he's a big teddy bear probably to know. He still is on the radio a lot even after the good song with J.Lo because he is a very talented performer. "I'm Real" is real ill.

4. Ozzy Osbourne, *Down to Earth*

He went crazy because he did so much drugs all the time. He sounds like he's slow but Max says he's smart. Max liked him because his last album was in 1994 on the same day Max was born. Brian [my older brother] said this album sounds like "old Sabbath" but I don't like hard rock so I don't care. I don't care about Brian's new girlfriend named Frankie.

5. We've never heard of Nickelback.

Then you're stupid—sorry, but true. Their video is always on. It's probably on right now. They are grunge. Even though "Good Times Gone" sounds like Staind they have a lot more singing. Max would always turn up the metal but I didn't like it, but I like this band because they have singing. If he was alive we would both like to rock our heads out to this.

**From Vol. 7, No. 3, April 2000

MUSIC, PARTYING, AND LOVE

The Holy Trinity of Raising Hell

by Andrew W.K.

In the same way Oasis was the composite of every British band ever made, Andrew WK is the musicfication of all American rockers—always, everywhere. His shows tear the place down every time and even though it's just him, a microphone, and a CD of himself playing every instrument, the crowd goes nuts. In a few short weeks he's gone from burnt-out speed metal drummer living in the ugliest part of Brooklyn to fancy-pants, high-art legend being flown first-class all over the world. The best thing about this one-man pop/metal band is that he is the real deal. The real rocking-out, partying-hard, getting-laid deal. Here's how he does it.

Music

So, like, dudes!!! How awesome is music??? Like, ALL music!!! Music is what makes your fucking world go 'round! Music is what cheers you up when your girl-friend sucks!!! You know?

I mean, let's say you have this one favorite band, and, like, all of their music is your favorite shit! Like, you know every song, all the words, everything about the band . . . You LOVE them!!! One day you hear that they're coming into town and they're going to play this big concert, you know? So, like, you're super excited and you immediately slam down your $25 to see this group!

So, like, the concert night is slowly approaching and every day you're thinking about how awesome it's going to be! I mean this is, like, YOUR *FAVORITE* BAND!!! You know? So finally after three weeks of waiting, it's concert night!! You get out of work early and head out to your friend's house to get ready for the show! Your friend is excited too, but not quite as excited as you because, like, this is your favorite band and you've never seen them in concert before!

So, like, there is a feeling of fucking in the air as the two of you drive out to the concert! You've got a mix tape of the band's best songs playing on the car stereo and you can hardly wait to get to the fucking place! Finally you pull into the parking lot! There are tons of other cars pulling in too, and you have trouble finding a park-ing space, but finally you get one near the end of the lot! You jump out of the car and start hightailing it to the fucking entrance! It's awesome cuz as you're running you can hear other people's stereos playing the band's songs, and other people talking about how awesome the band was last time they played!!! You can hardly wait to get into the fucking place, and after about ten minutes of waiting in line you finally get to the main concert space!!! AWESOME!!!

The excitement is at a blistering level now! There is an opening band playing, but no one really cares about them . . . YOU JUST WANT TO SEE THE MAIN ACT!!! THE BAND *YOU CAME TO SEE!!!* So finally the opening band packs up their shit and the stage is set for the headliner . . . There's a shitload of tension and the crowd can hardly contain themselves!!! All of a sudden the house lights go down and the band comes out!!! IT'S INSANE!!! They rip into your favorite song right off the bat!!! You completely lose your shit and start dancing around like a fucking madman, but it rules cuz, like, everyone else is going nuts too!!!

You go to a fucking music show to tear shit up and dance the fucking world into pieces!!! So, like, don't go to a show and like get pissed off become some awesome dude is acting like an idiot and running circles around you and your lame-ass, gay-ass friends while you stand there "trying to enjoy the music." FUCK THAT SHIT!!! I hope you get slam-danced into your grave you tired old soft-boy!!! LET'S GET A PARTY GOING!!! Every fucking show should be a fucking party!!!

Partying

When I say the word *party*, I don't mean your fucking twelve-year-old nephew's gay-ass birthday bash . . . I MEAN A *FUCKING PARTY*!!! I want to see people losing their shit!!! Let's have fucking ten punk bands, ten hip hop DJs, and ten auction-eers (you know, the fast talkers), and let's have them all do their shit ALL AT ONCE!!! So, like, it should be, like, total chaos!!!

Every great chaos-killer party should be, like, the fucking party they would have on December 31, 9999! You know what I mean?? Can you imagine the fucking vibe at that party? IT WOULD BE A FUCKING MIND-BENDING, EAR-BLASTING, CUM-DRINKING, STOMACH-CHURNING SKULL FUCK!!! Think of the fucking "rollover" on that night . . . from 9999 to what? 10,000!!! So, like, every fucking party should be like a New Year's Eve party for the year 9999! Just get a whole bunch of people together and lock them in your grandparents' basement, start blasting some music, and POW!!! It's like World War III!!!

Get some black people, some white people, and some, like, totally weird dude and make them all start fighting. Eventually they'll all get tired, so, like, have them bundle up in a blanket and roll around for a while!!! You know! And, like, everyone else should keep rolling them around for a while!!! You know! And, like, everyone else should keep rolling them around the room and, like, splashing water on them and blowing air-horns in their ears and stuff!!! And then, like, totally start playing music really loud and, like, running around and totally, like, breaking everything in sight and, like, just, like, SCREAMING AT THE TOP OF YOUR LUNGS!!! You know??? IT'S TIME TO PARTY!!!

Cuz life's too short. Like, I once read about this weird old woman who, like, had one true dream in life . . . and that dream was to have sex with a salmon fish. She bought a live salmon at a fish market, you know, and, like, took it home to have sex with it. This is where it gets weird, cuz like she was lying in the bathtub and, like, had the fish swim into her (where it counts). Then she, like, held it in there and, like, poked its eyes and shit so that it would wiggle all around and give her the pleasure that she was looking for!!! But she ended up dying from it cuz she bought a bad fish. The fish was infested with some kind of shrimp eggs and they got inside of her and grew up into shrimps and then she died because of it . . . But, hey, I mean, it's, like, totally gross to you and me, but, like, this is what this woman really liked to do . . . and she did it till death!!!

Like, if you try having sex with salmon fish and you get all fucked up and you end up dead with a fucking pussy full of shrimp, then at least you can look back at it all and think, "At least I tried all the stuff that I wanted to try," and you can be happy. But if you go through your whole life, like, all unsatisfied and all wound up, then you'll go to the grave and be all stressed out and unfulfilled. You know? LIFE is simply TOO SHORT!!!

It's a damn shame that we can't live forever, but if we did live forever imagine if you always saved all your cum!!! You know??? Like a big bottle with a vacuum top so that it wouldn't dry out. You would have like gallons and gallons!!! And think of how much someone would have to pay you to drink it all!!! Actually, you could make a living off of it!!!

Love
Dude, like, love is the total deal!!! It's the all-around package! Everything comes back to love! Music and love go hand in hand I think! Like, you love your parents (even if they suck), or you love your friends, or you love your girlfriend, or, like, you love your pet!!! You know? Like, a cool pet is, like, what . . . a dog? Fuck that shit, man, how about a fucking baby rabbit, man . . . how totally awesome are baby rabbits? Dude, is that gay? I'm telling you, anyone in their right mind cannot deny that pets are fucking cool. Like, fish, cats, dogs, spiders, lizards, birds, baby rabbits, mice and rats . . . you know?

Like, remember the first time you thought you were in love? It was like, "No way!!" But the other person was totally into you, you know? How awesome was that day!!!??? Nothing else in the world mattered cuz, like, you had this totally hot babe that was all into you and it just made your fucking life into the world's own joy!!! You know? And how cool is Girls' Own Juice too? Like, remember the first time you discovered that shit!!!??? When she comes she *really* comes into your world. That much we all know!!! She gets what she wants, she gets what she needs, I get what I need . . . I need your love. Dude, love rules!!!

CRIME

PHOTOS BY RYAN MCGINLEY UNLESS OTHERWISE SPECIFIED

**From Vol. 8, No. 3, April 2001

Estella Gomez
Hair Dye 8.19

VICE'S TOP TEN CRIMINALS OF ALL TIME

by Jesse Pearson

Important disclaimer: We do not wear Charles Manson T-shirts. Nor do we own Natural Born Killers on DVD. We don't care about serial killers and don't think violence is funny or cool. People who live outside the law, however, are fascinating—probably because we all wish that we could be them to some degree. After putting this list together, we were surprised that most of these cases had something, whether explicitly or not, to do with class. The ones that weren't about the struggles caused by evil capitalism were about straight-up fashion and how high class you can look when you're young and you're smart and you don't fucking care about a fucking thing!

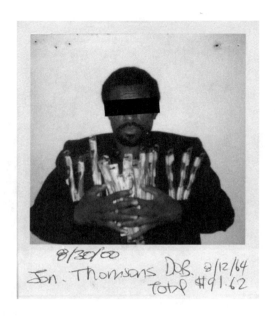

8/30/00
Jon. Thompsons DOB. 8/12/64
Total #91.62

1. Blackbeard

He always dressed head to toe in black and had a black beard, which means he gave as much thought to his image as the average drag queen. Before boarding another ship, he would tie his beard into pigtails and stick lit matches in it—the same matches used to light cannons. He also came strapped with six fully loaded pistols across his chest, two swords, and an ankle dagger. Blackbeard's prosperous career was put to an end in 1718 when, in a shoddy attempt to save face, a group of crooked Virginia politicians decided to go on a crusade to capture him and his crew of jolly pillagers. They faked him out by pretending to be fellow pirates and then, once aboard his ship, struck. It took five bullets and multiple sword slashes to take him down.

This was back in the days when bullets weren't streamlined marvels of design: They were lumpy chunks of lead. Legend has it that he was cocking one of his pistols as he fell. To celebrate killing Blackbeard, the politicians stuck his severed head on the front of their boat. After it rotted, they made a wine cup out of his skull.

2. Typhoid Mary

In an inventive take on class warfare, Mary Mallon made her body a weapon against the people who employed her as a cook. By the time her career was over, she'd infected at least fifty-one people with typhoid and caused at least three deaths.

Mary was born in 1870 in County Tyrone, Ireland. She came to the United States alone at the age of fourteen. She was a carrier, immune to the disease but able to transmit it. She added her special sauce to the dishes she prepared in a vacation home in Long Island, a private residence on Park Avenue, a sanitarium in New Jersey, and a maternity hospital in Manhattan. Also be sure to check out "Missouri's No. 1 Unsigned, All-Original Hard Rock Band" of the same name. Their motto: "World Domination Is at Hand."

3. Bill Clinton

He was the first American president who actually inhabited his body while he was in office. Sure, we found out that JFK was a big slut, but not until he was dead and safely ensconced in martyrdom. Bill went whole-hog while he was still the most watched leader in the world. We're really enamored with the fact that an incredibly brilliant scholar who was born a hillbilly could convince the world that he was just a good ol' boy, thereby getting away with adultery, sodomy, tax fraud, shady real-estate deals, and God knows what else.

4. The Baader-Meinhof Gang

German nuts who made terrorism sexy. Andreas Baader was a teenage petty thief who decided his true calling was to stick it to the man. After all, there were a lot of chances to hurt people and destroy things when you were a German student activist in the late 1960s. Andreas started out fire bombing department stores in Frankfurt. He got sent to jail in 1970, but was sprung by a fan of his work, the prominent left-ist journalist Ulrike Meinhof. For the next two years, the two built an army of almost 100 terror-minded liberal German buddies and went on a spree of bombings, robberies, and cool photo-ops. The ringleaders of the gang were apprehended in 1972. Baader and his girlfriend, Gudrun Ensslin, committed suicide in their jail cells on October 18, 1977, a date they had creatively dubbed "Death Night." The Baader-Meinhof gang dressed the way you wish your parents had: lots of large collars, suede jackets, and huge sunglasses.

5. Charles Starkweather

Gets on the list just because he was the inspiration for the movie *Badlands*. He was a nineteen-year-old Nebraska garbage man nicknamed Little Red for his stocky, bowlegged, ginger-haired appearance. He fancied himself more of a James Dean, and his favorite things were comic books, his .22 rifle, and his fourteen-year-old girlfriend, Caril Ann Fugate. When things started getting rocky between him and Caril Ann's parents, he took the logical step of killing them both and sticking a sign on the Fugates' door that read, "Sick with Flu—Stay Away." When the local cops got too nosey, Charlie and Caril Ann took off on a two-week spree of shooting and stabbing just for kicks. 1,200 cops took part in the hunt for Starkweather and Fugate. He fried.

6. Leopold and Loeb

In 1924, Richard Loeb, the nineteen-year-old son of a Sears-Roebuck exec, was a student at the law school of the University of Chicago. His lover, Nathan Leopold, was an ornithology buff. At nineteen, he was recognized as the top authority on the rare Kirtland's warbler. When these two upper-crust boys weren't secretly necking, they pursued their common interest: Nietzsche. Leopold and Loeb were especially into the concept of the übermensch, a man so evolved intellectually that he transcends the boundaries of morality and law. Leopold and Loeb decided the perfect übermensch crime for them would be to kidnap, sodomize, and kill a neighborhood boy.

Bird genius Leopold left his one-of-a-kind eyeglasses next to the kid's body, so it took the cops about five seconds to find the two killers. Way to go, überman. Loeb was killed in a prison razor fight in 1936. The more ambitious Leopold mastered twenty-seven languages during his thirty-four-year prison stay. Though he claimed to still be in love with Richard Loeb, Nathan Leopold married a woman (of all things!) after his release from Joliet.

7. French Students, 1968

If we ran J. Crew, we'd put together a *Paris 1968* line NOW. The rumpled khakis, dark V-neck sweaters, unfiltered Gauloises, and stained flannel suit jackets just screamed, "I'm too busy trying to undermine the spectacle to wash my hair." Plus, these kids came up with gems like, "Under the paving stones, the beach."

8. Unabomber

Speaking of class warfare, how about some homemade, organic nailbombs mailed to the heads of nature-destroying corporations? Sounds good! Too bad this guy was too fucking stupid to get the addresses right or whatever, thereby maiming and killing innocent people who happened upon his handiwork. On the fashion side of things, he inadvertently gave the world its most iconic and bad-ass police sketch ever. Those cop shades he was rocking were way fashion-forward at the time!

9. Jack Kevorkian

"Christ. Was that a dignified death? Do you think it's dignified to hang from wood with nails through your hands and feet? Had Christ died in my van, with people around him who loved him, it would be far more dignified."
—Jack Kevorkian, July 7, 1996, National Press Club Speech

Dr. Death is responsible for more than forty fatalities during the last fifteen years. His first few victims were put to death using the "Mercitron," a device of his own invention, made from a toy car, scrap metal, and a bunch of syringes. When this setup proved too complex, he resorted to carbon-monoxide gas for the rest of his patients, which "often produced a rosy color that makes the victim look better as a corpse." The law eventually took notice and what started as a hearty, all-American adventure in medical experimentation became a spree of media-protected, self-assisted suicides in the back of a van. After five murder acquittals, the powers that be finally put an end to Kevorkian's career. If he had been successful with his last court case, America could have become the breeding ground for franchised Disney Death-Worlds where the lost souls of society could snuff themselves out in any number of ways.

10. Patty Hearst
We all know that John Waters has mined her for basically all she's worth, but can you please take one more look at the now infamous shot of her in her full Symbionese Army brainwashed glory?!? So rad looking. This is where the young designers of today are getting all their inspiration.

Now pardoned by criminal #3, Patty Hearst was a nineteen-year-old college student in Berkeley, California and the heiress to the Hearst newspaper empire when she was kidnapped by the Symbionese Liberation Army in 1974. The SLA's motto was "Death to the fascist insect that preys upon the life of the people." Awesome! They held Patty for $2 million while they indoctrinated her with radical rhetoric. Some of it must have sunk in because before you could say "Power to the People," Patty had metamorphosed into "Tania" and was toting a rifle in Symbionese-led bank robberies. She took her pseudonym from the name of a woman who had been close to Che Guevara. When the SLA was reduced to rubble by the authorities, Tania/Patty went underground. A year later, in 1975, she was arrested in San Francisco. At her trial, she pleaded brainwashing, but she got thrown in jail for a couple of years anyway. Now she's a happy wife and mother in Connecticut, but we really hope that now and again she looks at that shot of herself in revolution-mode and says, "I used to fucking rule."

**From Vol. 7, No. 5, June 2000

The original article featured two newspaper clippings about the robbery: Reid below the headline, "Author faces 10 counts in brazen robbery" and Musgrave below, "He went mad, poet says."

THE LAST KISS

Notorious Poet Susan Musgrave and the Bank Robbery That Put Her Husband Stephen Reid in Jail

by Susan Musgrave and Stephen Reid

Susan: It's almost a year since I had celibacy thrust upon me. A year of living, as Butch Cassidy called it, in a state of single cussedness. My sex life went into remission the day my partner, dressed as a transvestite Barbie, failed to rob the Royal Bank in the peaceful Cook Street Village in Victoria, British Columbia.

Stephen Reid, who used to lead the Stopwatch Gang (who always made it in and out of banks in less than a minute and forty-three seconds) before turning family man with a part-time heroin habit, spent four minutes taking down that bank. "I could have taken out a loan in less time," he told me later.

Stephen: June 9, 1999, 9:15 AM, Pacific Standard Time. Well, maybe it was standard for the rest of the Pacific Rim, but for me, standing outside a Shell station with my hand gripping a hubcap-sized reminder to return the washroom key to the attendant, this AM

SHOOTOUT IN JAMES BAY
He went mad, poet s

Victoria poet Susan Musgrave pauses to reflect Friday outside the Vancouver Island Regional Correctional Centre

Husband's in jail, she's in hell after crime :

would be anything but standard. I had just fixed a spoonful of courage, the blood spot on the inside of my elbow was still wet, and there were four long blocks between me and the bank robbery. A light breeze caused the leaves to tremble and the shadows on the sidewalks became like little fishes kissing. For that one moment I saw how absurd this all was, how crazy I had become behind the coke. It almost jolted me back into sanity.

But sanity for Stephen had become sticking a needle in his arm every fifteen minutes, shooting up a heroin and cocaine cocktail. Still, he wasn't too wired to have a plan. It went something like, "Aha! A bank! Let's rob it." Another part of his fantasy was to take a ghetto blaster into the bank, stick in Pearl Jam's version of "Last Kiss," then stick the place up while he rock 'n' rolled.

I parked in the bank's rear lot, climbed out of the car, and fumbled with enough artillery to light up a small country. Wearing a clear plastic mask, with sweat pouring down my face, crudely rouged lips, and a forty-pound weight loss, I burst through the front doors, shotgun held in sergeant-at-arms position, and threw the place up in the air, tossing a duffel bag to the manager. He filled it from the ATMs and hustled me out the back door. He was in a hurry to get this maniac out of his bank.

Every time I take off my underwear I think of June the ninth. I kissed Stephen goodbye that morning and reminded him to pick up dog food on his way home from work (i.e., scoring dope). "Right after I knock off the First National," he said. A family joke.

Instead of going to my office first thing the way I usually do, I polished the wood-stove with stove-black, using a bunch of old rags that used to be my favorite pair of Stephen's Joe Boxers. After the stove was black, and the rags were black, I tossed them in the washing machine. Waste not, want everything, that's my motto. You never know when the world might be hit with a rag shortage, for instance.

I also had some underwear—a white bra and panties—in the laundry basket, and so as not to waste water on two separate loads I threw these in with the rags and added a cup of Cheer. I grew up in a family where frugality was next to cleanliness. My mother washes her Saran Wrap and reuses the same piece of dental floss until it, and most of her teeth, have fallen apart. I hoard the elastic bands that hold together the bunches of broccoli I buy at Thrifty's and still pick up beer bottles in the ditches to subsidize my poetry habit. Stephen and I have been married for thirteen years but have never found a way of marrying our differences over the management of our finances. When it comes to obscene amounts of money, he believes "There is always more where that came from" (i.e., the bank); I *deposit* money and leave it to work for me at a quarter percent interest per annum.

So on June 9, 1999, while he was withdrawing $92,000 from an ATM, I was saving rags and dyeing my underwear at the same time. And after that I went to my office to work on a poem:

Loneliness
takes the good out of all of our goodbyes,
more permanent than the sadness you know
when your lover drives away having lost
interest in everything about you, especially
your suffering. Love's a blip, a glitch,
but loneliness signs on for the duration,
one gunshot wound to the head is all it takes
to assure your allotted space in today's
News of the World

The police were already there, confronting me from a three-point stance before I even got out of the parking lot. They yelled, "STOP!" but I thought they said, "DUCK!" and kept going, barreling along the narrow streets and into Beacon Hill Park, firing a shotgun back at my pursuers. We careened through the park, dodging horse-drawn carriages, flying over stone bridges, knocking out barriers, and doing a four-wheel slide into the traffic and down the streets of James Bay. My pursuers stuck and stayed.

Finally I abandoned the car, climbed over fences and through backyards, staggering out onto Michigan Street. I was exhausted and surrounded, coughing up pools of green fluids and waiting for that nine-millimeter slug to catch me between the shoulder blades: I had attracted a crowd of uniforms by then.

CONTINUES AFTER DO'S AND DONT'S

VICE'S
DOs AND DON'Ts

In the past eight years of critiquing street fashion we have run about 800 DOs and DON'Ts. Here's our favorite ones (DON'Ts on the right hand pages DOs on the left).

OK, DUDE! I don't know about these guys that are playing soccer with you. Maybe they're blind. Maybe they're so into the game they don't care who they play with. But, shit, I fucking care. Look at you. You little Rikki-tikki-tavi in blue trunks, snaking all over the place like a Julian Lennon video. It's not Nazi Germany, don't get me wrong, but COME THE FUCK ON! Can we not have a modicum of decorum? Why don't you just put on some harlequin face paint while you're at it? FUCK!

This is something we like to call "Only in Quebec." Only in a nation where people have been receiving two decades of free grant money to promote their own culture (no matter how gay that culture may be) could you have this fucking clown being totally serious.

Step on me with those. I'm a worm.

Fedoras are really hard to pull off. Most of the time you end up looking like a foppish nerd who wants to solve crimes and be invisible. The only way you can pull it off is to be a stoned, bad-ass nice guy with weird tattoos and something really important to do later on, like this guy.

I hope dude is for sale because I am buying him to hang out at my house. What a piece of eye candy. He could just be sitting on your couch eating biscuits and drinking tea and you'd think to yourself, The sun is shining.

Holy shit, it's a *This Is Your Life* babe. She has the Linda Ronstadt hair your babysitter had in the 70s, the Olivia Newton-John pants your friend's sister had in the 80s, and that Gwen Stefani top your first girlfriend had in the 90s. You've been jerking off about this girl for 25 years.

Don't ever show us your gay-ass tongue piercing again. We live on a planet where men like Mortiis permanently change their faces and women convert their entire bodies into lightning-bolt tiger prints. Anything less is a joke.

Oh my god. Punch me in the face with your ass, why don't you? Haul off and lay me out with those two perfect fucking POW! POW!s of an ass. Like we need the red piping to drive the blows even farther home. "Gee us a fu'n break, can you no'?" That's Scottish.

If we ever do a DON'Ts book, this will be the cover. It's the most self-explanatory DON'T ever made. If you haven't seen your dad in a long time, don't bother finding him. He's wearing a gold hoop earring and has a knuckle tattoo that says "Ozzy."

Your curly purple mullet looks like you're wearing a cluster of grapes as an earring.

Who the fuck are these people? Are they five years old? Do they have a fort under the stairs and curse the streetlights for coming on because it means bedtime? Do they "hate Craig's guts?"

You didn't hear about dirtbag fops? It's the new thing in Italy: fancy lads who drink Pabst Blue Ribbon, listen to classical, and smell their balls. We call them "grunge chappies."

"Let me see here. What am I going to put on my dangling ball? Some kind of wee hat ... a paper cup? Ooooh, a golf-club cozy! Perfect."

He's waiting for a cab to take him back to DON'T headquarters where he sits in a huge throne and has everyone else on this page drop to their knees and pray to him.

Remember that part in *Animal House* when the Playboy Bunny falls through the window of that kid's room and he goes, "Thank you, God"? That's what it was like combing the city for three hours yesterday trying to find a DO and then running into this. What is she — a drawing!?

When you're having trouble getting laid and you want your friends to know it's getting on your nerves but you don't want her to know, invent some kind of way that your friends can see what's going on without her noticing. Then everybody wins.

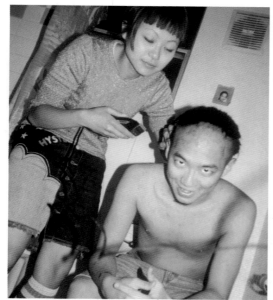

Cute chicks in striped tube socks and disco denim are so right on you'd be willing to let them cut your hair into a retarded-monk-with-AIDS look that will take years to grow back. How sweet would it be to have her outfit in a pile next to your bed?

Could you be more of a fucking babe, please? How could you be more of a babe? I guess you could fly. That would be hot. Or you could be the president of Russia or something but, HOLY SHIT, what a babe.

The only people that dress worse than teenagers are middle-aged rich guys. This one has the trophy wife and the Radiohead CD, but most importantly he's got his trademark "hope I die 'fore I get old" leather pants.

Paris! New York! Tokyo! London! Rome! Los Angeles! Paris! New York! Tokyo! London! Rome! Los Angeles! Paris! New York! Tokyo! London! Rome! Los Angeles! Paris! New York! Tokyo! London! Rome! Los Angeles!

Look at these meatheads. They are homophobic homosexuals who hate women and talk about fucking women all day. I'd love to just take a carpet knife to one of those Achille's tendons and hear the "SNAP!!!" That would be really satisfying.

Someone has to tell American girls and girls from Toronto that drag queens took over boas, Kiss boots, and '60s slut kitsch a long time ago. You basically have a dick right now, lady.

Dutch metalheads think they're so tough, but they play with their hair like Fabio and spend hours and hours putting studs in their coats. That's the exact same as knitting, you realize. (They do it in front of the TV.)

No matter where you go there will always be some Piglet walking around in a shirt that's longer than his Speedos like some girl making you coffee after a one-night stand. BTW we were eating breakfast and he kept walking by us with the bottom of his cheeks poking out and zits on his ass. Thanks, pal.

When this little treasure passed us by, everyone turned into Lenny and Squiggy and bit their fists. We're not sure what it is but those black socks are so fucking raunchy they make your chest tight with horniness. Can you imagine if this was your wife?

I smoked crack with this guy (not kidding).

Some people accuse this column of just being "Babes & Not Babes" and that we don't really have anything to say about the outfits which is totally unfair.

Not until you dive into punk whole hog do you realize how laid you get. It's a pain in the ass getting your hair ready every morning, but every rich girl in school wants to punish her parents by letting you punish her ass. That flag has never been more literal.

You can't really go wrong with mod clothes. They're a timeless combination of sharp hipness and virgin innocence. The kind of thing that goes really well with gigantic bazooms.

I'm no fag, but when you see a cute loner guy with great style in Nike Uptowns and a parka you're like, "Maybe I'd let him lick my balls."

They don't have video games down in Fraggle Rock so occasionally some of the bigger ones will come up here and blast off a few rounds. It's actually good luck to see one.

Is it just me or do you get the feeling that everyone into speed metal was either beaten by their uncle or molested by their stepdad?

"I love this logo. This is my 'team'. Players change every year and half of them aren't even from the same country as me, but this is my logo no matter what." Sports fans are basically just graphic-design groupies.

"You know what I like about you, Barbara? You're like me but with a cunt."

Whoa, it's the walking police sketch. Do you purposely set out to look like the personification of rape or is that a look that sort of just toppled out of the closet on to your head?

Nice fucking purple track pants, you fat bitch. What are you, the fucking Michelin Man? Nice gay hat, too, you fucking little loser bitch.

Not only are they best friends but they make their own clothes and they drink Blue Ribbon and dance to every song. I don't know if I want to fuck them or be them.

The best way for men to age so gracefully they can still fuck twenty-year-olds is to: be incredibly rich, be a tiny bit racist, have an eight ball in some oak box you picked up in Malaysia, enjoy cooking pheasant, know a lot about guns and hunting, slick your hair back, and wear an expensive suit at all times (even Sundays).

How hot is this bitch? She cuts her Jordaches off so we can see those cool lines girls have at the top of their hips and then she yanks them up her ass with suspenders. Dude.

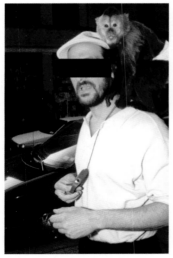

That's cool — a diapered monkey as a pet. Why don't you just ride around town on a unicorn and dig your spurs into it every time it gets tired? Why don't you put a rainbow in a jar while you're at it?

"Hey nigger! Wanna date? Hey! What's the matter? I thought you liked white women. What's the matter? You can't handle it? I'm too much for you? Hey! I'm talking to you! You want this or not? Hey? Hell-oooo!"

If you have a wet fart at your girlfriend's house you can't just grab her Saturday-night slacks and go to the opening anyway like it ain't no thang. We know you shit your pants, you asshole.

This fuckface weightlifter meathead is standing there like he's Benicio del Toro about to get picked up. No, dude. You are an ugly little rapist wearing a maroon dress, pajamas, and a hat that makes you look like a 13-year-old with cancer.

This literal and figurative clown had us on our knees and pissing in our pants. He was inviting everyone to a "collaborative paint jam" and we couldn't stop thinking about the exact moment the idea to do this popped into his stupid fucking head.

There's something real special about looking at a beautiful landscape and seeing a nice lady also looking at a beautiful landscape with a big, beautiful landscape embroidered on her back. Oops, where'd she go? I can't see her anymore.

Fuck wearing loose pants. If you've got a good quality bulge, let it show. Why are women the only ones that get to show off their shiznit?

Montreal just exudes sex. It pops out of tops and sits perched on high heel boots. After a few days there it gets to the point where you have to walk around in Depends just to keep the cum from soaking through your pants.

This dapper beer drinker looks so smooth and casual in his Triple 5 Soul t-shirt they should pay him $20/hr just for looking so good. Notice to white people: do not try the fishing beard thing at home. You will look like Henry Fonda with AIDS.

We're not sure about the next president of the United States being a woman but the mayor of babesville certainly will be.

After you haven't had it for about five months, there's nothing like getting a real good fucking. One of those workhorse types that is going to last more than an hour and pummel you so thoroughly the bladder infection feels totally worth it.

Accessorizing is important. Some stop at making sure their socks match their shirt while others are willing to incorporate: 10-ft stuffed animals, hair, lipstick, shoes, pubes and even their own fucking nipples into the overall color scheme.

You know the fascinating thing is that magic was considered "the work of sorcerers" a hundred years ago. If you were caught even making an egg disappear (which I just did) you would have your hair burnt off and your hands blackened. Now people would kill to see a good musician, I mean, magician but they can't ... hello!? Are you even fucking listening to me?

"Aw fuck, Zorf was totally wrong. Earthlings don't dress like geriatric gay Italians."
"Will you shut up and just relax. We're fine."

Whoa.
You probably don't know this but there's this thing that moose hunters get where they see the beast but are too awestruck to shoot it. They just sit there frozen until it walks away. Luckily, Neil Simonton of Byron Bay, Australia was man enough to aim his camera and catch this buck, (possibly the heaviest DON'T in the history of *VICE Magazine*) in mid-stride. "My heart was pounding after I caught him" said Neil in a recent email, "it was a huge adrenaline rush."

No weird shredded shirt or stupid tiny purse, just the bracelets and the hair thing and her favorite T-shirt and that's it. How fucking New York City is that?

Falling asleep on the train is relatively safe but with the clever stacking of those dreads and that perfect facial hair, don't be surprised to wake up and feel four wet pussies rubbing up and down your legs in a state of panic.

This fucker is starting a whole new thing. Soon these "Willy Wonka punks" are going to be all over New York, drowning German kids in chocolate rivers and getting shit-faced in Loompaland and stuff.

When did ten year-old kids get so cool? Look at her breezin' along with a potato in her hand, just a singing and a dancing cuz the sun's shining.

Maybe I'm a lesbian but how great are chicks who just put any old shirt on and are ready to go in one minute? Assuming the bush is well-kempt that's basically the perfect girlfriend.

Something tells me this girl has an incredible amount of willpower and would be able to resist you so there's no sense hitting on her. All you can do is make a mental note of her outfit and beg your girlfriend to copy it.

Did a 13 year-old girl spill a big glass of bad ideas all over you? I think it's time to cram your flowery headband, red sunglasses and terrible dog into that homo Guatemalan bag and just whip everything into the East River.

We know it's just a cheesy hippie but isn't there something princely about his demeanor? Like he regales her with stories of his father's kingdom while Zamfir dances in and out of his path playing the flute. He has a sword, you know.

Is this guy trying to pick up those 12 year old girls that are obsessed with horses? Dude, If you really want them to brush your long mane and hold you close why don't you glue a big horn onto your forehead and hang around mountain tops?

I bet you you just said, "Oh shit."
Me too. We've got a gold scarf ponytail-holder, a receding dye job, no pants, a woman's winter coat, black leather gloves, and 11 alligator horns. He is Grandma Man gone crazy gay Hollywood.

Wanted: Bassist with bad ass attitude. Influences include: Walking around town looking like a total dickhead.

Men can't wear dresses. We don't care if you're this huge, muscular black guy with some exotic Thai wrap. Dresses are for girls and drag queens. Hey Mr. Gender Free, why don't you go glue a plastic baby's head to your asshole and pretend you can give birth too.

Oh sway Mya. Sway back and forth like you just kissed the love of your life because you are so wet and naked -ugh.

Dude is just chilling. He's unflappable. You could be like, "Humpty what if nobody shows up to our party?" and he'd be all "Don't worry about it doood."

What makes this guy even better is that he's British. He's fucking British and his Muppet moustache is totally real. How are you going to compete with that? You can't. Just step aside and let the fucker DANCE!

Graffiti kids tagging bums is a level of marketing genius that people get paid $450,000 a year to think of. It costs a buck, lasts for years, and tours the entire city 24 hours a day.

What a fucking treat. What are those called, "pull me down" shorts? And the sockless Wallabes. Way to prove that girls are better than boys. Your feet don't sweat. You don't poo.
She's even got kind of a native vibe.

The results for the Cutest Motherfucker in the World just came in and that four-year-old, Japanese punk kid that was in our "Summer Kids" issue (pictured here) is sweeping up every category. It's almost dangerous because girls scream and pinch him so hard it hurts him a bit. Geez.

JOE STRUMMER'S DOs AND DON'Ts

The following DOs and DON'Ts were done with the help of that guy from The Clash. When we first printed it we thought it would be obvious that the red type was him and the black type was us but a lot of people got confused. People are stupid.

Joe: There's a certain American kind of wearing shorts that is absolutely awful and it's the same as the Spanish men. They stuff their shirts into their shorts, with a belt, with the loops out there- It's not on. *VICE*: We call it belt pride. This guy's obviously wearing the same shorts he's had since he was a baby.

This is a bit too heavy of a contrast. It's a very New York thing this look. She's like an aerobic shopper. This is an intense machine. Shopping, aerobics and talking on the phone. All at the same time. There's a bloody mobile tapped into her ear there. It's the black tights into the white shoes that really does it.

We have this disease in England because we go to a lot of those Glastonbury festivals where they sell that gear. Like those bloody jester's hats from the middle ages and the pants. These pants are specifically for jugglers. There's some correlation in the brain between juggling and sartorial loss of style.

This is a guy in Calgary. You can't see it here but he has this really giggly strut like the end of Saturday Night Fever in ffwd. Look at his helmet. The guy is tiny.

This is what we call a techno hoser. There's no more rock shows in Canada so they're taking over all the clubs. When we were doing *Earthquake Weather* in 1989 we got addicted to Bob & Doug Mackenzie reruns. It got so that everyone in the control room was a hoser. I've never dropped the use of that word but I never even knew what it meant until today.

Fanny packs are impossible to pull off. OK we've got a big problem here. It couldn't be worse really. Appalling. And we're the ones that have to look at it. He's medieval but without the panty hose. "Get some hose on you hoser!"

Illustration by Joe

You can't rock the biker look with fucking sandals. It's hypocrisy. He looks like Lemmy on the beach. That would be a good fashion shoot. Sandals are always a DON'T. The Stone Roses had a vibe-master. A dancer named Cressa that made them rich. He is my sandal guru. He's been the only person that could ever convince me to consider wearing those horrible things. I've been in the most vile conditions with him and he always has them on and they look all right. He says your feet are like your lungs. I'd like to think I could pull that off but I can't. I haven't got the guts.

This girl just knows what she's doing. If she wants to fuck you she will. It's not up to you. You know that her pad is in order and the kitchen looks good. There's no filthy piles of newspapers stacked everywhere. She'd cool us down if we were too high on blow. We could stop gripping the table with our teeth and we'd be in an oasis of tranquility. Another 100 out of 100. She's got a real stride going on here with a most difficult footwear apparatus. Sometimes I'm glad not to be a woman because I hate having foot impediments strapped to the end of my extremities. This bird is going very far and moving dead fast.

At one o'clock I went into the house and checked my machine for messages. There was one, from a pay phone, an unidentified caller: "You may want to do a bit of housekeeping. Stephen might be in a bit of a sticky situation." My first thought was "Housekeeping! Haven't I just polished the woodstove and done a load of laundry . . ." but then the "sticky situation" bit began to sink in. Any minute now the police might arrive to do the kind of housecleaning your house never recovers from.

I unlocked my front door, though I've heard drug dealers say the police like to break down the door even if you leave it wide open for them, and waited. When I didn't hear sirens, only the sound of my lonely 38D being tumbled dry, I went back to my poem:

The cure for loneliness, they say, is solitude,
trust everybody but cut the cards, take your delight
in momentariness. . .

I forced my way into an apartment building, began pounding on doors, working my way towards the rear of the building. I could hear the police outside. I was outflanked, cut off, and outnumbered. Like any trapped animal, I began to climb. An elderly woman opened the door to her second-floor apartment. I went inside and stashed my gun in a back bedroom. My presence no doubt frightened and confused them, yet John rolled me a smoke and Kathy told me my life was not over, that God worked in mysterious ways. They agreed to help me hide. When the police finally did pound on the door and pulled the couple out, they never entered the apartment or called for me to surrender.

I sat for hours, my hands on my knees, waiting for them to come. I thought of retrieving my gun, by then convinced the police were not going to let me walk out of this one. I thought I would save them the trouble. I must have nodded off; I woke up when four men in black padded uniforms, visored helmets, high boots, and Plexiglas shields—like the casting call to a *Star Wars* flick—stormed the room. They were all over me before I could rub the sleep out of my eyes.

The media made a pretty big deal out of the botched robbery. (You're considered a criminal in this town if you water your lawn on the wrong alternate day.) Even so, the way everyone was acting, you'd think he'd robbed a *food* bank. The papers called it the James Bay Shoot-out. The Jesse James Bay. They reported, too, that I was standing by my man, though I would have rather been lying underneath him. Or on top of him. Depending. Jesse James, I've read, never cheated on his wife. I like that in a man.

Three days after Stephen's arrest I got out of bed and into my gray nun underwear. My first prison visit was to take place "under glass" in a sensory deprivation booth made of concrete and Plexiglas. Walls a timid off-cream, the trim around the windows mental-hospital green. All else puce, and the graffiti misspelled: LOOPY IS A NECOFILIAC.

It was familiar decor. Stephen and I were married in prison, in 1986, when he was serving the last months of a twenty-year sentence for bank robbery. He was paroled thirteen years ago, almost to this day. But prison is not a place easy to escape, even if they release you. When the door to the prisoner's booth finally opened, the man I was supposed to be standing beside was not the one standing in front of me. The guard picked up his telephone, I picked up mine. "He's refusing the visit," he said. Point-blank.

I knew Stephen would be going through withdrawal, so I wasn't surprised. Part of me, though, felt betrayed. When we got married we vowed to be there for one another, *in sickness and in health*.

My hands are broken, my ribs are broken, and I'm dope sick beyond belief, but I know the real pain is in the mail, deeper than broken bones. It's about broken promises, broken hearts, and broken lives. The headlines in the newspapers are as black and bold as gunpowder: THE JACKRABBIT STUMBLES. After thirteen years of freedom, thirteen years of a publicly redeemed life, I had gotten myself wired, robbed a bank, shot at policemen, and held two people hostage, a nightmare I can't imagine away nor hide from in sleep. Behind my eyelids life has become everything I can't get back.

I see a clear plastic laundry bag lying in a corner of my cell. I keep it clutched in my hand for five days as I lie fetal, curled around that empty hold that others call the center of their being. I lie down with the pain and I sweat and I weep. Every five minutes I gather enough strength to do it, to place that bag over my head, wind it tight, airtight, at the neck, and every five minutes and one second I gather enough strength not to do it.

When they first brought Stephen to jail, his lawyer insisted he be examined by the medical staff. "If it's a question of his health, or security here, he dies," the warden told the nurse.

By the weekend I can sit up. Another inmate brings me a plate of congealed stew with a biscuit. I manage to swallow a forkful of the stew, but not for long. I charge for the toilet and sell a Buick all over the corner of my cell. The guy who brought my dinner helps me clean up. That evening I sit on the edge of my bunk, sip a cup of water, and this time keep the biscuit down. I glance over at the plastic bag, now filled with sweaty socks and underwear. Who'd want to be sticking their head into that?

Next time I visited, Stephen had come down. I told him we should try to focus on what was *good* about our situation. Most couples didn't get to spend an hour a day, face to face, talking intimately, even if the conversation was over a monitored telephone, "under glass." At least now I knew where he was all the time, that he wouldn't kill himself driving down the white line on the highway. We'd save money, too: He wouldn't be able to blow $1,000 a day getting wasted. I brought him other good news: His novel, *Jackrabbit Parole*, was being reprinted and my own novel, after eight years, was finally off to the printer's. "It's about a woman visiting a man in prison, so it's timely," I said.

"Well, it's going to be timely for a very long time," Stephen replied.

Susan visits. She's been here before but I couldn't get up to see her the other time. All we can do is sit there and watch each other weep through that scratched-up sheet of Plexiglas.

She begins to visit every day. Our words come slowly; the trembling of my face, of my hands, lessens. One day my lawyer shows up: With my bones back in my body, my will to live barely restored, it is already time for me to help him to form a narrative of the crime. As I walk through it with him, recollecting the carnage, it is the faces that emerge most clearly. Bank employees, bewildered customers, innocent bystanders, the elderly couple in the apartment. And finally, the masked and goggled Emergency Response Team. I didn't ever see the actual faces of the ERT officers, but their feet left a lasting impression.

The soldiers from the Empire broke his ribs and crushed his hands when they took him down, lying on the couch, where he'd been sleeping for two hours, with the door to the apartment wide open. "Don't be mad at them," he told me. "It's just cops, they're doing their job. In Toronto they would have killed me."

A month after his arrest, we were granted an "open visit." Even though we were no longer "under glass," there was still glass, nose-high, between us, and a sign saying PASSAGE OF ARTICLES OR PERSONAL CONTACT PROHIBITED. Instead of having personal contact we tried making as many words as we could out of the word *prohibited. Debt. Debit. Rob.*

It was a humbling experience, visiting Stephen in prison again. But at least *I* could leave. They kept him Hannibal Lectered in a high-security ward with a bunch of criminally insane garden-gnome thieves who stole his mail to get the names of writers who could help publish their memoirs and addressed the Crown as "Satan's Whore Mother."

Stephen was sentenced on December 22. The judge gave him eighteen Christmases. Our first conjugal visit is coming up. There will be just the two of us, alone, for seventy-two hours in a soundproof trailer. For the first minute and forty-three seconds at least, I'll be wearing my stove-black underwear.

**From Vol. 3, No. 9, September 1996

These are the two harshest pages of Debbie's book.

DADDY'S LITTLE SLUT

by Christi Bradnox

Debbie Dreschler's comic novel Daddy's Girl *was banned all over Canada and the States because it tells a true story of incest and pedophilia. Where most victims of child abuse choose to repress their memories, Dreschler has put together an incredibly graphic and disturbing story that is impossible to put down. We tracked Debbie down in Santa Rosa and asked her to talk more about the subjects no one will talk about.*

VICE: Why are you doing cartoons now, Debbie? I thought you were an illustrator.
Debbie Dreschler: I have this environmental disease—actually the current hip name is Multiple Chemical Sensitivity, or MCS. I think I got it a few years ago when I moved to this small cottage near the California vineyards where they were spraying all the time. Ironically, moving to the country from the city is what did me in. Anyway, I was doing illustration work and I discovered I was allergic to most of the art supplies I was using. After I switched to scratchboard and ink I got into comics and I haven't gone back since.

So if we were sitting in McDonald's right now and I was wearing a polyester suit and you were on your third Big Mac, what would your symptoms be?
Oh, God. The polyester suit would be okay, but the laundry soap would kill me, especially if it was Tide. If you had mousse in your hair or aftershave or cologne I couldn't take it. I'd have breathing trouble and neurological problems like hand-eye coordination for up to ten days. One time I couldn't even make my hand dial the phone number I wanted.

Could this be your father's abuse manifesting itself as a physical disease after all these years? Could it be psychosomatic?
It's not like I haven't thought about it, because a large percentage of people with MCS have had some sort of childhood trauma, but I just don't know. All I know is I have this disease and it has real symptoms and the only thing that seems to be helping it is time.

How does what happened to you as a kid affect your life today?
I did three or four years of therapy, which drastically changes the way I deal with those memories.

What about that phenomenon where people invent these experiences as a scapegoat to justify all their problems?
There's a lot of questions about all of that now and I still have doubts myself. But it was actually my sister that helped bring these memories forth. She remembers my father coming into my room and forcing himself on me. I mean, I didn't know these things had happened to me for a long time and some days I think I might have made this whole thing up. But then I think, what is my motive to make this stuff up? I know this sounds crazy after reading the book, but I still don't have really clear memories of it. My memories are really disjointed and they didn't start appearing until I was in my thirties. Well, that's not entirely true. They did start appearing, but I just had no idea what to do with them and there was nobody I could talk to. I used to have terrible nightmares, but all I ever got was, "Oh, you have an active imagination."

Now, who can we blame for that? Is it you or your friends or your family?
First and foremost it's my family. It's in my parents' best interests not to remember. I think my mother knew, but she stopped speaking to me since I started to talk about it. Actually, one of my three sisters is the only one that will speak to me these days. Their philosophy is that I moved to California, got crazy, and that's it. My mother's arguments are always a little weird, you know? It's like she protests too much. And it's weird because our family really prides themselves on being able to talk about things. My sister and I have been ostracized by the rest of the family for talking about things.

How do you feel about your father? Do you see him as a poor, sick man or as an evil ogre?
Oh, somewhere in between. He denies everything, but as an adult I did have the sense that he loved me. And if he was a brute that treated us all really badly I would understand, but I can't. I don't understand him, but I can only assume he was one of many on a long list of child-abuse victims. I don't know if he's truly forgotten or if he's so slimy he can pretend to be innocent, but at some point you have to take responsibility for your actions.

Your book will probably help a lot of kids who feel like this kind of thing only happens to them.
Well, the question is how many kids will read the book. With all these censorship issues going on, it will probably be more adults that will read it.

Have your parents seen it?
I'm prepared for that but I really don't want it to happen.

You can't forget how esoteric comics are.
I've actually had a lot of adults tell me they really enjoyed it because it helped them

deal with their stuff, and I was surprised to see the number of men that wrote to me saying they enjoyed it. I was sure no man would ever want to talk to me again because of the way I portrayed my father.

I heard about some of the cartoonists at *Screw* magazine putting together a book called *Daddy's Little Slut*.
(laughs) That doesn't surprise me. I mean, that's more the kind of reaction I expected.

I guess men have more trouble relating to child abuse than women do.
Well, it's not just girls. I've met a lot of boys that have been molested also, and that's even more shameful. Girls kind of expect it. It's expected that bad things happen to women around sex. Culturally there's that message. Women expect it so they're more prepared to deal with it. We're always taught, "Don't be too provocative." And for boys, they're taught they're the ones who should be doing it, it shouldn't be done to them. This may sound vastly oversimplified, but if you think about it, it makes sense. It's harder for boys to be vocal about it because there's the shame of being molested and then there's the shame that you're weak or the implication you're a homosexual.

Is it only men that molest children?
No, women molest differently than men do. It's not as sexualized. It's harder to distinguish but there's a lot of women out there molesting boys and girls.

Why did you put this book together?
Simply because I had a burning desire to tell my life story. I strived for emotional truth and added a few lies to make it more interesting.

Did this book help you piece together what happened, and was that a cathartic experience?
All the stories came to me and I'm still not totally clear about what happened. I just wanted to do real stories from the child's perspective without that bitter and jaded adult narrative. It may look like I'm stuck in my teen years, but I don't have a choice. The comics just turn out this way.

I think you've done a lot more by just telling the truth than someone with an agenda would do.
Well, that would be a whole other interview, you know? What makes people want to do art? I think pain is a big factor.

**From Volume 8 No. 3, April 2001

Brian Azakus

THE VICE GUIDE
TO NEW YORK GRAFFITI

by Bruce LaBruce

New York's graffiti scene is made up of some of the most reckless drug users in America. Their crew is called Irak. They are rude, illegal, sometimes gay, and always on the verge of losing their lives. We like to write about people who get fucked up, but this is better: Spacer, Semen, and Earsnot are more than most wanted on NYPD's hit list. They are what New York looks like. If you close your eyes and think of this city, you see the work of Irak and its peers. With this much hedonism getting this much credibility, it was time VICE put together the supreme guide to what, where, when, why, and who is painting on the fifth-biggest city in the world. We knew notorious fag filmmaker Bruce LaBruce hung out with them so we flew him down to blow it wide open. We asked him to live with them for a week, go bombing with them, get Ryan McGinley to photograph everything, and then research the history of this fucked-up form of indigenous art. He said sure, but then he got too wasted.

This isn't an article about graffiti. If you want to read a definitive piece of journalism on throwing up (and I'm not talking about Karen Carpenter), go to your local library and hunt down the *Rolling Stone* article "Mean Streaks," dated February 9, 1995. In it Kevin Heldman, a real journalist, trails a couple of spray painters around New York (following them into subway tunnels to stand breathless by their side as the trains barrel past; clambering up the Manhattan Bridge to observe them hanging from their knees to bomb or tag the mammoth structure) and generally lays out the whole historical and sociological context of urban graffiti.

Fuck that shit. I ain't no kamikaze reporter fresh from covering the events in the war-torn Republic of Chechnya; nor am I any kind of expert on the graffiti scene. I do, however, enjoy getting blotto with a couple of the most unusual and gifted kids currently bombing New York. When I was asked to do this story I had hopes, but all I ended up getting was high. It isn't easy trying to write about vandals when you're getting fucked up with them.

I arrive on a Saturday with my long johns under my clothes, having just escaped from a twenty-below-zero Toronto cold snap. I stomp sweatily up the five-floor East Village walk-up with my heavy bags. Ryan McGinley answers the door. This young cutie, who follows writers everywhere fanatically taking pictures, is just now saying goodbye to Marc, his model boyfriend. They seem like they're really stoned, which I soon discover is because Tyrone, Ryan's best friend (a corporate headhunter and part-time "rum-runner"), has acquired some opium, a rare treat that comes along only a couple times a year.

Ryan and I buy some beers and settle on the couch in the small, shabby living room in front of Tyrone's widescreen digital TV with pirated cable, and watch the inauguration of America's latest figurehead, Dubya. We get ridiculously high, like Withnail and I, in time to witness Latin queen Ricky Martin do his queenly routine. He's followed by a gays-in-the-military faggot who belts out "God Bless America" as if she's in a Broadway revival of Neil Simon's *The Star-Spangled Girl*.

I'm flying high on the opium magic carpet, my kundalini shooting through the top of my head into space, while trying to concentrate on Dubya's speech and Tyrone and Ryan's repartee. With his choked pauses and clipped phrasing, Dubya seems like an automaton. I half expect white liquid to start dripping out of the corners of his mouth. He talks in vague, populist homilies that don't really mean anything, like Mao. I'm convinced in my altered state that Iraq is going to drop the bomb on him right here and now, which would be appropriate since the name of the graffiti crew I'm here to observe is called Irak (not the country, silly—"I rak" as in "I shoplift").

As a Canadian in the land of the Yanks, the ascent of the Texas travesty unfolding before our eyes is stirring up my old political punk leanings, but strangely I will soon discover that Ryan and the graffiti kids he will be photographing, despite their radical pursuits and flagrant disregard for the law, such as racking and mopping on a daily basis and ragging and throwing up wherever they go (crimes against property, in this new era of hypercapitalism, are the worst you can commit), are surprisingly apolitical. The only thing they seem to want to boycott is talking to me seriously about graffiti. Nikes, new or vintage, are ubiquitous amongst the crew (what sweatshops?), and any conversation regarding the motivation behind spray painting is devoid of any specific political or even anarchistic socialist rhetoric. Sure, they often destroy mass media billboards and mall-like chains, but it's not ad-busting. It's wrecking something to "ups fame" (an Earsnotism). The general impression is "après moi, le déluge." Things are so fucked up at this point in history, so monumentally surreal, that only the impulsive moment counts—the rush of adrenaline garnered from racking or tagging, the natural high.

But believe me, the unnatural high for these kids isn't chopped liver either. The amount of opiates and pharmaceutical powders and pills that courses through their veins would put Judy Garland herself to shame. Lucky for me, it fits right in with my new diet regime: no food and tons of drugs. I'm so high at this point, the last thing I want to do is interview someone, but I do my duty and try to contact the graffiti kids. Nobody's answering his cell phone. *VICE* wants me to profile the real legends.

Sacer. He's the guy you read about in the *New York Times* who did the ultimate throw up: the Brooklyn Bridge. This is a large deal for two reasons. One, when you do the bridge, there's only a very tiny ledge separating you from the black water below, making the odds of death by falling so high that it makes me nauseous thinking about it. Two, vandalizing a national monument is a felony, which means if you do it more than twice you go to jail for life or longer. Shortly after the bridge incident, he made the news again after throwing etching cream on a slew of high-end boutiques and pretentious galleries.

Earsnot. He's more than one of the most prevalent tags in New York; he's an infamous thief who often walks out of a store with three $400 North Face jackets. His crimes are popular with the press, too. So much that he's had several two-week stays at Riker's.

And Semen. Semen is the one who draws those little sperms on every single door and window in New York. Once you start to look for them, it becomes a challenge to find a block that hasn't been hit.

These are the people I'm here to profile, but do I have to do it now? Anyway, I hear a rumor that Sacer has fled to Texas, where Dubya stands on the TV in front of me.

As we watch the Knicks game, a stream of Jersey boys revolves through the apartment. They all talk in advanced homese, so sometimes I feel like a visitor from a foreign country, which I suppose I am. Whenever the door buzzer rings, you have to be careful to see who it is. A couple of weeks ago the cops busted in during the night and dragged Ryan down to central booking for some outstanding warrants. He got into a little altercation during his day-and-a-half jail visit, from which he is still sporting a bandage on his hand, and says he doesn't want to ever repeat the experience.

We finally drag ourselves out of the apartment at 3:00 AM and go to a neighborhood dive gay bar where we encounter a fag who works for *Honcho*, the porn mag to which I frequently contribute. That's where my memory ends.

The next day I go to the excellent fag novelist Bruce Benderson's annual Martin Luther King Jr. party, but I'm pretty burned out so I leave around 11:00 AM. On my arrival back at the apartment, whom should I find but Ryan, Sacer, Earsnot, and Marc, all in full party mode. The first thing that catches your eye when you see these kids is gold. Gold fronts, gold chains with gold tanks hanging off them, and gold rings. Bling bling. After that it's an expensive combination of high-end Gucci hats and low-end Nike Uptowns. They are all very high. Well, when in Rome, do coke, Special K, Vicodin, and Budweiser, I always say.

Semen drops by and, as it's his birthday, we're compelled to get even higher. We're watching the patterns you can create by playing CDs on a Sega Playstation. I was just reading in the newspaper that this option was developed in cahoots with NASA scientists to control the brainwaves of hyperactive children, which most if not all graffiti writers surely are. The song we're playing, appropriately, is "Paint It Black."

I decide it's time to clean up their act, so with a shaky hand I reshave Sacer's hair into a Mr. T—modified Mohawk in the bathroom as Ryan snaps photos. Sacer is nineteen, married, diminutive, and cute as a fucking button, with epic tattooage and a killer smile. The first night I met him, he and Earsnot snuck me into a very exclusive Ford model party at Lotus, where Kate Moss was spinning (she was also DJing). Sacer bought me drinks and told me about his tragic life, something about his parents dying in a bizarre ritualistic murder/suicide when he was a kid. Earsnot also filled me in on his sordid past, but I got the feeling that their personal bios are as fluid and transient as their tags. Earsnot is tall and handsome and has a big smile, but has been passed out about 73 percent of the time I've seen him. He's a fag and has a preference for that burly, hairy, forty-plus subgenus known as "the bear." He hibernates in the Bronx with just such a noble creature.

The fact that both Ryan and Earsnot are openly fag in the circles in which they travel is pretty remarkable, but it's something you don't really think about when you hang with them because they are so unfaggy. There's a certain amount of machismo in the graffiti world. If you paint over another writer's tag or write "toy" over it (the ultimate diss), you better be prepared to drop your paint cans and put up your dukes. And most writers aren't really down with the gay thing, so it's pretty brave for this crew to be so "fuck you" about it even though only one of their members is a card-carrying faggot.

Sacer and Ryan and I amble on up to the roof to get some fresh air. Ryan is covered in a multicolored Indian blanket, looking like a cross between Howard Beale, Tiny Tim, and the cutest white homeboy ever. Sacer is in camouflage, and with his Mr. T do resembles a hot militia member. With a can of Bud in his hand, Sacer jumps up on the front ledge of the building and peers seven floors down into the black abyss as Ryan and I snap pictures. As Sacer dances and prances and does a jig on the precipice of death, I discover I don't have the stomach for this. For a moment I think it's a classic case of the Heisenberg principle—the presence of a journalist influencing the behavior of his subject, causing him to take risks in a way he normally wouldn't—but then I realize I'm flattering myself. The adrenaline, the flirtation with death or jail or bodily harm, is as natural for these kids as peeing. Sacer is poised to lob a snowball at a passing car fifty feet below and as I fear that the momentum of the throw will send him over, I retreat back to the apartment. I wait in anticipation for Ryan to come running down from the roof yelling that Sacer has gone over, is gone forever, but after a few minutes the two of them come stumbling into the room laughing. Ha ha.

The next night we all end up at a trendy place where at various points in the evening I see George Stephanopoulos, a woman who looks like Catherine Deneuve in *The Hunger*, three Hell's Angels with some loose models, and a bunch of young artists and spray painters. Sacer is underage, but he's drinking for free and we're doing lines right off the tables. Believe it or not, there's a whole lot of other stuff going on that I can't even write about, but ultimately on the way home a member of Irak who shall remain nameless accidentally on purpose torches a huge bundle of Christmas trees propped up on the street in front of the bar. The flames are shooting twenty or thirty feet high as Ryan and I snap photos. It doesn't seem like that big of a deal to me, but after someone calls 911, Ryan convinces us that we should bust out fast so we hop in a cab and book. Dismissing the little incident as a harmless prank, we go to a friend's restaurant and drink wine till the wee hours. At one point I get all weepy thinking of Sacer last night on the roof, plummeting into the void, supernova-ing. He pats my shoulder consolingly. He's too beautiful a soul in an ugly world to burn out like that, but I suppose that's why his life has to be constantly on the verge of sacrifice to make that point.

The next day, Ryan and I go to check out the damage outside the bar. Apparently a car caught fire and may have slightly exploded or something. It does look a little charred, like something you might have seen in Beirut in the 1970s. The Irak crewmember in question has to get out of town before sundown, heading appropriately south of the border into the sunset. So I guess that's the end of my reportage.

I have accompanied the kids on bombing expeditions before and it's pretty much what you might expect. Every square inch of the city is a potential target for their tags, every store a wealth of free goods. At this point their behavior is compulsive, an addiction and definitely not something that they can articulate, nor should they be expected to. I see them as antibodies attacking the infections of the modern world: corporatism, materialism, brainwashing, conformity, mass indifference. Graffiti is one of the last forms of rebellion left, and it looks pretty, so shut up.

I call the refugee Irak pyromaniac in Texas and he's having a helluva time. He's bombed some major billboards and at least sixty railroad cars. And he's bringing me back a pillowcase full of pills from Mexico.

**From Vol. 6, No. 6, July/August 1999

CORPORATE JUDGEMENT DAY

Write a Subversive CV and You Can Play God Too

by Tracie McMillan

We all know that life in the corporate world sucks. Who doesn't set out on a job search without thinking: "Good God, am I destined to spend the rest of my life rotting away in some depressing gray cubicle?" But just how low will the average personnel director go? VICE sent a daring ingenue, cover letter in hand, to find out just how slimy corporate scumbags really are.

Customer Service Cocksucker
To whom it may concern,

I am writing to apply for the customer service position advertised in the *Village Voice*.

CANDY BAR 5 14

MIGUEL FUENTES
7/31/97 F. 60

I have very little experience in the actual customer service field. I am, however, a great cocksucker, and really willing to please. Given the nature of customer service, I feel that this skill will cross over nicely.

I am also into women and can eat pussy pretty well. Not as good as with the dick, but good enough. I figure an orgasm is an orgasm, right?

If necessary, I can bring knee pads to the interview. Just let me know in advance.

Letters sent out: 9
Number of callbacks: 1
Response: One week after the letters were sent out, a man called around 10:00 PM. At first reluctant to identify himself, he would only say that he wanted to speak with me about my cover letter. After conferring with a colleague, he told my roommate that he was calling from a company called Subtlety and left a number. Phone calls to that number were answered at a Manhattan correctional facility.

Corporate Nazi Bitch from Hell
To whom it may concern,

I am writing to apply for the administrative assistant position advertised in the *Village Voice*.

I have had some experience in the exciting administrative assistant field and I love it. I would truly be a great asset to you as an enthusiastic employee, ready to screw over all the little people in the company if they even look at the boss wrong. I am obedient and willing to please in any way possible, and am very responsible when necessary. If you need any reckless office terror, I can do that too. It helps keep the temps in line, eh? And unions? Fuck unions. I hate unions. Anyone mentions unions, they get my high heel right in their eye. That'll shut them up.

If you like a tight ship, I'm the bitch for you.

Letters sent out: 21
Number of callbacks: 10
Selected responses: A reputable bicoastal entertainment law firm, which has represented artists as big as Hole and regularly participates in charities, made no mention of the letter. The interviewer appeared more concerned with confirming that I had indeed worked at MTV (blatant lie) and that I would be content with part-time employment. Taken aback by my aggressive salary demands ($8/hour), they chose someone else for the position.

A prominent SoHo gallery called for an interview the same day I sent my letters out. Despite the fact that my cover letter sat pertly atop a clipboard in the interviewer's lap, he made no mention of my offers to brutalize lazy employees. My self-confessed love of office work was, however, duly noted. At deadline, I was still in the pool of possible candidates. Score one for the Corporate Nazi Bitch from Hell.

White and Proud
To whom it may concern,

I am writing to apply for the clerical position advertised in the *Village Voice.*

My résumé shows why I'm good for the job. Why don't I tell you about me? The last good book I read examined why we shouldn't feel guilty about wealth. Two of my favorite writers are Charles Murray and Dinesh D'Souza—they're the only authors I know who really take racism against whites seriously. The liberals make it so we're supposed to feel guilty about being rich and white, but I say who gives a fuck? It's not my fault I was born this way.

Give me a chance and I'll knock your socks off.

Letters sent out: 8
Number of callbacks: 1
Response: Just before deadline, this message was left on my machine: "Tracie, I'm calling from [a reputable Manhattan investment firm]. Just got your résumé and cover letter—looks good. Give me a call when you get this message and we'll set up an interview." Who says racism is dead?

** From Vol. 9., No. 4, May 2002

Jeff Rodgers   D.O.B. 8/2/50
9/2/99   Total $250

YOU CAN'T
HANDLE THE TRUTH

VICE's Favorite Lies

by Anthony Lappé, Executive Editor, GNN. tv

Say "conspiracy theory" and most people imagine a lonely white guy who mastur-
bates about alien probes and eats Krispy Kreme donuts in front of a film loop of
JFK's brains splattering on the back of a limo.

The fact is, however, that many so-called conspiracies may actually be true. Ask
around. There are Harvard professors who believe in alien contact and even Nixon
thought the Warren Commission was full of shit. It's not hard to find ample evidence that much of what is dismissed by the powers-that-be as a "conspiracy theory" just might have some basis in truth, even alien butt plugs and shooters on
grassy knolls. The CIA does have little chips they can implant in your head, and
while Skull & Bones may just be a bunch of rich nerds at Yale living out pseudo-

homo fantasies, the club's rolls do read like a who's who of the masters of the universe. Is it a conspiracy that America is able to use up a third of the world's natural resources with only 5 percent of its population? That Bill Gates is richer than the GNP of fifty nations, yet Windows 98 still sucks? That chemical companies genetically engineer corn with DNA from a toxin-producing bacterium and no one tells you it ended up in your Fritos? That illicit drug sales make up 10 percent of the world's economy, yet we still believe we are fighting a war on drugs?

The problem with so-called conspiracies is that one nut's paranoid fantasy gets lumped together with someone else's legitimate search for the truth, and it all becomes grist for the infotainment mill, thus getting neutralized.

The rumor that 4,000 Jews got a warning to stay away from the World Trade Center is a perfect example. It was widely reported as fact across the Arab world, where millions still think the Mossad was the real mastermind behind the attacks. The rumor appears to have started when an Israeli newspaper reported on September 12 that 4,000 Israelis were unaccounted for. Of course, the phones were out in NYC so any Israeli, Californian, or whatever in the city couldn't call home. An Arab paper decided the ever-so-tricky Jews must have been warned, and the rumor spread like wildfire.

Another whacked-out theory is that the planes were flown via remote control and the hijackers never existed. Also, some French fruitcakes claim that a plane wasn't what blew a hole in the Pentagon—it was a bomb. Where the people on Flight 77 are supposed to have gone is not exactly clear. The point is, people are actually taking these theories seriously. They have websites, documents, even photographic "evidence."

The problem is that these idiot theories obscure a lot of evidence suggesting that the Bush administration and/or the US intelligence agencies knew something was coming and chose to ignore it. Numerous European news organizations have reported that both Israeli and German intelligence warned the CIA that Middle Eastern terrorist cells were planning something big, soon. BBC reporter Greg Palast reports he was told by a member of a US intelligence agency that prior to 9/11, "the agencies were told to 'back off' investigating the bin Ladens and Saudi royals."

Some of the most damning evidence that someone, somewhere, knew something was going down was a spate of short trading just prior to September 11 on stocks like United Airlines, American Airlines, Morgan Stanley, Merrill Lynch, Swiss Reinsurance, and Citigroup—all companies severely hit by the attacks. As investigator Mike Ruppert has pointed out, American Airlines alone experienced put options (betting the stock would go down) sixty times above normal on the Friday before the attacks (CBS News, September 26). United had put options ninety times above normal between September 6 and 10, and 285 times higher than average on the Thursday before the attack. Tens of millions of dollars of earnings on these trades were never cashed in, and the government hasn't said boo about who the inside traders might be.

In April of this year, Rep. Cynthia McKinney (D-Ga.) called for a complete investigation of what the government knew and when they knew it. She has been branded a "traitor" and a "conspiracy nut" for even asking the question. That's what democracy smells like in wartime.

Alien sightings, on the other hand, manage to avoid any accusations of treason. It's an American industry despite the fishy fact that most ET sightings have come after WWII. That's coincidentally the same time the space program started, science fiction became a literary genre, and—most importantly—the military started flying hundreds of experimental aircraft in remote places like Roswell, New Mexico. The tiny desert outpost of Roswell is the UFO Graceland, where tens of thousands of saucerheads flock every year to pay homage to the place they believe the US military performed autopsies on the alien pilots of a downed craft. On further examination, the story falls apart like a teenager's condom. It's pretty well documented that the Army was testing shiny weather balloons in that area—balloons they were using to drop human-like dummies.

Roswell is a convenient diversion, say serious UFO-logists. There's a growing body of evidence that some sort of alien spacecraft is flying in our skies. For the last seven years, Dr. Steven Greer, director of the Disclosure Project, has been videotaping testimony from more than 400 military, intelligence, and scientific personnel who say they were involved in UFO-related incidents. More than 100 of them, Greer says, are willing to testify under oath in open Congressional hearings he is trying to arrange. The captain of a US missile silo says a UFO hovered over his launch site, rendering his ten Minuteman nuclear missiles temporarily inoperable; a senior flight controller at the Mexico City airport claims he has tracked scores of UFOs; a former Army sergeant says he was a member of a crack squad sent to cover up evidence at UFO crash sites. Greer sees his mission as nothing short of saving planet Earth. He claims alien technology could solve the world's energy crises if the US military would make public the technology it has reverse-engineered from downed alien spacecraft.

A scarier postwar trend is the CIA's interest in mind control. Immediately following V-Day, Truman launched a secret operation called Project Paperclip. Its goal: Bring back Nazi scientists to help in the new war against communism. Hundreds of Nazis went to NASA and the nuclear weapons programs, and a smaller number went into intelligence, and what is called "the mind sciences." In the 1950s, both the USSR and the United States were obsessed with creating the perfect spy. The United States, with the help of Nazi scientists, launched several secret operations to try to figure out how to control people's minds. Project Monarch tried to create a sex slave/spy. The spooky-sounding MKULTRA tested the use of drugs to control people's thought patterns. Dr. Ewen Cameron, then head of the American

Psychiatric Association, performed hundreds of tests on unwitting participants with the help of MKULTRA money. He injected them with LSD and other hallucinatory drugs. He made them listen to repetitive messages for days on end without sleep. Officially, the program stopped in the '60s, and was exposed by Congressional hearings in the '70s, forcing the CIA to settle with some of the victims for hundreds of thousands of dollars. Is it going on today? Given that US intelligence agencies now have billions of dollars at their disposal, computer chips the size of hangnails, and devices that use sound to make you shit your pants, lose your memory, and pass out, who the fuck knows what they're up to?

For all we know the CIA is still dealing drugs. It happened in Vietnam. It happened during the 1980s in Central America. The US Congress's own findings during the Iran-Contra hearings documented the CIA at the very least doing business with known traffickers to secretly pay for the Contra war in Nicaragua when Congress cut off funds. Even Republican Al D'Amato exclaimed, "We should be fighting this scum, not working with them." Twenty-two-year veteran DEA agent Cele Castillo documented flights out of Ilopango Air Force Base in El Salvador that were bringing coke into the United States via Mena, Arkansas, where a young governor named Billy Clinton was running the show. Even Ollie North admitted the whole "arms for hostages" line was a "cover-up upon a cover-up." As Senator Daniel K. Inouye commented during the Iran-Contra hearings, "There exists a shadowy government with its own Air Force, its own Navy, its own fundraising mechanism, and the ability to pursue its own ideas of national interest, free from all checks and balances, and free from the law itself." Think the CIA's nose is clean now? Our War on Terror just reinstalled the world's biggest heroin suppliers in power in Afghanistan. "There's no such thing as the War on Drugs," says Castillo. "There never has been. We have more drugs today than we ever did thirty years ago."

Once you get into the CIA and the FBI's evil doings the shit water starts gushing out of the bowl. What about Oklahoma? Was Timmy McVeigh a patsy? It's a theory no mainstream news organization has touched with a ten-foot pole, but when you examine the facts, the idea that the Oklahoma City bombing was the work of two white power enthusiasts with a Ryder truck full of manure seems rather ridiculous. No fertilizer bomb sitting in the parking lot could do that kind of damage. As Gore Vidal wrote in *Vanity Fair*, "Timothy Samuel Cohen, father of the neutron bomb and formerly of the Manhattan Project, wrote an Oklahoma state legislator, 'It would have been absolutely impossible and against the laws of nature for a truck full of fertilizer and fuel oil . . . no matter how much was used . . . to bring the building down.'" In the March 20, 1996, issue of the *Strategic Investment* newsletter, it was reported that "a classified report prepared by two independent Pentagon experts has concluded that the destruction of the Federal building in Oklahoma City last April was caused by five separate bombs." Sources close to the study say that Timothy McVeigh did play a role in the bombing but "peripherally," as a "useful idiot."

Day-of reports from numerous local journalists talk about bomb squads finding other devices, and an FBI-authorized APB was issued for "two Middle Eastern–looking men seen speeding away from the blast area in a brown Chevy pickup with tinted windows and a bug shield" (*IndyStar*, Feb. 17, 2002). In fact, numerous witnesses report seeing a so-called John Doe #2 but their testimony, along with tens of thousands of pages of evidence that were conveniently "lost" by the FBI, never made it to trial. A local news reporter from KFOR-TV collected testimony from the staff of a motel near downtown Oklahoma City stating that they saw McVeigh with a number of Middle Eastern men at the site in the months before the bombing. "The motel witnesses also said they saw several of the Iraqis moving large barrels around in the back of an old white truck. The barrels, they alleged, emanated a strong smell of diesel fuel, one of the key ingredients used in the Oklahoma City bomb."

In fact, the more you dig the higher you climb. And it all stops at the presidency. The Bush family's theft of the 2000 election should go down in history as one of the most successful conspiracies in modern history—so successful that even when presented with damning evidence, the people don't seem to care. "We're at war, that's unpatriotic!" Even Al Gore can't muster enough balls to admit the fact that he got jacked. In his new book, *The Best Democracy Money Can Buy*, the BBC's Greg Palast documents just how Bush & Co. pulled it off. Forget the hanging chads and butterfly ballots, the outcome of this election was determined way before any old Jews in Palm Beach mistakenly voted for Pat Buchanan. In the months leading up to the election, brother Jeb and his secretary of state Katherine Harris hired a Republican-connected computer consulting firm to generate a phony list of convicted felons (some 57,700) to "scrub" thousands of people from the state's voter rolls. Eighty percent of the "scrubbed" voters were blacks, who vote almost exclusively Democratic. By many calculations, Gore should have won the state by more than 20,000 votes. Instead, Harris blocked a statewide recount and declared Bush the victor by 537 votes—a move upheld by one of the most corrupt US Supreme Court decisions ever. Ask any Brit or Frenchman who they think won the election and they'll tell you Gore. This story is all over Europe, but most Americans are either too lazy, too stupid, or too busy looking at Britney Spears to give a fuck that they are being ruled by a semiliterate con man.

That may be the biggest conspiracy of them all.

DOB: 7-13-74

5-19-99 STEPHANIE BRUNET $37.50
12:33pm

**From Vol. 7., No. 6, July 2000
Updated June 11, 2003

THE VICE GUIDE TO EVIL

by Adam Gollner

Afghanistan: A chick-haters' paradise. Afghanistan is a place where a woman will bleed to death in a dark kitchen (no sunlight allowed) because she couldn't find the mandatory male-family-member escort to take her to the hospital. Men divorce women at random, but if a woman so much as kisses another man, the locals turn into psycho evil people and stone her to death. Nice.*
Runners-up: Attila the Hun, AIDS in mosquitoes, arson by preteens, Australians, Anton LaVey, antidisestablishmentarianism.

Brazilian Funk Balls: In Rio's favelas, hundreds of ghetto kids are taking "There's a party over here, fuck you over there" to another level. Every month they have these

* When this article was originally published (see date above), Afghanistan was known by very few people as "the worst place on earth." We deemed it so but nobody would listen. Then the shit hit the fan. Listen to us next time.

D.O.B 7-12-66 10:30AM

D. BEDECK
6-15-95 $86.59

big warehouse parties and play hardcore techno they call "funk." The evil part comes when they split the room into two groups, with a "corridor of death" in between the opposing factions. Periodically, a macho show-off from one side kicks, punches, or shoves a member of the other side. If someone slips into the corridor and gets dragged into the other crowd, he or she is beaten, maimed, and cut. So far twenty-four kids have been killed, including one young lad who had his eyes cut out and was left there to bleed all night.

Runners-up: Beelzebub, brain lesions, bone cancer.

Child Armies: Legions of brainwashed African kids with spears and AK-47s are killing so many soldiers with such *Matrix*-like efficiency that even white people are getting scared. They wear amulets that they think will dissolve bullets and their reign of terror now includes Papua New Guinea, Chad, and Sudan. What the fuck are we going to do if they learn how to fly planes?

Runners-up: Cossacks, communists, Catherine the Great, chemotherapy, the Chinese government (especially the Three Gorges Dam Project), castration, cock blocking.

Dr. Octopus: With eight interchangeable tentacle-arms made of reinforced stainless steel, Dr. Octopus is one of Spider-Man's toughest enemies. Actually, all those supervillains are bad. Darth Vader, the Mysterions, the Joker, and the like want to

take over the world, not to party, but to more effectively spread misery and gloom and death.
Runners-up: Damian, death, Danzig, Discover cards, death squads.

Evil Eyes: Evil eyes are the universal bad. In Turkey, parents keep their babies wrapped in gauze for forty days so nobody will give them the evil eye, and in India women wear eyeliner to prevent them from accidentally giving the evil eye to their friends. Every time we give an evil eye, we open a channel that goes from the center of the evil within, out the eyes, and into the enemy's soul. When you give an evil eye you are wishing cancer and violence and death on someone and you have the power to do that because giving a good evil eye means becoming evil while doing it.
Runners-up: Envy (which is derived from the Latin *invidere*, meaning "to see into"), evil itself, elves, *E. coli*, Evel Knievel, entertainment reporters (and all you other sycophantic slags; you know who you are), entropy.

Florida: From defective electric chairs that flicker on and off for a prolonged death sentence to plain old fucked-up date-rapist creeps with long blond hair, Florida is a real shitty place. We also know this girl in Florida who lives in this big house and in the basement of the house she found all these photos taken by the KKK of tons of black men being lynched on the big tree in her front yard.
Runners-up: Fast food, fake tits, fat chick humor.

Guy from *Mask* Who Asks Rocky to Take off His Mask Because It's not Halloween: Fuck you, dick. The guy has craniodiaphyseal dysplasia and it's his first day of high school. How could you say that?
Runners-up: Gypsies, Goliath, girls, gabber techno, getting dumped, geeks who collect records based on serial numbers.

Homolka and Bernardo: Sexual torturers who filmed themselves raping, torturing, and killing a bunch of teenage girls. They thought the whole thing was funny and Paul Bernardo wrote rap songs about it.
Runners-up: Hallucination-inducing Hungarian peach palinka, Hitler, Hellfire Club (old British royalty who would ride around on horses and when they found a homeless person on the side of the road, up to thirty of them would cut holes in the wretched bum's body and then have sex with the wounds).

Islamic Organ Trade: In the Sudan and Yemen, Islamic groups have taken to selling criminals' organs to other countries. It's gone from the odd liver and kidney to dinks and vaginas. Now you have Brazilian perverts walking around with black women's clits sewn onto their dicks (a song called "Amo Voce Clito Negro" is climbing up Rio's charts). There's even snuff movies of the gory organ removal (they just cut off the guy's dink and let him bleed to death), and they are selling better than *Baywatch*.

Runners-up: Insane people, Idi Amin (the African Hitler who ate kids), Ivan the Terrible, individualism.

Jewelry: The government's most lucrative stupid tax. The diamond trade in Sierra Leone is causing tens of thousands of deaths and gold miners in Nigeria are dying every day. Here in New York, prostitutes will wiggle their tongues and say, "I'm gonna suck your dick and you're gonna fuck me in my ass," while they surreptitiously remove a $500 gold chain from your neck. Even Jay-Z admits that "bitches kill for it." That shit be evil.

Runners-up: Jesus, jocks, juniper (when you fall in it), jazz musicians, Jiminy Cricket (dick).

Korean Horse Fighting: In South Korea they use horses for medicine and food and racing, and now killing. The sport involves getting two badly matched stallions hyped up and ready to die for a mare in heat. The big one pounds the smaller one with its heels and teeth until it is dead, and the fiercer it is the louder the crowd screams. Fuck cockfights, this is the next-level shit.

Runners-up: K-holes (Special K paralysis), kids (kids are cruel), killer bees, Keef Richards' blood.

LSD Overdoses: After three hits on a camping trip in the Rockies, our friend Craig went from being a good-looking young black man to a vegetable for life. He became convinced he was Jesus and, after surviving a treacherous jump off Montreal's Champlain Bridge, went on to think he was God. Now he lives in an insane asylum with everyone else who's done more than twenty hits in one lifetime and his lover is a forty-six-year-old woman with a goiter. She looks like Robin Hood and wears pointy shoes.

Runners-up: Liver spots, Lex Luthor, lover's nuts (more commonly known as blue balls), liars, leprechauns.

Meat Industry: Meat farmers are exempt from the Humane Slaughter Act, the Animal Welfare Act, and even the Clean Water Act. Thanks to this we have chickens born so deformed they aren't chickens, cows born with pencil legs that don't work, pigs dying in their own shit, and hundreds of species of fish on the endangered list. We also have bone cancer and five-year-old girls with huge tits, but the meat industry is still killing eight billion animals a year because that's how they do.

Runners-up: Mass suicide, Medusa, mimes, militias (whatever happened to them, anyway?), models, millionaires.

Norwegian Black Metal: When all of those corpse-paint-wearing Scandinavian black metal dudes decided that burning churches and killing people and eating their brains (no joke) while playing blistering Nazi vomit-core wasn't evil enough, they decided to go back to their prehuman roots. Mortiis (the most evil person in the world today) had himself surgically altered to look like a 600-year-old elf with tons of wrinkles, a long witch's nose, and pointy ears. He replaced metal with songs that sound like roly-poly chamber music and he added an extra finger to the metal salute to symbolize "witchery."
Runners-up: Nosferatu, Narnia, nuns, nannies, Nervous Norvus, Never-Never Land, Namibian headhunters, Nancy from *The Craft*.

Olestra: The evil fat substitute. It's kind of like NutraSweet, only instead of shrinking your balls it causes anal leakage and uncontrollable bowel movements.
Runners-up: Oreos (reverse wiggers), obituaries (who reads those?), omens, Ouija boards.

Pedophiles, Especially Female Ones: "Short eyes" are the ubiquitous evil that everybody agrees on, but what about the female ones? Though only 15 percent of pedophiles are female, a mother who molests her kids is way scarier than a man because . . . just because (gross). Men are treated with castration or an electrical ring that gives shocks to bad erections, but what can you do about evil vaginas? Run.
Runners-up: Paper cuts, Premarin (the menopause drug made from mare urine), progressive trance, pigeons, power, prudes, people who love purple.

Quake: Every mass-murdering high school kid from Columbine to Danforth played Quake. That's why they peg off jocks with such straight-to-the-head, Navy SEALs accuracy even though they've never touched a gun before. OK, maybe it's not so evil.
Runners-up: Queefs, Quaaludes (nonavailability of), Mayor Quimby, Quincy Jones.

Rats and Roaches: What started out as a few pests on German boats have evolved into 4,000 species of roaches and a vermin that attacks thousands of people daily (264 New Yorkers last year). We're putting them here in one category because they are both evil in the exact same way. They eat their young, have small eyes, shit in their pants, and won't stop spreading misery and disease until they take over the whole planet.
Runners-up: Rock 'n' roll music, Rumplestiltskin, raisins, Resistance (the Nazi record company that made $3 million last year), Rasputin (the blood-drinking Russian pedophile who seduced the czar's wife and started communism), religion (heaven is here on earth, you losers. It's called heroin).

Sports: It takes up half the news and consumes over $100 billion of American cash each year, but it is totally boring and irrelevant. The unavoidability of sports is basically saying, "Ha ha, we are men and we rule the whole world and there's nothing you can do about it, because we made the whole planet a big living room for us to do whatever we want."
Runners-up: Snuff movies, smegma, Scatman, schizophrenia, Sodom (and Gomorrah too), spinal taps, sex accidents, Spam (the e-mail kind).

Testicular Cancer: Prostate cancer is for old people. Fuck that, we're scared of ball cancer. What happens is they go in through your stomach, remove your intestines, and start haphazardly ripping at your ball. Sure, they might kill the ejaculation muscles that allow you to cum, but whatever, they have to get the lump. Ugh.
Runners-up: Tamil Tigers in Sri Lanka, Twisted Sister, Toronto, toenails, tampons with chemicals that promote more bleeding.

Ugandan Cults: The Twinomujuni cult (a.k.a. The Movement for the Restoration of the Ten Commandments of God), for example, had this deal where you would give the main guy all your worldly possessions and in exchange for your sacrifice you could go to heaven via being blown up. Ugandan authorities got the situation under control after 470 charred bodies were discovered in a Roman Catholic church.
Runners-up: The universe, ugliness, the Ubangi Stomp, underwear (men's).

Venereal Warts: Sixty percent of sexually active college students between the ages of twenty-two and twenty-five have VWs. You can take all the antibiotics you want but the only way to get rid of them is two years of blasting with liquid nitrogen (a liquid that is approximately one million degrees below zero and hurts like hell). There are hundreds of different strains so it's almost impossible to find a cure, and even wearing a condom doesn't help because when it rides up you can get it on your labia or shaft.
Runners-up: Vlad the Impaler (a.k.a. Dracula), Veronica Lodge, vagina dentata, Venom (the band and the poison).

Windows: Microsoft is doing shit now that will lock your computer down and basically they can do anything they want without your approval (rights management built right into the computer chip) and if you want to use a PC for email and internet, have fun with viruses and trojans. You'll need to spend the whole first day installing anti-virus shit.
Also, when you get Windows you need to invest in a special program that can find all the spyware and bullshit hidden in your computer and stop it from changing your shit to their versions. And Windows XP is gay. It's like Tampax and Fisher Price

got together to make the most patronizing operating system they could. As our IT guy put it, "My bosses Window XP machine (newly installed) can't even print or use the net because the power went out and it all went to shit. I haven't a clue how to fix the endless assortment of problems with Windows."

Burn in hell, you fuckers.

Runners-up: White South Africans, wimps, white people in general, Westernizing everything, wiggers ("Come correct, brother. I'm flossing and cold, cold lampin'!"), Wal-Mart.

X-Treme Television Shows: From the X Games on ESPN to *The World's Deadliest Police Chases* to shows where insurance agents investigate fraudulent claims, X-treme television viewing has become church for people with low IQs. Fox's *Faces of Death* is just around the corner.

Runners-up: Xanadu and all its related temptations, X-ing people that don't deserve it, X-rays (ultrasound rocks).

Yugoslavia: As if 3,000 years of ethnic cleansing wasn't enough, madmen in the former Yugoslavia have decided to bring their legacy of rape, hatred, and turf warfare right into the new millennium. As a bonus, the Yugo organized crime ring is now all over Eastern Europe controlling human slavery and child pornography. When they get bored, they force peasants to run through the forest chased by starving and rabid pit bulls for entertainment. The peasants have no choice. It's that or be killed by a fat bald Serbo-Croat-Herzegovinian-Macedonian-Greek-Muslim-Slav.

Runner-up: You.

Zappers: The cops in *Logan's Run* that used to zap people were so scary the police decided to make some 500,000-volt guns of their own. They keep losing their badges for going overboard, but there's something irresistible about interrupting neurological impulses and giving people epileptic spasms until shit flies out their ass.

Runners-up: Zipped sack skin, zebra poachers who only take the tusks and leave the rest, Zenophobes.

**From Vol. 8, No. 3, April 2001

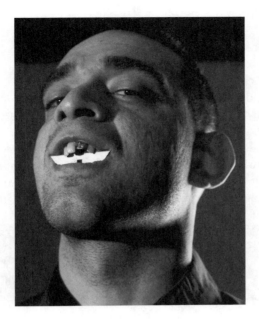

LIFE IN HELL

by Christi Bradnox; Photos by Sarah A. Friedman

Twenty years ago, the Lower East Side was a drug dealer's paradise. A good day meant a heroin supplier was looking at $100,000 pure profit. Even the runners, advertisers, and lookouts were getting several thousand dollars a shift. There was more money than the thugs knew what to do with, and there were enough addicts to make the supply go on forever. Then, in the mid-'80s, a crackdown began that landed everyone from Avenue A to the East River in prison.

When people first started arriving in New York state prisons things were lax. You could show up with two huge gym bags of books, clothes, bathroom supplies, and even drugs. As the population of the prisons doubled, and then tripled, shit got heated. The prison guards were forced to revoke all rights and freedoms to keep gang violence under control. Today a first-day inmate is lucky to get a bible filled with phone numbers past the guards. This overpopulation has led to less funding per prisoner and, subsequently, fewer rehabilitation programs. In 2001 life in the hole is all about sleeping, staring at the wall, and making sure your shoes are tied.

And the revolving door of New York's prison system gets worse every day.

Underwear: Phat Farm
Shoes: Clark's
State Greens: Cor Craft

Used to be, Kings could wear their gold bandannas, Bloods could wear red, Crips could wear blue, and Netas could wear white. Now all gang identification is banned. Not that there's anything else to do. New York state prisons can no longer afford their successful prerelease programs, and there are no more college training courses. With no skills to offer new employers and a parole system that forces a grown man to be home by 7:00 PM, the ex-con has no choice but to commit more crimes. Only this time he's looking at a much tougher sentence so he's going to do everything in his power not to get caught again. Even if that means killing the witness.

Underwear: Hanes
Shoes: FUBU
State Greens: Cor Craft

With no one allowed to wear gang colors, the only way to identify a member is by his tattoos. A tattoo gun is made by hooking up a Walkman motor to a pen casing with a guitar string for a needle. The ink is made by burning black chess pieces. It is forbidden to do tattoos, but the motors are quiet enough that a guest in your cell can get a few good hours of work done without getting caught. Just tell the porter to leave your cell open so you can clean it, and after the guard has made his rounds, your tattoo shop is open for business.

Track Pants: Cor Craft
T-shirt: D-Gital Systems
Shiv Proof Vest: *National Geographic*

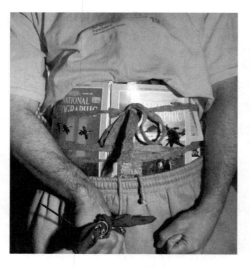

You have to wear your greens everywhere in the facility. The only exception is when it's time to go out in the yard. In the yard you can wear the state track pants and a T-shirt that is not gray, blue, orange, or black. Gray and blue are reserved for officers. Orange is reserved for the Orange Crush (the special task force used to break up riots). And black is forbidden because it makes the inmates harder to see. The T-shirt must be free of logos and designs.

If you have a beef with someone the best way to get prepared is to tie magazines around your torso. It takes sixteen magazines to make the vest because they have to be two deep. The first eight (four in the front and four in the back) are stuffed down your pants and the next eight are tucked into the first eight. The magazines can't go higher than that or they impede your movement. The shiv is best hidden with a bandanna.

Pants: Triple 5 Soul

Fifi towel: A Fifi towel is a homemade vagina. Simply take a small towel, fold it in half, and roll it into a tight cylinder. Then keep it that way using elastic bands. To make the vagina realistic, inmates insert a rubber glove into one of the ends. The wrist of the glove is folded over the edge of the towel and tucked under the elastic bands. After it is secure, the glove is filled with hot water. A second glove filled with Vaseline is then inserted into the first glove and tucked under the same elastic. The hot water melts the Vaseline and makes it feel warm and soft. Like a woman.

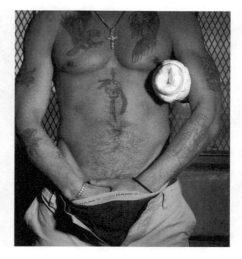

State Greens: Cor Craft

Back in 1981 there was so much heroin going around that lineups to dealers' apartments would span five flights of stairs. Thieves could make $10,000 by robbing the dealer and all the addicts waiting to score. Now the same heist isn't going to bring you more than $500. New York's heroin crackdown has inadvertently made the Lower East Side a well-respected and well-represented segment of New York state prisons. No matter where you are there will be fifteen to twenty LES thugs throwing up the "L." Often it's someone from another gang showing respect.

Towel: State-issued
Jeans: X-Large

"Prison air conditioning" is a wet towel with a large hole in it draped over the torso. Only people in county jails are allowed to wear jeans. Female prisoners up in Bedford Hills make their own brand of jeans for state prisons but they are not to be worn inside. The jeans are for inmates who can't afford to buy civilian clothes for their release day. The female prisoner fashion line is called Cor Craft and it also includes socks, underwear, shirts, and the state greens featured earlier.

**From Vol. 8, No. 9, November 2001

THE VICE GUIDE TO FOREIGN POLICY

by Anthony Lappé, Executive Editor, GNN. tv

Dear World,

We know you are sick of Americana. We know you grew up with everything from the Fonz to the word *couch* rammed down your throat and you see the American flag as a giant sports icon for jocks, but you're wrong. The average American has nothing to do with your plight. If you trace the blame for US foreign policy, for example, you end up going past Americans, through most of their elected representatives, through the CIA, and into the lap of a small cabal of corporate-connected leaders who have little regard for the democratic principles most Americans think their country stands for. As world-renowned Mr. Nice Guy, the Dalai Lama, said following 9/11, "As far as domestic policy is concerned, they think democracy, democracy, democracy, but American foreign policy is not very concerned with democratic principles." When fundamentalists and moderates alike talk about "evil

dob 3/13/75

Dan Morrison $63.18

America," they are talking about a handful of corporate-influenced crimes most Americans know nothing about. And the reason average Americans don't know anything about it is that they're working too hard. When we see the American flag, we see construction workers and waitresses busting their asses and going into debt trying to make things better for their families. They get home too tired to read the paper and get their world news from late-night comedians.

Before September 11 the deal was this: The American people agree to work their asses off and not ask questions about what the government is up to as long as the government promises to continue to provide the American way of life. As Ollie North put it, "The American people don't want to know." Then on September 11, everything changed. A group of lunatics had been using foreign-policy blunders abroad to vilify America and start a war. All Americans became victims of wrongdoings that none of them had anything to do with, and the American way of life became threatened.

For the first time in decades the American people want to know what's been going on behind their backs, and the answers are not pretty.

Philippines

The 1899 Filipino-American War is one of those nasty little conflicts that you won't find a lot about in your high school history textbook. Call it the first Vietnam. During the 1898 Spanish-American War, the United States help the Filipinos gain independence from Spain. Then they declare the country an American colony, and a brutal war follows. Many of the scorched-earth tactics used in Vietnam are first used here. More than 100,000 Filipinos die. A large anti-imperialism movement starts in the United States. "We do not intend to free, but subjugate the people of the Philippines. We have gone there to conquer, not to redeem," writes early celebrity activist Mark Twain. In 1945, the Americans come back to the Philippines. Even though they have a common enemy (Japan), America fights left-ist forces known as Huks. The United States defeats the Huks and installs a series of puppet presidents, culminating in the absurdly corrupt Ferdinand Marcos. He and his high-heel-obsessed wife milk the poverty-ridden country dry for three decades before retiring comfortably in Hawaii.

Iran
The CIA's first big takedown, in 1953. The democratically elected prime minister Mossadegh had to go. He was talking crazy talk, like nationalizing Iran's oil. A CIA-sponsored coup ousts him and restores the Shah to absolute power that begins twenty-five years of repression and torture. Iran's oil is returned to its rightful owners, the Americans and the British. This, of course, sets the stage for a radical Islamic rev-olution in 1979, when the Ayatollah Khomeini takes over, holds Americans hostage, burns many American flags, and pisses off rednecks across America.

Guatemala
1953: Jacobo Arbenz also had to go. The progressive, democratically elected presi-dent was also talking that crazy talk—you know, land reform, civil liberties, nation-alizing the Washington-connected United Fruit Company. The CIA organizes a massive disinformation campaign and coup. Next up: forty years of bad, bad things you don't even want to think about—American-trained death squads, torture, dis-appearances, mass executions. Victims: 100,000.

Middle East
In the '50s, the Eisenhower Doctrine stated the United States "is prepared to use armed forces to assist" any Middle East country "requesting assistance against armed aggression from any country controlled by international communism." In other words, no one is allowed to fuck around in the Middle East or its oil fields except the United States. The United States tries to overthrow the Syrian govern-ment (twice), lands 14,000 troops in Lebanon, and conspires to overthrow and assassinate Arab nationalist Nasser in Egypt. America supports Israel with billions of dollars of aid, despite its harsh treatment of Palestinians and massacres in Lebanon.

Indonesia
1957: President Sukarno is another troublemaker. He takes back Indonesian com-

panies from their former colonial masters, the Dutch. He takes a trip to Moscow. He refuses to crack down on communists. The CIA launches a disinformation campaign, tries to blackmail him with a fake sex film, plots his assassination, and hooks up with dissident military officers to start a full-scale war against the government. Sukarno, unlike many on the Agency's hit list, somehow survives. 1965: Sukarno is finally overthrown by General Suharto. The United States helps him track down anyone suspected of being communist. The *New York Times* calls what follows "one of the most savage mass slayings of modern political history." Up to one million die.

Cuba

1959: When Fidel Castro rolls into Havana on New Year's Day he isn't a commie— he is a nationalist and an opportunist. But he does take over Cuba's national industries. And that, as we've learned, is something the United States doesn't look kindly on. The Americans begin a comically disastrous campaign to oust Castro. They help launch a full-scale invasion at the Bay of Pigs and are crushed. They launch gunboat attacks, bombings, and biological warfare. New evidence has just come out that the CIA even considered committing terrorist acts and then blaming them on Cuba as a pretext to invade again. They try to send Castro exploding cigars and spray poison on his beard. The United States also issues sanctions and a trade embargo that, more than anything, ensure that Castro remains in power.

The Congo/Zaire

1960: Patrice Lumumba becomes the Congo's first prime minister after independence from Belgium. But the Belgians don't quite leave. They keep their hands on the vast mineral wealth in Katanga province, where the Americans also have a piece of the action. Lumumba is defiant, calling for the Congo's economic and political liberation. In other words, he is doomed. In January 1961, he is assassinated with help from the CIA, under orders from Eisenhower himself. His body is chopped up into little pieces and burned in acid. Mobutu Sese Seko takes over, renames the country Zaire, and begins one of the most corrupt and bloody dictatorships in modern times. Even his CIA handlers are amazed at his cruelty. Thirty years later, despite its rich natural resources, the people of the Congo are still dirt-poor, Mobutu is a multibillionaire, and the country is in chaos. In 1997, Mobutu is overthrown and retires to the Côte d'Azur. The country slides into a civil war that has killed more than one million.

Vietnam

After watching the French get their asses kicked halfway to Montparnasse, the United States gets embroiled in a civil war pitting communist nationalist forces against a corrupt, pro-West government. In 1961, the first young American men start arriving home in body bags. Before it's over, more than one million Vietnamese and 50,000 Americans will die, Jimi Hendrix will play Woodstock, the Beatles will form and break up, and the American psyche will be radically transformed. In 1975, the United States finally admits defeat, forever dooming it to the need to overcome the "Vietnam Syndrome" (see *Rambo*).

Cambodia

1969: Nixon and Kissinger begin their secret "carpet bombing" of Cambodia. They say it is to kill Vietcong hiding out in the Cambodian jungle. Hundreds of thousands of Cambodian civilians die. 1970: Washington finally helps overthrow troublesome Prince Sihanouk in a coup. The United States enlists the genocidal maniac Pol Pot and his Khmer Rouge to help fight the Vietcong. Five years later, Pol Pot takes over, declares "Year Zero," kills anyone with an education (or even wearing glasses), and sends everyone to the countryside to work in agricultural labor camps. More than two million die in his "killing fields" (see *The Killing Fields*).

Chile

1973: Salvador Allende was a "dangerous" man. He was popular, democratically elected, and a leftist. Against the objections of many inside the US State Department, the CIA, pushed by Kissinger, helps the military overthrow the government. Allende is killed. General Pinochet closes off the country to the outside world. Tanks roll in, soldiers round up students, stadiums turn into execution grounds, and the country is gripped by fear. For two decades, Pinochet rules with a brutal hand, and thousands of students, union organizers, and other bad apples are "disappeared" (see the movie *Missing*).

East Timor

December 1975: Indonesia invades the other half of the small island of East Timor, which had proclaimed its independence after Portugal left. The day before, US president Ford and Secretary of State Kissinger are in Indonesia meeting with Indonesian president Suharto. Amnesty International estimates that by 1989, Indonesian troops had killed 200,000 people out of a population of between 600,000 and 700,000. The United States supplies Indonesia with aid, guns, and training throughout.

Nicaragua

1978: The leftist Sandinistas overthrow the US-backed Somoza dictatorship. Reagan becomes obsessed with taking out the Cuba-and-Soviet-friendly government, enlisting an army of mercenaries, drug dealers, and ex-Somoza National Guardsmen. The Contras attack schools and medical clinics, raping, torturing, mining harbors, and bombing. When Congress cuts off funds, Reagan's "freedom fighters" are financed by CIA drug dealing and secret arms sales to Iran in what comes to be known as the Iran-Contra Affair.

Afghanistan
Beginning in the 1970s, the United States pours billions of dollars into overthrowing the pro-Soviet government. The CIA funds, trains, and arms a guerrilla army of Islamic extremists known as the mujahideen. The Soviets are driven out, in their own version of Vietnam. More than a million Afghans are killed, three million disabled, and five million made refugees. The country slides into a civil war in which an even more radical group of Pakistan-educated students and uneducated hillbillies known as the Taliban take over. The country becomes a haven for anti-American terrorist groups and woman-haters. Lies flourish. While outwardly criticizing the Taliban, behind the scenes the CIA and American oil companies jockey for leverage to build a pipeline across the country.

El Salvador
During El Salvador's bloody civil war (1980–92), the United States funds, trains, and secretly fights alongside a military that operates less like a traditional army than like a loose confederation of homicidal fraternities. By the end of the war, 75,000 Salvadorans are dead.

Panama
During the '80s, Manny Noriega was George Bush's nigga. On the CIA payroll, he helped the United States run drugs, launder money, and ship arms to its operations in Nicaragua and El Salvador. But ol' Pineapple Face became a problem. Turns out he was helping Castro, laundering money for Pablo Escobar, and talking smack about US imperialism. Plus he knew way too much about the whole Iran-Contra scandal. Dude had to go. In December 1989, Bush sends in the Green Berets to arrest him for drug dealing. A whole Panama City barrio is leveled. The official body count is 500-something; others say 3,000. Noriega sits in a Florida jail feeling confused.

Iraq
In the '80s, Saddam Hussein is America's ally. The United States sends him weapons and money as he fights a seemingly endless war against Iran, murders his political opponents, and gasses the Kurds. In 1991, Saddam is pissed off at neighboring Kuwait (a country invented by Britain) for undercutting the price of oil. He invades. The United States forms an international coalition to "liberate" Kuwait; Saddam sends an army of barefoot conscripts. For more than forty days and nights,

177 million pounds of bombs fall on Iraq—the most concentrated aerial onslaught in the history of the world. The US troops use cancer-causing depleted uranium weapons; they bury soldiers alive; they bomb retreating troops and civilians. At the war's end, the United States turns its back on the Kurds and other anti-Saddam forces (see *Three Kings*). While Saddam remains in power, US sanctions and continued bombing keep food, medicine, and clean water from everyday Iraqis. According to the UN, over one million Iraqis have died, half of them children.

Yugoslavia

1999: After the Serbs start "ethnic cleansing" Albanians in the Yugoslavian province of Kosovo, the United States and NATO launch seventy days of air strikes against Serbia. Thousands of Serbs are killed. The ethnic Albanian KLA guerrilla army, a drug-dealing group of thugs who were first accused of ethnic cleansing Serbs by the *New York Times* back in 1982, starts an open season on Serbs living in Kosovo. The bombs stop, and Serb demagogue Slobodan Milosevic is driven from power by a popular movement.

Colombia

2001: Colombia's three-decade-old civil war is still going strong, despite or, one might say, as a result of $1.4 billion of US military aid. The country is a chaotic death trap. Marxist rebels hold large portions of the country; American mercenaries and Defense Department front companies like DynCorp covertly help the inept Colombian military; right-wing paramilitaries massacre civilians; and everyone has their hands in the super-lucrative drug trade. Most people don't know that American forces have been around for a while. In the early '90s, a secret group code-named Centra Spike launches a covert operation to take out Pablo Escobar, a major cocaine lord who made the fatal mistake of giving money to the poor and talking shit about American imperialism. The Colombian government and the secret American unit go into business with Escobar's rival, the Cali Cartel. Escobar is finally killed. The Cali Cartel's power is solidified and the flow of cocaine into the United States only increases.

**From Vol. 9, No. 3, April 2002

The original article featured photos of the bomb. That's the weapons expert in the background.

DIRTY DEEDS

Black Market Nuclear Bombs Are Dirt Cheap

by Carlo McCormick

The biggest security threat to the international community isn't a runaway jumbo jet, a can of powdered anthrax, or even a Korean ICBM. The thing that's going to kill us all within the next five years is a dirty bomb: a small, portable, self-detonating nuclear device, usually fueled with misappropriated post-Soviet-era radioactive materials. As an Arab student in Egypt recently explained to the *New York Times*, "With just eight suitcase-sized nuclear bombs, the whole problem of Israel could be eliminated." Weapons of mass destruction are becoming so much smaller and so much cheaper, it won't be long before this student gets one of his eight bombs. Israel is only the beginning.

When the Soviet Union collapsed in 1990, various sources of radioactive materials from around the crumbling empire were suddenly huge security problems for the international community. Everything from weapons-grade plutonium to radiotherapy isotopes started to disappear. Most of the newly independent former Soviet states were barely able to pay for important things like toilet paper and cabbage, so the whereabouts of pint-sized lead canisters of strontium, iridium, and uranium 235 just didn't register. A lot of it ended up on the Eastern European black market, fashioned into lightweight explosive devices by disgruntled, unemployed, ex-Soviet government scientists who were desperate to make a fast buck. Now anyone can buy one.

The truth is that we've known about these dirty bombs for a long time. In early March of this year, the US National Intelligence Council was forced to admit, "Weapons-grade and weapons-usable nuclear materials have been stolen from some Russian institutes. We are concerned about the total amount of material that could have been diverted over the last ten years." The Russians deny this, of course. Defense Minister Sergei Ivanov says, "There is not a single case that any Russian weapons-grade nuclear material has been stolen, sold, or something like that," but admits they cannot account for ex-Soviet satellite republics. That's where the bombs are born.

While Bush and Cheney empty the coffers of the billions they'll need to create Reagan's Star Wars missile shield in order to protect us from death from above, crafty, black-market gangsters are buying and selling nuclear bombs small enough to overnight ship in a FedEx poster tube. Just about anyone can buy a bomb: a good Christian who really wants to teach that abortion clinic a lesson, your average local survivalist or patriot, or that weird guy who keeps to himself in the shack down the road. Even an overzealous journalist desperately seeking the undercover scoop of the century can get hold of a nuclear weapon. Take French journalist Alex Jordanov, for example.

Right now Jordanov is running for his life. He left Paris after numerous death threats and endless interrogations by police and government officials because he bought a nuclear bomb. His nightmare began when he was working for French TV network Canal Plus. A small, unsubstantiated story came in over the AFP news wire about a Bulgarian who was recruiting personnel for the Bin Laden Corporation in Dubai. The story reported that the Bulgarian had met with Osama and his associates before September 11, and that they had inquired about procuring nuclear waste or other by-products from Bulgaria. Within days of the AFP story, Jordanov decided to fly to Bulgaria to meet this shady character and find out why the deal went sour. "I decided to go look for this guy," Jordanov told us during a three-day stop here in New York, "but I didn't know where to find him. I had no real contact, and no one knew, or was telling if they did." After days of dead ends, a friend of the Bulgarian's arranged a few cautious meetings. It was at the third meeting that the Bulgarian finally decided to explain the deal with bin Laden.

In early 2001, the Bulgarian was contacted by bin Laden's Al Qaeda operatives once it was revealed that his Bulgarian "import/export" business put him within reach of nuclear material that had been floating around on the fringes of legality. It was clear to bin Laden then, as it has been to the CIA, Interpol, and MI5, that this nuclear material was up for grabs out there in the post-Soviet ether. The Bulgarian agreed to a meeting, and in May 2001 was flown to Pakistan and shuttled through Islamabad in Humvee Safaris by an Al Qaeda entourage. They put him up in a villa, wined and dined him, and brought him to a Muslim rally where he was told he would be meeting Osama himself. The crowd was whipped into a frenzy but Osama never appeared. Instead, the Bulgarian was tucked into a minivan and driven into the mountains. His eventual meeting with bin Laden was brief, simple, but bewilderingly inconclusive: They bowed, talked about the weather, and shook on the vague promise of doing something together in the future. It wasn't until the next day, back at the villa in Islamabad, that the envoy asked bluntly if the Bulgarian could supply some nuclear by-products. As a first-rate black marketeer, a sort of latter-day Harry Lime working in the most replete, corrupt, dangerous, and profitable black market in the world, the Bulgarian knew that he could easily fill the order. The Bulgarian upped the ante for the Al Qaeda operatives: "Why bother getting nuclear waste when you can buy the finished product? Why not buy a warhead?" His hosts jumped at the idea and offered $250,000 for the dirty bomb, but within a day or so the magnitude of the deal had sparked some semblance of scruples in the Bulgarian. He backed out of the deal and flew back to Bulgaria.

Jordanov was skeptical about this story and prodded the Bulgarian for some proof of his ability to acquire a finished, working dirty bomb. The Bulgarian proudly defended himself, explaining that it was easy to find a dirty bomb on the black market, but every time that Jordanov pushed him for some evidence he balked, backing out as he had done with bin Laden before. What followed were several weeks of bribing officials and wandering down dirt roads marked with signs like "We shoot without warning." They went to Russian slums and talked to ex-colonels and came up with nothing. Eventually the Bulgarian left Jordanov to pursue leads on his own.

Jordanov came close a few times, but eventually was forced to give up too and return to Paris. Canal Plus had canned the whole story, but about a week later, the Bulgarian emailed Jordanov out of the blue, itemizing a number of arms he had stumbled upon for sale. On that list was a nuclear device called the Howitzer 152 mm artillery tactical shell. Jordanov assembled 25K, traveling expenses, and an edgy bomb expert named Franz, who had designed most of the Soviet bloc tactical weapons. Franz had seen this done back in 1993 when the Ukraine returned its nuclear arsenal to Russia. He was sure one of them would be killed, but couldn't resist the adventure.

Jordanov and a cameraman flew to Sofia where they met up with Franz, who was coming in from East Germany rather than his home in Russia. Franz was hostile, however, and told them how stupid they were. Jordanov panicked, believing that Franz was part of a sting operation of some kind, but once Jordanov put Franz and the Bulgarian together to sniff each other out and talk the military-jargoned minutiae of weaponry, they reached a consensus to head east the next morning. After an eight-hour drive in which the Bulgarian and Franz talked shop in fluent Russian the whole way, they found themselves in Drobic, a depressing hellhole of a Russian slum. There they met an entirely new contact, with no explanation as to what had happened to the former connection. Another typically sudden change of plans had their scheduled meeting at a villa moved to the Hotel Bulgaria, where they waited twenty minutes in a shady bar peopled by a clientele of thugs with gold teeth and leather jackets and cheap hookers in ripped stockings. "It wasn't supposed to go down that way," Jordanov says, as if still reliving the mind-blowing shock and sphincter-clenching terror of that afternoon. "Suddenly they pull up in a car and drop the bomb into the front seat of our car. We all just freaked and jumped out of the car as fast as we could. It was like looking at the face of God. You suddenly realize you're facing something beyond comprehension."

Franz the expert had to decide if this was the real deal, and he was getting paid whether or not it was actually a nuclear bomb. He checked it out, and reported that the device was the detonator for a nuclear missile. It was the top of three component parts and it contained by far the most deadly payload, filled with pure plutonium rather than the uranium nuclear blend that would make up the rest of the missile. Knowing that this wasn't the best moment to pull out their camera and start filming, Jordanov improvised, showing the arms dealers his cash and asking for some time with his partner to talk things over. They privately shot some video of the bomb, which gave Jordanov time to hatch a plan. When the group of Bulgarians returned, he gave over the $25,000, asking them to keep the money and hold on to the bomb while he and his partner went back to Sofia to get money to buy a second device. It was too good an offer to refuse, and Jordanov, his cameraman, and Franz drove all night back to Sofia.

Upon arriving, they did a quick interview with Franz in which he carefully explained for the television audience what it was that they had bought. They agreed to meet in the morning before leaving, but they discovered the next morning that Franz was not taking the late morning flight to Germany. He had already checked out and grabbed the very first flight out of Bulgaria, a dawn departure to Greece. It seems that the Bulgarian had dropped by the hotel with their original contact carrying a suitcase full of uranium bars for sale in addition to the second nuclear device. Franz panicked and fled. With nowhere to run if the Bulgarian mob were waiting for him at the airport, a whole lot of videotape that he hardly wanted to be caught holding, and a very long wait until their flight, in which anything could happen, Jordanov decided to call a reporter for Bulgarian Television he knew and offer her the rights to the story if she would just come get him at the hotel and get him to the airport alive.

Back in Paris, Canal Plus was torn apart by infighting over what to do with the story. Many did not want to run it at all, while others argued for a major media promotion. With a lot of outside pressure on the network, concerns were once again raised as to whether Jordanov had wittingly or unwittingly taken part in some grand hoax. Again the search went forth for more experts, a long and winding road that eventually brought not only Franz (unidentified and with his face hidden) on camera, but a second expert, Feodor Pachenko, former head of the Soviet Atomic Program. Pachenko more than validated the assertion that this was indeed a bomb, and he carefully explained before the cameras every terrifying aspect of just what Jordanov had bought and subsequently abandoned. In the meantime, however, the French government swung into action. When the Ministry of Defense came into Canal Plus to seize the tapes, Alex and his coworkers were stunned. They had been trying for weeks to give them these tapes to verify them and gladly turned over copies.

At first the Defense Department asked them to wait, maintaining that it would take them six months to authenticate the bomb. But with so much evidence already accumulated, Jordanov's show, *Le Vrai Journal*, felt confident enough not to wait for such approval. The day before the program was to air, a spokesman from the Ministry of Defense called the network executives to put pressure on them not to show Jordanov's footage, assuring them that they had been fooled. Of course, at the same time they were asking Jordanov if he would be willing to go back to Bulgaria accompanied by some of their agents. And as if he didn't have enough problems, just four days back in Paris Jordanov received a desperate phone call from the Bulgarian. He was in Paris and was not pleased. It was around this time that the Bulgarian journalist who had saved Jordanov's life decided to air the story on a Bulgarian news show.

By the end of that show, Jordanov had received a call from his father in Germany saying that a bunch of Bulgarian mobsters had just threatened to blow him up in his car. Twenty minutes later Jordanov received a call on his mobile threatening to break his neck "like a rabbit." It was the last call Jordanov got in France. He took the next flight to New York.

Today Jordanov could be anywhere. Just before this story went to press he called our office and said he was working on a way of getting in touch with the surviving Al Qaeda leadership. Then he hung up. The story on the nuclear bomb did finally run on Canal Plus, but the French and Bulgarian authorities have been busily denying the whole affair ever since. Jordanov is not deterred. In fact, the past year's events have inspired him to go for bigger game. Maybe it's his tenacity that gets him these incredible stories. Maybe it's really difficult to buy a nuclear weapon and Jordanov is the best research journalist in the world. Or maybe it's easy and we're all going to fucking die.

JONGS JEFF, B
7-3-95 $15.89

THE VICE GUIDE
TO SURVIVAL IN PRISON

by Robbie Dillon

Jack Murray isn't the smartest guy in the world, but he knows how to do time without getting into trouble, and that's no small task. The thirty-five-year old ex-con's penchant for armed robbery and drug abuse has given him an intimate knowledge of the penal system. At the moment, however, he's trying to put an end to a string of prison sentences that began when he was a teenager.

Murray was nineteen when he started his first five-year prison term. On the third day of his sentence, a younger, longhaired inmate approached him in the showers. "This kid walked right up to me and said, 'I'm going to suck your cock,'" says Murray. "So I punched him in the mouth. The next thing I saw was this 300-pound naked guy coming towards me in a rage." Convinced that he was about to be sodomized either before or after his imminent murder, Murray threw up his hands and explained to the fat guy as loudly as possible: "This guy said he was going to suck my cock so I punched him in the mouth!" The furious lifer charged close enough for Murray to inspect the tattoos on his face. At the last second, he turned and grabbed a handful of the younger inmate's hair and dragged his "kid" out of the shower with arm. Just before the two disappeared, the big guy called back to Murray warning him to "stay away from her!"

"I thought I'd seen everything," says Murray. "But that's when I realized that prison is a completely different world."

It's a world that more than 200,000 Canadians enter every year. Although most of them finish their sentences relatively unharmed, an unfortunate handful are targeted from their first day inside. Failure to understand the rules and norms that govern prison life can turn a simple jail sentence into a nightmare of violence, blackmail, and sexual harassment. "Most people don't plan on going to prison, and that's the biggest problem," says Murray. Over the years, he's seen dozens of inmates seriously hurt and even killed over easily avoided jailhouse faux pas.

Some of these breaches of etiquette would seem comical if the stakes weren't so high. In Ontario, for example, "goof" is a serious insult that can get you killed. In Nova Scotia, an inmate who didn't like country music was stabbed to death when he tried to change stations on the cellblock radio. The list goes on. "Every prison has its own little rules," says Murray. "When you first get there, the best thing you can do is keep your mouth shut. Take the time to observe your situation and figure out what you can get away with."

Hopefully, you'll never experience the pleasures of a "Club Fed vacation," but odds are more than a thousand *VICE* readers will end up there, so you may want to memorize these helpful prison hints just in case. They could ensure you a safe and happy incarceration.

1. Don't Be a Rat
Rats are inmates who inform on or steal from their fellow prisoners. Along with diddlers (child molesters), they occupy the lowest rung of the prison hierarchy. If other prisoners discover you are a rat, you will be either tortured and killed or chased into protective custody. Protective custody means doing all your time with perverts, rapists, and other assorted scum. Once you go PC, you are labeled a "punk" and can never return to the regular prison population.

2. Just Say No
Next to being a rat, the surest way to get your head kicked in is to owe someone money. With hash going for upwards of $50 a gram, the first-time inmate can quickly find himself in heavy debt. Your best bet is to avoid drugs altogether. If you can find no other way to handle the tedium of prison life, don't front.

3. Choose Your Friends Carefully

Every convict's reputation depends on whom he associates with. Usually, when you start your sentence, no one will talk to you. They need to see what kind of person you are first. Use the time to figure out where you fit in. Eventually, you'll find the right clique.

You may be approached by a smiley, nervous character who offers you cigarettes and wants to show you around. Don't talk to this guy. He needs to be your friend because everyone else hates his guy. If you hang out with him, they will hate you too.

4. Don't Play the Role

Prison is a pretty confusing place. If you're scared, you can't show it because people will walk all over you. On the other hand, acting like a tough guy in a place that is full of angry, violent criminals is just stupid. Some of these guys are just waiting for an excuse to fuck you up. Don't give them one.

5. Keep Quiet

Don't whistle. Not "blowing the whistle," but literally whistling. According to prison lore, only birds (i.e., stool pigeons) whistle. Whether or not you believe this, the fact is it's a stupid habit that usually provokes a violent reaction. Marc Jessup, an inmate who liked to whistle as he mopped the floors, once had an entire deadlocked wing literally clawing at the walls of their cells. When the doors finally opened, eight guys tripped over each other trying to be the first to beat him. They smashed his head in with the metal wringer from his bucket and rammed a mop down his throat while everyone cheered.

Other noises, like laughing and shouting, can be just as deadly. All that steel and concrete magnifies annoying sounds until they drill right into the heads of stressed-out convicts. An inmate who's shaking it rough doesn't need to hear you giggling like a baboon.

N.B. If you follow these guidelines, respect yourself, and use a little common sense, you should be able to do time like a pro. Remember, prison can be a great place to reflect, think about your mistakes, and figure out how to be a better criminal. As for all that stuff about being sodomized by gangs of glue-sniffing brutes, "It isn't true," says Murray. "Everyone knows they sniff paint thinner."

*From Vol. 9, No. 10, Nov. 2002

The original article featured photos of the author on stage, shortly before he strangled someone.

THE VICE GUIDE TO GETTING BEATEN UP

by Eugene Robinson

Don't be a victim. If some huge fucking Coke machine of a guy tries to attack you, grab his right arm with the forefinger of your left hand, then twist it behind his back and kick in the back of his knees from behind. If he has a knife, use your elbows as side fists and smash his temples at 45 degrees until his pupils dilate. If he gets you into some kind of a headlock, then sit down on one knee so that he's forced to sit on your lap and then implode his kidneys using the heel of your left palm against your right forearm... blah blah "nose bone into his brain" yadda yadda yadda.

Yeah, right.

If a huge fucking Coke machine of a guy tries to attack you, that's it. You're dead. He is going to break your nose and you'll be lucky to escape without head trauma. Any attempt to use some bullshit fighting tips you read in *FHM* or *Maxim* is only going to add to the

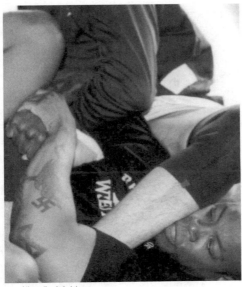
... and the author in training.

humiliation. Professional street-fighting tips are for professional street fighters. What about us 90-pound weaklings?

After watching the singer of Oxbow (the greatest art-rock band of all time) strangle a heckler into unconsciousness at a recent Leicester show, we had him write a *VICE* Guide that deals with the reality of fighting, i.e. how to minimize the inevitable pounding you are about to receive.

Here's what he sent us. (It's totally unedited because we were told that making any changes would result in having our bodies "twisted into a ball of misery.")

IT'S NOT SO BAD
First of all, let's cut the bullshit. Getting fucked up really bad isn't that bad. Thanks to the anesthetizing tendencies of adrenaline it's not even that painful. It's more a pain in the ass than anything. You know as soon as that nose bone cartilage snaps you are looking at a long and boring 12-hour wait in the emergency room. When someone says, "I am going to fucking kill you," think of it more as "I am going to audit you," because all he's really doing is adding a huge mundane thing to deal with into your next 24 hours. The truth is, the three-week-long pain of regretting that you pussied out is a hell of a lot worse than the dull nonpain of getting in a fight, so there's no need to be scared. And hey, if you're that calm you might even win.

DON'T GO CRAZY
More fights are lost from the biophysical functioning of stress-induced fatigue

than they are from inferior technique. In other words, relax. Exhale. Like you would for a bicycle crash or an anal rape. If you can fight with as much brio after five minutes (an eternity in fight time) as you can after 20 seconds, you will probably win.

STAY INSIDE

Bar fights are typically fought by drinkers. That is, drunks. Play the odds: Boris might actually be drunker than you and the limitations of indoor fights can't be underestimated. There's the errant barstool either swung or tripped over to mix things up a bit, the strategic positioning of reliable friends who can move in if you're losing, and finally, the simple truth that it's going to be broken up in less than 10 seconds, leaving you free to posture, scream imprecations, and hope to god nobody takes you seriously when you shout, "Let me go! Let me go!"

CHOOSE YOUR BATTLES

You want to lose a fight? Start one. Every single fight I've picked I've lost. No one picks a fight they think they can lose, and overconfidence is your worst enemy in a battle. If someone gooses your sister and you *have* to start a fight, try to avoid men with scarring around the eyes and the ears. Men sporting cauliflower ears and scar tissue on their eyebrows only get that way from training.

BE INTO IT

The most important thing about fighting is to feel passionate about it. That's why you had all those sick fantasies about that skinhead Pat O'Connor punching your mom in the stomach. You realized a brawl based simply on boots wasn't enough to get you sufficiently amped. If you just accidentally burned him with a cigarette, fucked his old lady, and smashed into his car, you might want to let this one go. He's got at least three good reasons to kick your ass and you have... well, none actually.

DON'T MAKE THAT STUPID
POST-FIGHT FACE

That fake smile guys do after they've been Ass-Kicked has got to go. It's the same face guys make when their girlfriend catches them cheating. It's the face of "The Complete and Total Inability to Deal With The Fact That You Might Be Thought to Be a Pussy." The most notable thing about this face is what the guy says as he's making it—"Did you see that? The fucking guy sucker-punched me. What a bitch." Then, four hours later, you come back to the bar and you hear the guy boring some other poor bastard to death with "The fucking guy sucker-punched me. Did you see that?" Get over it. All you should do after the fight is quietly call him a piece of shit and then go get a drink. You're not going to be able to talk normally (feel your heart) for at least another three minutes, so don't bother trying.

DON'T GO TO THE HOSPITAL

Unless he removed one of your fingers, do not let the word out that you pissed off some guy so bad he put you in the hospital. Have a beer and settle down. Accept a fake phone call on your cell and pretend you have to go. Shit, pretend you have to leave to go find him but you have to do it on your own. Just make sure that NOBODY finds out you actually went to the hospital instead. If you get stitches, cover them with a huge Band-Aid and say you had to put it there because you were getting blood on your food.

RUN FROM ANGRY GIRLS

What the fuck are you going to do—pound her? Unless you are also a female, you should run away covering your head if a girl has a problem with you. It looks kind of cool, actually. Like you're a heartbreaking bad boy. If she wants to take you on and you stand there defending yourself, there are two possible scenarios: 1) she beats the shit out of you in front of the whole party and you leave with a black eye and a future as laughingstock of your town; 2) you beat the shit out of her, and you're forever remembered as the guy who sat on Linda's chest pounding her bloody head into the ground as the crowd looked on in total and utter disbelief.

HOPE FOR THE BEST, EXPECT THE WORST

I know you've been told that people who are willing to say anything are not likely to do anything, but that's bullshit. Most humans who are not psychotic use a psychological technique called ramping immediately prior to conflict. Through a series of words, or language structures, they get themselves warmed into the prospect of violent activity until, voilá, they've arrived at Fight Time. Get there before they do. Pop him one early. Which brings us to our next section...

ACTUAL PLAUSIBLE MOVES

OK, it's going down. You are a little Timmy. What to do? We're not going to bore you with impossibly ninjistic moves you'll never have the gumption to use. We're going to give you invaluable little tips, like how you should repeat the words "kill, kill, kill" in your head before it goes down. Things like:

THE HEADBUTT

Headbutts are great because they take almost no accuracy and the risk of accidentally hurting yourself is nil. The secret to smashing open his nose is to focus your attention on his two front teeth on the way in. If you're in North America, he will be totally taken by surprise.

Drawback: As it is for sharks, you can't see what's going on as you hit him, so you're never sure if you really got him.

THE KNEE TO THE HEAD

Most people never think of this, because most people haven't taken the deadly

Southeast Asian art of Muay Thai, and your knee seems too far away from his head for this move to come naturally. Wrap your hands around the back of his head, yank down with an authoritative snap, and leap upward knee first. As you leap your downward snap will meet the rising of your knee, and when his head and your knee meet? Well, it's nothing short of magic.

Drawback: You have to do it fast because people tend to figure out something's up when you grab the back of their head.

THE REAR NAKED CHOKE

If, by any sheer luck, you end up standing behind him, it's time to choke the fucker. Wrap your right arm around his throat, and squeeze it closed by grabbing your left shoulder. Now with your other hand you can push his head into the hold thereby squeezing his neck even tighter. The best part of it is you can talk to him the whole time.

Drawback: You could easily kill him, in which case there'd be "a whole lot of splaining to do."

THE UPPERCUT

If someone is delivering a knockout punch, nine times out of ten, it's the uppercut. I don't know whether it's the sharp clicking together of the jaw or the stimulation of some sort of nerve bundle, but this punch is relatively easy to do and guaranteed to slip him into sleep. Throw your whole body into it and keep it tight against yourself at the beginning, like a jack-in-the-boxspring. A great way to administer this blow is to be waving your left hand in his face saying something like, "Whoa, whoa, I don't want any trouble. This is all a big misunderstanding," and then POW with the right.

Drawback: If your hand speed is slow, don't even THINK about trying this one.

THE MAD COUNTER

You are going to think this is strange, but it works every time. You tell the guy you're going to count to five. You don't say why. You just do it. "ONE," then, while apparently inhaling for "TWO," you fucking tear out of there and run as fast as you can. No idea why this works, it just does. There's a three-second interval where he's thinking, "Hey, he said he was going to count to five," and that is all you need to make your getaway.

Drawback: You will be known as a pussy if there's even a remote possibility you could have won.

Robinson has a street fight record of 0 wins and 3 losses for fights that he's started, 6 wins and 0 losses for fights he hasn't, eight years of Kenpo Karate, two of Muay Thai, one of Brazilian Jiu Jitsu, three of wrestling, and ten with his fight-prone band Oxbow (www.theoxbow.com). Their latest album, An Evil Heat, has been out for months but it hasn't exactly made a dent on the charts, so go and get it. This month, Oxbow will release a movie, Music For Adults, which contains lots of footage of Eugene strangling people on tour in Europe.

**From Vol. 7, No. 6, July 2000

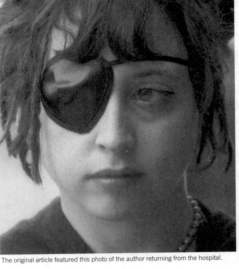

The original article featured this photo of the author returning from the hospital.

MY MOM SHOT ME

by Teresa "T. Dawg" McWhirter

The worst trip I've ever been on in my whole life was a couple of months ago when I went back to visit my family in Fruitvale, British Columbia. Fruitvale is a small village in the West Kootenays of interior BC where they brew Kokanee beer. When I went to parties in high school anyone who showed up without Kokanee got called "fag" or "pussy" and then got beat up.

Me and my mom and Chuck (my new dad) started drinking early at my brother's house. Later everyone went outside for some target practice, which is how we celebrate all major holidays. My brother has seven rifles and says he'll be damned if the government is gonna get their hands on them. I'm not that paranoid even after a gram of coke to myself. Chuck believes it's the feminists in Quebec making all the fuss about gun control.

Not one to be labeled the p-word, my mom pumped up her air rifle four times and took a shot at the target. CRA-ACK! I was standing ten feet from it so it was easy to see that she missed. I thought to myself, "Ha ha," and then had this nanosecond of realization that something large and black was about to hit my eye. After it hit, I screamed as loud as I could, clutching my face. My mom had shot me in the eye. The pain was unreal.

Almost immediately my vision clouded over with a thick white fog. We rushed to the car and I swear I heard Chuck ask about dinner. That made me think of the time my ex-boyfriend said feeling up a girl was like sticking your hand between two pieces of ham. I knew my mom felt bad so I really played it up, writhing and moaning in the backseat. I figured if I was blind I might be able to get a scooter. I passed out pretty quickly from the pain, but somewhere around Rock Creek there was a giant thud and I jerked awake. We had hit a deer. "Keep going," my mom screamed, "it's already dead!"

The Mum in question.

At the hospital the admitting nurse rushed us right in. Another nurse came and put some freezing drops in my eye. Then she wanted me to explain how the pellet ricocheted off the target into my eye.

"I did it," my mom said meekly.

"I thought it was a bunch of teenagers messing around," the nurse said. "Nice going."

We sat and waited for the doctor in the emergency room. The man in the bed beside us was trying to pass a gallstone and the grunts were inhuman. Finally the doctor came and examined me. He said my pupil was an irregular shape and that meant very bad things. He had creamed corn on his tie. After, like, an eternity of tests, he said that there is still hope down the road, but basically I'm blind in one eye.

Back in the car I let my mom have it. All the way home I shot her dirty looks from the backseat with my good eye.

These days, things are better between us. Even though I look like a pirate with this leather eye patch I will probably be wearing until I die, I still love her because at least she didn't kill me.

CRIME

SOMEONE THREATENS TO SUE YOU

SETTLE
You pay out $5,000 cash (unless you're *The New York Times* that's probably all you have).

THEY'RE HAPPY WITH THAT
They leave with your $5,000 and then word gets out that you give out money and everyone with the slightest beef files a claim.

BANKRUPT

THEY WANT MORE
Often original claims will ask for upwards of $250,000. You'll look up historical cases and they'll say 1% of that but that doesn't seem to matter. $5,000 is an insult to someone that asks for 50 times that so they're going to want more.

FIGHT IT
You can either give the money to a stranger and get a reputation as a cash cow or you can give it to your lawyer — an employee of the company that's saved your ass several times in the past.

PAY IT
Whose budget can spare more than a $5,000 hiccup?

BANKRUPT

IT GOES TO COURT
Your lawyer needs $25,000 just to show up.

IT KEEPS DRAGGING ON
You only have $5,000 to play with. If they send more than, say, five letters, your retainer is going to run out and you're done.

THEY GIVE UP
Once they realize the magazine is an actual business and not some vanity project funded by an eccentric millionaire they will probably give up. If you had a retainer bigger than $5,000 you could last longer and, hence, this scenario would be more likely.

THEY WIN
They "get" $45,000 (98% of which goes to their lawyer) and your lawyer still needs $25,000.

THEY LOSE
Good for you, but you still owe your lawyer $25,000.

BANKRUPT

BANKRUPT

BANKRUPT

YOUR ONLY OPTION

THE VICE GUIDE TO LEGAL DEFENSE

Over the years we have had at least 13 court cases threatened against us. They range from kind of valid to totally absurd. We've had a Jamaican guy try to sue us for being in the DOs ("what if you had photographed me while I was committing a crime?") and a Wall Street broker that claimed, "since the publication of this article my wife and I have been ostracized both in our community and in our individual workplaces" – yeah right. In every case the only people with any hope of getting money are the lawyers so we thought, "fuck it." Magazines suffer when they make up fake names and try to play it safe. That is why we've decided to go for broke, never settle and say whatever we want about whatever we want. If it means we go bankrupt at lease we die with our boots on.

SPECIAL PEOPLE

PHOTOS BY BRUCE LABRUCE UNLESS OTHERWISE SPECIFIED

**From Vol. 9, No. 11, Dec. 2003

MY WAR

CP Thinks That It's My Friend But It's One of Them

by Paul Remy

My debut in the world 48 years ago, spasticity and involuntary movements due to cerebral palsy have been the dictators of my body. These twin Saddams constantly fight for control of my legs, arms, and throat muscles, creating a never-ending battle that forbids me from walking, properly using my hands, and talking clearly. Muscles in my left arm can become so tight that I can't extend or bend it at all, while at other times it moves wildly in the air. My right arm never completely defected to the other side, but it refuses to feed me and help me perform daily tasks. Despite this, I've been living in my own apartment for the past 14 years with the assistance of personal care attendants, who come in for several hours at a time throughout the day.

Depending upon how much control the evildoers in my brain have over me at any given time, I can type between two and five words a minute using a pointer

These photos by Terry Richardson.

attached to a helmet on my head. There are times when spasms invade my neck muscles, causing jerky movements that prevent me from striking keys. I guess entering a speed-typing contest is out of the question. However, my pointer has helped me accomplish many things in life, such as getting my college degree. It is now allowing me to pursue a career as a freelance writer. Sometimes frustration and sadness consume me—it takes a week or two of poking keys to produce a single article, and I cannot financially support myself at that pace. Therefore, I'm forced to survive on welfare. I wouldn't consider myself disabled if I could type 60—90 words a minute, but I can't escape the grip that prohibits me from accomplishing this feat. Regardless of this, I get paid handsomely in other ways—knowing that I am well-respected for my hard work and, more importantly, believing that my articles might help others understand.

Meeting new acquaintances can be difficult. Some automatically assume that I'm mentally retarded because I use a wheelchair and have speech impairment. When people have this impression of me, I get frustrated, wanting so desperately to tell them I'm just as intelligent (if not more so) than they are. I do sometimes win battles in this area: While in college I took a course in political science, and at first the professor wouldn't pay any attention to me. Perhaps he thought I didn't have the IQ required for his class. During one session, however, I presented him with a piece of paper containing questions, which I had typed the night before, pertaining to his previous lecture. After reading and answering them, he became convinced that I fully understood the material. He ended up giving me a B+ for the course.

My disability doesn't stop me from fully enjoying life. I've even gone windsurfing and horseback-riding using adaptive equipment. Several years ago, a friend invited

me to Oregon to go skiing, and I had a hell of a lot of fun. Many times in my life people have told me I can't do this or that because of my physical limitations—some believe that the disabled can't accept failure, and want to protect us from it. But I'm not afraid of getting hurt once in a while. Failure is a part of life and being overprotected is far worse than having a disability.

Everyone wants to believe that people with physical disabilities are asexual. I can tell you that this is idiotic thinking, because I am a full-fledged sexual being. It outrages me when some nondisabled person attempts to persuade the disabled not to develop relationships, thinking we're unable to handle the ones that go wrong. I can vividly remember one friend telling me, "Relationships aren't all they're cracked up to be." If she truly holds this belief, I'm still mystified as to why she got married several years later.

Being a wheelchair user and having a severe speech impairment make it very difficult to meet new female acquaintances for possible friendships and intimacy. Thoughts sometimes rumble though my mind of getting a call girl. Maybe this is immoral and illegal, but I know other disabled people who resort to that type of service to fulfill some of their fancies. It's a difficult decision. What would you do if you were, God forbid, in the same situation?

I have wonderful women friends, and their companionship means so much. I know that asking them about the possibility of making compassionate love with me could tear us apart. I'm hoping to eventually find a close friend who is also willing to occasionally make love sleep with me. I don't know if I'll ever get married and have children, but I would be just as happy to have a life partner and lover.

This is Sean and Bobby. They are part of the *How's Your News?* crew mentioned in the next piece. Photo by Terry Richardson.

**From Vol. 9, No. 11, Dec. 2003

Photo of the author by Terry Richardson.

HOW'S YOUR ATTITUDE?

Sue Harrington Makes Her Corrections Accordingly

by Sue Harrington

Good day Ladies and Gentlemen. My name is Susan Harrington. I am a 36-year-old woman who was born with Optic Nerve Hypoplasia. This basically means that I have nerve damage in my eyes. What I have not yet told you is that at birth I was unfortunately diagnosed as being legally blind. What I am extremely proud to tell all of you is that I have not at all let my vision condition at all impact my involvement in making films and doing my job. I live at home with my roommate in Plymouth, MA. I live in a group home with one roommate. I should also tell you that I have a regular full time job. I work as a receptionist for the Department of Mental Retardation. For the past twelve years I have been working for them as a receptionist.

Today I am here to talk to all of you about a very special project in which I have been thoroughly involved. The name of the project is *How's Your News?* It is a travelling news show where we talk to people on the street about what they're up to.

All of the reporters met at a camp for people with various disabilities. It all got started when my friend Sean Costello went into sports class, and asked other campers and counselors, "How's your sports?" Well, from this point forward, I can proudly tell you that *How's Your News?* was born.

When *How's Your News?* did get started the group's founder, Arthur Bradford, chose a few people to become a part of the official crew. At the time that I got the call, I was sitting at the front desk of the Department of Mental Retardation. I can tell you first hand that this was a call that I was very excited to answer. I was excited to answer it because it was my friend Arthur on the line and he was telling me about this project in which I was about to become thoroughly involved.

When I hung up I remember thinking to myself, OK Susan this is probably just a one shot deal. Well let me be the first to tell you that what I got was a very rude awakening because I was completely wrong. The fact that I was wrong is something that you will very seldom get me to admit, but in this case I am going to make an exception to the rule.

This voyage really marked the beginning of what has really become an amazing success story, for all of us that have become involved, myself included. It was during the first voyage, a road trip across America, that we were really able to put the Man on The Street interview idea to the test.

During this maiden voyage of *How's Your News?* all of us for ourselves made a little discovery. What we quickly discovered for ourselves was that the Man On The Street idea was one that, worked out very well for us. All of us liked this idea so much that we later came together and decided to keep this as the primary *How's Your News?* format. Well, about a year later we were entered into our very first film festival. We all saw this as the beginning of a whole new chapter in *How's Your News?* movie history. So as you can probably imagine, this was really very exciting for all of us. I personally have to admit that, for a couple of reasons I was quite nervous.

First and foremost I was nervous because I didn't know how well the audience would react to our film. I thought they would say, "Get these damn Yankees out of here." I was also nervous because our first screening in history was in Austin, TX, not in my hometown. Well, let me tell you first hand that the response was very different than anyone, myself included, expected.

Well, with that having been said, I now feel better that I did not leave out any of these important details. For the record, I was glad that I caught myself when I wrote this. What I was thinking to myself was, "Oh my god Susan, you can't be leaving out details such as these. Details such as these are something that, you should certainly include in this article." Well, let the record show that this is one of many corrections that have now been made accordingly. When it was time to come home all I remember thinking was, "Yahoo! *How's Your News?* has made a gigantic splash in Texas."

I should tell you that on three different occasions, we have actually traveled abroad for these events. So all of us have now begun to develop a little bit of world exposure. So far we have been able to do these screenings in Canada on two different occasions and guess what? You guessed it. We are about to hit the road again. We are about to take off for Amsterdam, Holland. We already went. Well, I can tell you that the Amsterdam response to our movie was much better than any of us anticipated. I should also tell you that during these trips we have also made some time for songwriting. We have already taken most of the songs that we've written and recorded one compact disc. And to that let me add that we already have enough music to make a new one. If there are any upcoming movie screenings, I will certainly make sure that all of you will get the word.

Well, in closing, I would like to thank all of you for allowing me to write this today. Live from Boston, Massachusetts, this is Susan Harrington reporting live for *VICE Magazine.*

**10 Reasons Why
It's Great to Be Alive**

10. Because I am a woman who enjoys her active lifestyle.

9. Because I enjoy getting up and coming to work each day.

8. Because at the office I have developed good friendships with everyone on staff.

7. Because I enjoy singing in the church choir every Sunday.

6. Because, for the last 22 years, I have been enjoying going on summer vacations to camp.

5. Because, with some of my friends from camp, I have greatly enjoyed being involved in *How's Your News?*

4. Because I look forward to going home and spending time with Josephine my roommate.

3. Because I greatly enjoy holiday gatherings with my family.

2. Because I enjoy spending time with my two nephews.

1. Because I have greatly enjoyed the many places that we have been able to do our *How's Your News?* movie screenings.

**10 Reasons Why
My Meds Aren't So Great**

10. I'm getting really sick of always being tired.

9. The drowsiness is making me very exhausted.

8. When I wake up I feel as if I could sleep for four days.

7. Makes me feel very lethargic.

6. The tiredness is getting to be extremely annoying and on most nights I have been going to bed two hours earlier than usual.

5. The drowsiness is affecting my work performance.

4. Not in the physical sense but I feel as if this med is knocking me down.

3. I am not getting a second wind by the end of the workday. I have found that I have absolutely no energy.

2. Most nights I am in my room and asleep a lot earlier than usual. This med is playing around with my body clock and I don't exactly like it.

1. Especially during my workday I am finding that I have no energy, which is really beginning to piss me off.

Attention Dr. Wells: above all of you will see exactly how I have been feeling on the Kepra.

**From Vol. 10, No. 4, May 2003

Illustrations by Johnny Ryan.

OUR TEN FAVORITE PSYCHOPATHS

Life in the Mental-Health Unit Is Fun as Hell

by Bobby Richards

You get to meet a lot of fucking psychopaths when working in the mental-health unit of an East Coast maximum-security prison. All of the inmates I worked with were post-trial (already sentenced). Some were permanently in the mental health unit because they were found Guilty but Mentally Ill (which is different from Not Guilty by Reason of Insanity—that lands you in a forensic hospital). Other prisoners were sent to the mental-health unit because their "quirks" made it dangerous for them to be living in the general population. In fact, lots of the guys I saw were faking mental illness for that very reason, to be out of the snake pit. My duties included counseling, assessment and testing, conducting intake interviews with new arrivals, and saying "How-lee shit" to myself about 50 times a day. Here are just a few of the guys I miss the most:

THE LITERAL HOMOPHOBE

John was a twenty-year-old man, sentenced to 50 years for killing an acquaintance who had the audacity to assume John was gay. The victim made a pass at John, which he allegedly declined. Upon reflection, John became so enraged and obsessed that while the man was sleeping that night, John strangled him to death. John then strangled the victim's cat to death because he believed the cat was gay too, and he was literally scared of anything fag. When asked why he felt the need to murder the kitty, John replied, "I don't do anything half-assed."

FARRAKHAN WHITEY KILLER

There are a few select men in prison who absolutely nobody fucks with—like a militant, Afrocentric, bipolar ex-boxer who legally changes his FIRST name to Farrakhan. This guy always seemed to be mopping, and that alone scared the shit out of me.

CHESTER THE MOLESTER

Close your eyes and imagine what a cliché mentally ill, middle-aged pedophile looks like. See him? Bingo! Carl had thick glasses, crooked teeth, greasy hair, and remarkably poor hygiene. Jailed on several counts of child molestation, Carl was genuinely talented at making arts and crafts out of cigarette boxes and packing tape. He would cut a box into tiny triangles, laminate them, and weave them together with thin strands of tape. We all marveled as Carl showed us the picture frames and cup holders he created. We all cringed when he showed us the baby shoes he made with his scarily nimble fingers. You haven't experienced creepy until you see a pedophile showing off a pair of handmade baby shoes.

THE JERK-OFF

Some inmates pass their time trying to piss other people off. These are the kind of guys who try studying law while they're locked up and then write letters to Norman Mailer about how fucked up the prison system is. Our most notorious letter-writer was a guy who penned a note to Bill Clinton about poor prison conditions, jerked off on said letter, and mailed it. It never made it out of the prison mailroom and the guy lost his television privileges for a month. Score one for the system.

TICKLES THE CLOWN

Perhaps the purest psychopath I came across while working in the prison, Paul was a notorious child rapist who existed solely to get under people's skin. His most shining moment was when he joyfully told a room of people evaluating him that he looked forward to getting out of jail one day and "working with children."

PIGPEN

Collins was the quintessential raving lunatic. The prototype. Like Charles Manson dipped in diarrhea. He was dirty, hairy, gaunt, wild-eyed, and covered in self-inflicted scars. He was also a chronic masturbator with a history of throwing feces. Collins had the ability to hurt himself with any article of clothing he was given. One time he swallowed a bunch of buttons; another time he used the leg of his jumpsuit to strangle himself. As a result, he was forced to dress in a paper outfit—basically a big paper towel with a hole cut out for the head. Krazy with a capital K.

BILLY CONQUEST

When I was four, my grandmother's mailman was named Todd Postman. I thought that was fucking hilarious. Less hilarious, but equally "funny," was a vicious serial rapist I encountered whose last name was Conquest. One night Conquest shaped little pieces of soap to look like pills. He called over a nurse and told her he was killing himself and swallowed a big handful of fake pills. He then made believe he was convulsing and was rushed to the infirmary. Once he was there, he leapt from the stretcher and went apeshit, attacking nurses and doctors. He got some good shots in before they restrained him. Only a man named Conquest could pull that shit off.

RELATIVIST WHITEY KILLER

Jamal had paranoid schizophrenia, and he hated white people. He countered every single thing I ever said to him by replying, "Yeah, but to what extent?" We didn't get very far in counseling.

EL GHOSTBUSTER

Alfredo was a Cuban refugee who started screaming in terror during an assessment, claiming in Spanish that the ghost of his murder victim was walking across the room even as we spoke. Alfredo was truly bonkers, but he was also a skillful and manipulative liar. To delay certain hearings, he had staff convinced that he spoke only his mother tongue. Then one day, seemingly out of nowhere and in perfectly coherent English, he asked me where I bought my sweater.

MOMMA'S BOY

Tommy was only nineteen and sentenced to life for killing his mother. He ended up in the mental-health unit by faking a bunch of symptoms, which is a common way to avoid the much more dangerous general population. But unlike most criminals who fake delusions and hallucinations, Tommy went old-school and tried faking shit that hadn't been diagnosed since the turn of the century, like hysterical blindness and glove paralysis. His acting was atrocious, and he soon confessed to his con. We let him stay for a while, though, because we knew he would be destroyed among the general population. Tommy was bright and sweet, and definitely my favorite patient ever. One day he wrote me a poem that included the line: "I don't want the world to see me. Because I don't think that they'd understand." At first I thought it was poignant—until a coworker pointed out that Tommy had plagiarized Goo Goo Dolls lyrics (or was it The Eels?).

**From Vol. 5, No. 9, November 1998

INTERVIEW
WITH A CRAZY GUY

by a Sane Guy

Tracking down a crazy guy is an enormously difficult thing. First of all, most of them don't like talking and even if they say they do, they won't ever show up for the interview. Basically, their pants are on fire and they're hanging on about thirteen million telephone lines all over the world. We did get one guy, though. His name is Glenn Bedford and he lives with his parents in Hamilton, Ontario, at the ripe old age of thirty-nine.

***VICE*: So you wash your hands a lot.**
Glenn Bedford: I wash my hands about sixty-four times per day. I use a mechanic's soap called Snap. Sometimes they bleed if I do it too much. I don't know why I do it. I just can't tolerate having shit in my nails and being greasy. It leaves finger-prints everywhere. I would never touch any of my books or records if I hadn't just washed my hands.

That's unthinkable.
It would never happen.

Why?
I don't know. It has to do with resale value. My books have to be kept in perfect condition. The bindings can have no cracks or anything like that. I used to bend them open in order to read them, but it's hard to read the words closer to the spine. I don't read them anymore. I'm at the point now where I can't even open most of my records.

What's wrong with breaking a spine or opening a record?
Opening records is all right; I just like to avoid it. I hate cracking the binding of a book. If I see the corner of one of my records is bent or a book binding has a white line going down it, my day is ruined. I don't have a panic attack or anything, it just really brings me down. I'll usually feel bad until I go buy a new copy.

Any other fears?
I hate children. Especially bratty kids that cry all day and give their mothers no peace. Their shit-filled diapers make me sick to my stomach. One time a fare [Glenn drives a cab for a living] gave me $10 and I couldn't even touch it. She was carrying a baby and I was sure she had shit all over her. I just left the ten on the seat until someone needed change and then had them pick it up themselves. I think I even washed the seat after that.

**From Vol. 4, No. 6, July 1997

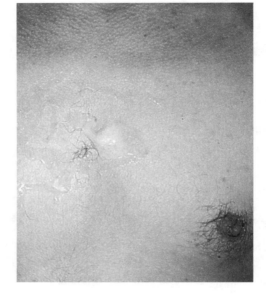

INTERVIEW
WITH A BIG HUGE FAT GUY

by a Skinny Guy

You know when you're walking down the street and you see one of those really fat guys, and you wonder, What's it like to be that fat? Well, being the hardcore investigative journalists that we are here at VICE, *we managed to get hold of a big huge fat guy named Peter Prusa and asked him all the questions you were too scared to ask. The interview took place at a local vegetarian restaurant, and in order to give the piece some kind of actual relevance, we invited an expert on Eastern medicine named Sylvie Lessard, who delivered some valuable insight and ate more than all of us.*

VICE: The word *fat* seems completely unlike *nigger* or *bitch* in that it is totally accepted as a valid criticism. Fat is synonymous with greedy or self-indulgent, and people have no problem criticizing overweight people to their face.
Peter: Hate hurts.

Be serious.
I've come across people that hate me solely because I'm fat, which is pretty funny. But it doesn't really bother me. I don't want to be any different, though sometimes I daydream about what it would be like to wake up skinny. I'm actually scared to be skinny. It would be like becoming another race.

You weigh about 360 pounds. Is that correct?
I think I might weigh more. Scales only go up to 360 pounds. Even doctor's scales.

Do you nod to other fat people you see on the street?
No, I laugh at them because they're fat.

Where do you get your clothes?
I got this T-shirt at Zellers. It's a 4X. I usually have to shop at places like George Richardson or Big and Tall. Jeans are more expensive, like about $70. A suit would cost me around $600.

What about your mom? Does she give you grief about your fatness?
All the time. She calls me up and tells me about the latest fat casualty, and I go, "It's all your fault. You're evil. You never loved me enough." She used to cook entirely with meat and grease. And so when I was a vegetarian, she couldn't cook for me.

What about having sex? Isn't that dangerous?
I don't lie on top of girls. Sometimes the girl will be on top of me, or I lay them on the bed, and I'll kneel on the floor. The only position I can't really do is missionary.

Why are you so fat? Is it a matter of metabolism?
Sylvie: (interrupting) No, it's not . . .
Peter: I've always been fat, and I don't eat that much. Yesterday, I got up and had no breakfast. I had two hot dogs and a Rice Krispie square for lunch, and for dinner I had a Caesar salad and some fries. I don't always eat the health food, but I don't pig out that often. I've been down to as little as 275 but the weight always comes back to the same number.

Sounds like fate.
Sylvie: It's not fate. It's his choice. Peter's problem is that he eats sugar at every meal, which hinders digestion. He's tied his colon into a knot by eating badly and there are piles of undigested waste blocked inside of him. It's the sugary soft drinks that kill him. Normally people carry about ten pounds of semi-digested meat with them. This meat becomes a hard rubber-like barrier that sits in his colon, giving

him this huge belly and preventing the other foods from being digested. Right now, this man is carrying about 100 pounds of undigested food. That's what's weighing down his entire system. He's actually starving to death.

Peter: Starving to death? Look at me!

Sylvie: You look at skinny little guys in Third-World countries. They're not really starving to death. People in America are. If you could just see the typical American colon, everything collects in this thick, black, rubbery substance and prevents them from being fed. Every animal on earth shoots water up their asses to keep their colons clean, but Western man is insane. He's scared of his ass—or too shy to talk about it—so the problem's never fixed.

So you perform enemas on yourself regularly?

Sylvie: Yes. It's simple. You lie on your back, relax, insert a tube a few inches into the anus, and the five-gallon container of water uses gravity to take care of the rest. You wouldn't believe the kind of horrible things inside of you. I've seen fluorescent blue, nuclear-colored waste come out of my body.

So if Peter took regular enemas and cut the sugar out, he wouldn't be fat anymore?

Sylvie: That's correct. But it would be very dangerous because of all of the toxins he's collected. He'd have to go on a macrobiotic diet and focus almost entirely on vegetables.

Are there any health risks you wouldn't normally think of?

Peter: Sometimes I get a shooting pain in my leg when I walk too much or when I stand around too much. Oh, there's chafing if I sit a certain way—my legs go to sleep. I've had two heart attacks and passed out quite a few times. Once I was late for work and was rushing around really nervous when my heart just stopped beating. I passed out, fell on my face, and broke my glasses.

Sylvie: If you feel his calves, they're probably pure muscle because he's walking around with a 200-pound weight around his waist. The veins bulge, the arteries get clogged.

What did your doctor say?

Peter : She was pretty nonchalant about it. Just took my blood pressure, which was normal.

Sylvie: And your doctor thought you were fine? Most Western doctors are maniacs with knives who can't wait to fill you full of pills. Peter's system is taxed to the extreme. His arteries get pinched and they can't move so they just die. The sad truth is that Peter is facing a huge variety of horrible deaths in his condition, and to call him healthy is pure ignorance.

Peter: I'm not hungry anymore.

**From Vol. 4, No. 7, August/September 199

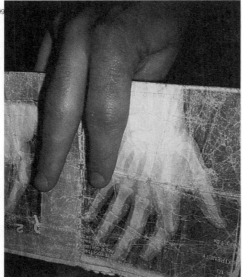

INTERVIEW
WITH A BLACK GUY

by a White Guy

Today a young hip hop head named Mark walked into our office and asked visiting Vancouver rep (and prominent Afro-Canadian) Derrick Beckles how he got so dark this summer. Mark was chastised and laughed at for not knowing that black people tan. But the sad truth is most of us don't know about colored folk because we're too scared to ask. Everyone's so busy saying "Asian," "West Indian," and "East Indian" that they don't know the difference between Taiwan and China or India and Pakistan or so on. Being the politically correct mavericks that we are, we asked Mr. Beckles if we could have a little of his dark-skinned time to inform our readers on what's it's like to be black.

VICE: So as Mark just asked, do black people tan?
Derrick Beckles: When I was a kid, I asked my brother why I was darker than all of

my friends, and he explained the concept of pigment to me. But when the kids in the school yard asked me why I was brown, I couldn't remember so I just said, "I have pygmies in my skin, you idiot!"

To answer your question, yes, there is a reaction to the sun. The really dark people aren't about to get sunburns or anything, but if you're light-skinned like me, you get really dark and can even burn in the summer.

Why is it bad to dress up in blackface? What's the matter with minstrels, Golliwogs, Amos and Andy, Sambo, and Uncle Tom?

The minstrels represent a time in black history when we were seen exclusively as clowns. Golliwogs portray blacks as cute furry toy savages. *Amos and Andy* was a 1950s show about two bumbling niggers. Sambo means "servant" and Uncle Tom comes from *Uncle Tom's Cabin*, which was about a doting old black guy who forgot about racism and told the white kids nice stories. Louis Armstrong is seen as Uncle Tom, for example, because of his "Wonderful World" persona.

What's a house nigger?

A house nigger was a well-spoken slave that didn't live in the house but could be in the house all day serving the white master. He would rat out the other slaves and be rewarded with better clothes and a higher standard of living.

What's "black time" or "island time"?

Blacks have a reputation for being later than whites, because when we're late we do it in style so people remember it better.

Why are black people usually better dancers and dressers than white people?

When blacks are about two years old, there's a two-month period where our parents get us drunk during sacrifices and teach the children how to dance. We kill goats and dogs and stuff, and the children are smeared in the blood and taught how to get down via good music and great outfits. It's happening around North America as we speak, which I think is a beautiful thing.

What do you think of the Canadian reggae greats like Canajah?

They're great. As a Canadian black, they really speak to me. I can hear things in the music that white people will never hear.

Do you like the Rolling Stones and Led Zeppelin? How do you feel when you hear Robert Palmer, or whatever his name is, crooning away in that bluesy accent or Mick Jagger doing the "Harlem Shuffle"?

At first it's kind of offensive to hear them appropriate black culture, but then I think no black person could ever sound as authentic as Robert Plant, or Robert Palmer, for that matter. The amazing thing about so many white people is the only blacks they'll have in their homes are on vinyl. In the 1950s, they used to have to put drawings of the black artist on records or people wouldn't buy them. It's essentially the same today.

Do you ever have white hip hop heads come up to you going, "Yo, nigger, wussup?"
That never happens to me. I talk like a white weatherman because I was born in Scarborough, so most of these rapper kids sound way blacker than I do. To most of them, it's a game. The only people that can afford to be black are rich white kids. It's really insulting because it's like, "Here's the black experience: dressing like this, talking like this, and wearing these clothes."

Let's go through the racism meter in Canada, starting with Vancouver.
Blacks are still a novelty there right now, so they're still figuring out how to be racist. But they're learning. They're preoccupied with the Asians right now, so the other races don't get the attention.

Calgary and Edmonton are, for the most part, out of control. They are isolated for a reason. Montreal and all of French Canada can be pretty ignorant about racism, but at least they can identify with the feeling of being second-class citizens. They have sex a lot and eat good food, as do blacks, so we both feel isolated from white English Canada for the same reasons.

Toronto has had bad dreads. Being white is a state of mind. When you get to the blues bars, there's all these white people shamelessly getting funky.

Halifax and the east coast had a lot of open doors after slavery. There were entire areas in Halifax that the underground railroad led to, but today there's America-like poverty there. Rural ghettos. It's like the southern states of Canada—a huge black community with heavy racial tension.

Do you nod to other blacks when you pass them on the street?
Yes. It's something I grew up doing. My grandfather did it. My father did it. It's an acknowledgement. It's just a subtle form of social interaction.

How often do you go through verbal and physical abuse for being black?
When I was tree-planting in northern Ontario recently, we went into a bar to play pool because the MNR [Ministry of Natural Resources] guys were late. After about a ten-minute staring problem, some redneck got up. The people I was with were white, and they didn't see the warning signs that I saw. When we came in, for example, Hank Williams was on, and they turned it up really loud. After feeling his glare for about ten minutes, we had a mutual staring problem that wasn't very romantic. Anyway, after the stare, he starts yelling, "What are you looking at, nigger?" It was at this point my friends finally realized we were in a bad scene. All I could do was laugh and we walked out.

The problem with these warning signs is once you start looking out for them, you can become obsessed and see everything as the beginning of a potentially serious problem. If I completely ignored all bad scenes, never took myself out of a situation, and treated the world as my oyster, I'd get called a nigger about once every six months. But you have to remember, when someone verbalizes it, they're at the point where they're willing to get into a fight because they hate you so much.

A lot of white kids, especially boys, go through a phase where they want to be black. Did you ever want to be white?
I never wanted to be white. Why would anyone want to be a part of such a shitty culture? I don't get that persecution complex thing where white kids wish they were black. I guess some whites feel guilty because a large majority have it easier and being persecuted looks like it would have some cool martyr status. In Vancouver some of the cooler white kids will dress as pimps and drive around in funky pimp hats with huge gold rings. As much as I love that gag and would like to change the interior of my Plymouth Valiant to zebra skin, I can't do that kind of irony because of all the racist connotations. There is no retro for blacks. If we want to do more than fuckin' put on clothes, we have to do it alone or in a room with other blacks with one guy constantly watching the windows.

With all the different blacks in this country, I don't understand how a Canadian can say, "I'm proud to be black." I mean, what does a Jamaican have in common with a Haitian, an American black, or a Bermudan?
To be proud of your race is really a reaction to the self-doubt you get from being bombarded with antiblack messages all day. It's a defense against racism that is just another way of saying, "I'm happy with who I am." What it is to be black, the thing that unifies us all, is pretty elusive. I'm still figuring it out now so I can't sum it up in a few minutes more than saying black pride is the opposite of black shame.

Do you feel cooler when you're in a room filled with blacks?
I like going to black clubs with white people. About half of them don't notice and the other half sit there squirming in their chairs. I grew up constantly surrounded by white people, so when I'm in New York or something like that, it can be a thrill to be surrounded by blacks. Not the sort of African safari thrill white people get when they're around blacks, but more like a sense of belonging. I don't want to exaggerate that, however. Most of the time when I'm in a room of blacks, I forget about it after a few minutes because there's nothing going on there that isn't going on in another club.

Is there a novelty factor with being black? People think it's cool to hang out with the black guy—jungle fever and all that.
If you look at porno videos, you have the lesbian section, the fat section and then you'll have black and white. The mentality is, "Here's two different races having

sex. Can you believe we filmed that?" But people don't really think blacks are cool. The image of blackness your average Canadian has isn't Sticks from *Happy Days* [Fonzie's cool friend that played the drums]. It's the guy lying face-down from the last episode of *Cops.*

Did that "woman grabbing her purse when you're alone with her in the elevator" thing ever happen to you?
That happened to me recently in Europe. I was checking out this exhibit on international press photos, and after I accidentally brushed up against this woman, she clutched her purse against her body. After that, every time I came near her, she'd move over dramatically, so I ended up spending most of my time going near her. I even considered taking her purse just to punish her, but I'd have to live out that joke for the next twenty years in some European jail.

Your granddad emigrated to Canada in the 1930s. What was it like for him?
He was a well-educated Barbados man with a photographic memory who came here to go to school, but McGill University wouldn't let him in so he ended up being a porter on the trains his whole life. He was a fairly big guy, but he'd get harassed all the time. He'd be waiting for the streetcar in Toronto, and guys would start shoving him around. Even my dad went through tons of shit. When he was a kid, businessmen used to come up and rub him on the head because it was good luck to "rub a Negro on the way to work." Even when he got to be a teenager, things were insane. He went on a date with a white girl once, and she asked him if he had a tail. I'm not kidding. This was Toronto in the 1950s.

**From Vol. 9, No. 2, March 2002

LATINO IS THE NEW BLACK

Exposing the Spanish Myth

by Jose X. Martinez

The Spanish CNN used for airlines is presently showing three main stories: a woman in Argentina who makes aprons and is doing well despite economic collapse; a lake in Chile where American astronomers go to get a good view; and a tequila bar in Tequila, Mexico, that represents how popular the drink is becoming. What the fuck do these stories have in common? Somehow the fact that 500 million people (251 million of whom live in poverty, according to the UN) speak the same language has made them into a demographic worth marketing—but it makes no sense. You might as well have the redhead channel or the left-handed channel.

In the last few years Latino culture has been processed, packaged, and promoted by every entertainment conglomerate, PR firm, advocacy group, and local TV channel in the United States. Since the ascension of Ricky Martin, J.Lo, and Marc Anthony to pop stardom, Latino culture has been given the stamp of approval by corporate America. The current media image is a commodified, artificial, and undifferentiated pseudocultural gloss that tells us nothing of the realities of the communities it supposedly represents. It's as authentic as Taco Bell and as culturally significant as Speedy Gonzales, Charo, or the Macarena.

The sheer numbers make it clear why the corporations want to exploit anything even remotely Latino-flavored: Latinos are the fastest-growing minority in America. Within ten to fifteen years they'll outnumber the black population, and by 2050, if current rates of growth are sustained, they'll eclipse the white population. But although you could say that Latinos are the new blacks, they're trying to create a different historical trajectory for themselves. Latinos are aware that they must be more than consumers if they are to avoid the fate of other minority groups. That's why there's such a strong affinity to entrepreneurship in the community. One of the easiest ways to become a respected Latino is to have your own business, or excel at climbing an otherwise white corporate ladder. All ethnic groups salivate over this kind of economic success, but for the Latino community, owning a piece is a way of making sure that the Latinos become the new Jews, not the new blacks.

That's why the American Latino community has relished any media attention, accepting even simplified representations of themselves rather uncritically. Their goal is to present themselves as a stable market force and entrepreneurial class rather than a cultural challenge to North American hegemony. Rather than critique, the general response is economic opportunism. But the worst part of this prepackaged artificial culture is the fact that the entire Latino community is given one face, one voice, and one identity. This is bullshit. The only thing all Spanish-speaking people have in common is that they all speak Spanish. They are as racist, classist, and judgmental of each other as everyone else is.

White Europeans Still on Top

During 500 years of colonial rule in the Americas, the intermixing of the three main racial groups (Amerindian of Mongoloid derivation, African Negroid, and European Caucasoid) led to a Byzantine system of racial prejudice and hierarchy. The Spanish, who wanted to keep track of the way that estates could be inherited by family lines born in the New World, legislated their own classification system in order to figure out how to settle rights while keeping the landowning class as purely European as possible. But race mixing was actually encouraged by the Spanish since their goal was the progressive "whitening"—*blanqueamiento*—and Europeanization of the region.

The effects of colonial racism still persist. In Latin countries race is articulated according to a color continuum where differences are related in shades like a paint-store color palette. For instance, when the Brazilian Institute of Geography and Statistics (IBGE) conducted a survey asking people to identify their own skin type, they received over 134 different descriptions of distinct skin-color groups: everything from *acastanhada* (cashewlike tint, caramel-colored) to *vermelha* (reddish).

But everyone is trying to be as white as possible. Just look at the contestants of this year's Miss Latin America pageant. Approximately 150 million black-skinned Latinos, in over a dozen countries, and only one is selected to represent?

Or look at the current heads of state of Latin countries. Vicente Fox looks like Charlton Heston pretending to be a Mexican in Orson Welles' *Touch of Evil*. Countries like Mexico were ruled by Spanish, British, or French patrons until revolutions and declarations of independence managed to install more Spanish, English, and French and, in the case of Peru, even a Japanese president.

If you take the percentage of population by racial category and index that to percentage of population by economic category, you get a picture of how race and economic class break down in Latin America. It's not a unified front that can all watch Spanish CNN together. It is a tangled web that is far too complicated to be understood by mortal man. See chart below.

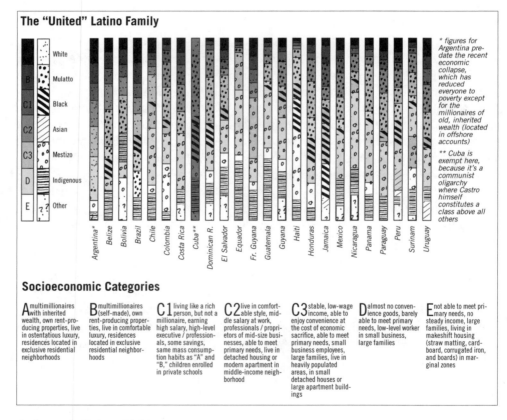

The "United" Latino Family

White
Mulatto
Black
Asian
Mestizo
Indigenous
Other

Argentina Belize Bolivia Brazil Chile Colombia Costa Rica Cuba** Dominican R. El Salvador Equador Fr. Guyana Guatemala Guyana Haiti Honduras Jamaica Mexico Nicaragua Panama Paraguay Peru Surinam Uruguay

* figures for Argentina pre-date the recent economic collapse, which has reduced everyone to poverty except for the millionaires of old, inherited wealth (located in offshore accounts)

** Cuba is exempt here, because it's a communist oligarchy where Castro himself constitutes a class above all others

Socioeconomic Categories

A multimillionaires with inherited wealth, own rent-producing properties, live in ostentatious luxury, residences located in exclusive residential neighborhoods

B multimillionaires (self-made), own rent-producing properties, live in comfortable luxury, residences located in exclusive residential neighborhoods

C1 living like a rich person, but not a millionaire, earning high salary, high-level executive / professionals, some savings, same mass consumption habits as "A" and "B," children enrolled in private schools

C2 live in comfortable style, middle salary at work, professionals / proprietors of mid-size businesses, able to meet primary needs, live in detached housing or modern apartment in middle-income neighborhood

C3 stable, low-wage income, able to enjoy convenience at the cost of economic sacrifice, able to meet primary needs, small business employees, large families, live in heavily populated areas, in small detached houses or large apartment buildings

D almost no convenience goods, barely able to meet primary needs, low-level worker in small business, large families

E not able to meet primary needs, no steady income, large families, living in makeshift housing (straw matting, cardboard, corrugated iron, and boards) in marginal zones

Nations of Millions Divided

If it once constituted a relatively homogenous region where "nations" were established by a handful of European land barons who belonged to the same social clubs and business guilds back home, today Latin American society has sprawled into a myriad of factions, each with its own agenda. Argentina, once the crown jewel of the Americas, and by far the most white and Eurocentric country, prided itself on having the most robust economy in the region and looked down on the fiscally inferior nations that surrounded it. Migrant laborers traveling to find work in Argentina from all over Central and South America often encountered social barriers to integration. Being a Bolivian migrant worker in Argentina was about as socially advantageous as being an Indian housemaid in Argentina. And if you want to see how bloated, pseudo-aristocratic, bourgeois middle-class Argentines are still mistreating Indians, even as they are rapidly becoming part of the poorest 50 percent of Latinos, you have to see the new film *La Ciénaga* (The Swamp) by Argentine director Lucrecia Martel. The film is being hailed at festivals all over the world for its artsy portrayal of the decay of a middle-class family, but no one has had the balls to point out that these classist, racist, arrogant elitists probably deserve the economic crisis they are currently enduring. There's a reason the Nazis flocked to Argentina after World War II: They felt right at home.

The problem for the outsider is formidable, however. National and racial tensions carve Latin American society into so many subsets that the naïve tourist cannot grasp its intricacies at first sight. That's why so many hippie travelers (ironically, mostly from Europe) are drawn to Central and South America: The complexity of its classism is such that it encourages oversimplification. Optimistic, happy, leftist tourists who come with a revolutionary zeal and who have already been brainwashed by the media myth of "the Latino" fail to understand the deep disparities that exist. What the hippie sees is a beautiful miscegenation of races distributed liberally across an unspoiled landscape whose political borders are more virtual than actual. They don't see that Costa Ricans see themselves as the elite of Central America and that they think the Nicaraguans and the Panamanians are scum; or that the Panamanians think they're the shit because they now have proprietorship over the canal, even though the whole region (and the whole world) doesn't have any confidence that they'll know how to run it. The tourist in Puerto Rico will never realize how much disdain the islanders have for their New York counterparts—the Neoricans—for not being Puerto Rican enough (not even J.Lo escapes their criticism), how everyone in the region calls the Dominicans the "niggers of the Latin world," or how property rights are threatened on a daily basis by squatters and overzealous landowners.

The problems of racial and class inequity in Latin America need to be broken down even further. It's far more complicated and viciously real than any charts or economic indicators can suggest. Ultimately, the promotion of a fake Latino identity in the media that tries to cover up the gross differences between these groups just perpetuates the long history of their oppression. There is no such thing as "the Latino," and any media stereotype that tries to suggest one is pure hype.

**From Vol.6, No. 1, February 1999

HEY NIGGER!

The *VICE* Guide to Bad Words

by Robbie Dillon

Here at *VICE*, we like to prance around the office calling each other things like "faggot," "chink," and "paki." That's because most of us are white, straight, and male, which means the worst thing anyone can call us is "honky," and that doesn't bother us at all. We also like to talk about something called "the reappropriation of language." A lot of smart people have written really boring books about this, but basically it comes down to dancing around in a circle and singing, "Sticks and stones may break my bones but words will never hurt me."

Words do hurt people, of course, but only because we let them. Call an Italian a gook, for example, and he'll just laugh at you. We offer this guide because as writers, we think that people shouldn't be so scared of, like, language and stuff. Examining the inane and ridiculous origins of slurs shows how stupid they actually are. So go ahead, take a good look. They're only words, for Chrissakes.

Nigger: This word is considered so offensive that some people would like to take it out of the dictionary, load it onto a rocket, and shoot it into outer space where it can never hurt anyone again. Originally pronounced "nigrah" by slave owners in the Old South, *nigger* is directly descended from *nigra*, the Latin word for "black." The unfortunate linking of blackness with everything evil can be seen in words like *denigrate*, which once meant simply "to blacken, as with ashes."

Wop: Most of the Italian immigrants who arrived in America at the turn of the century were peasants who carried little or no documentation. According to popular legend, immigration officials would record their lack of papers with the notation "WOP," short for "without a passport." Scholars have also argued that *wop* comes from *guappo* (pronounced "wappo"), the Italian word for a swaggering, loud-mouthed man.

Kike: Because they were illiterate, many of the Jewish peasants who came to America were unable to write their names on their immigration papers. Refusing to sign with an X, which in their eyes resembled the Christian cross, they marked a circle instead, the Yiddish word for which is *kikel.*

Faggot: Most dictionaries list the primary definition of *faggot* as a bundle of twigs or sticks. If you're like most people, you've probably wondered what, if anything, that has to do with figure skating or blowing a bunch of guys dressed up as sailors. In

English public schools (which are actually exclusive private schools) like Eton and Rugby, freshmen were usually paired as roommates with older upperclassmen. The younger boys were expected to perform menial tasks that included fetching firewood and—boys being boys—providing sexual gratification. Until recently, "Hey, fag!" was a friendly greeting at places like Sandhurst and Oxford.

Cunt: Derived from *cunnus*, the Latin term for a woman's genitalia, *cunt* has carried negative connotations from its very beginnings. In his 2000-year-old instructions to orators, Cicero cautioned speakers to avoid using it in public. In Grose's *Dictionary of the Vulgar Tongue*, it was printed as "c**t" and defined as "a dirty word for a dirty thing." It is considered one of the foulest words in the English language and was still being censored long after words like "fuck" and "shit" were widely accepted.

Spic: Although today this term refers to people of Hispanic or Latin American origins, it was originally used to ridicule Italian-Americans for the way they said, "No spika da English."

Wogs: A derogatory term used by the British to describe the natives of various colonies including East Indians, Arabs, and Australian Aborigines. Although it was later reinterpreted as an acronym for "Westernized Oriental Gentleman," *wog* was originally derived from the letters stenciled on the shirts of native laborers who were Working On Government Service.

Slut: From the Scandinavian *slodge* and the Middle English *slutch*, meaning "muck or soggy mud," *slut* refers to unclean or promiscuous women who have "dirtied" themselves by having sex or otherwise rolling in the gutter of depravity.

Honky: After centuries of being murdered, enslaved, and stripped of their humanity by an incredibly sick form of skin worship known as racism, black people decided to fight back and started calling white people "honkies." "You may be a disgusting race with a history of glaring moral flaws," they said. "But we have decided to avenge centuries of oppression by making fun of the fact that you talk through your noses and therefore will never be able to re-create the sweet, soulful sounds of artists like Barry White and Isaac Hayes." So far, white people have responded by continuing to act like assholes.

**From Vol. 9, No. 9, Oct. 2002

Photos by the author.

THE DAY I JOINED THE KKK

Was Super Fucking Gay

by Lisa Puley

In the summer of 1989, I joined the KKK. I never formally quit, so I guess technically I'm still a member. Shit, I never thought of that. I'm in the KKK.

The 80s was an interesting time for TV news media, the end of an era. News magazine shows were about a fresh angle on the news. A more in-depth and sometimes dangerous angle. It's not easy to get advertising when you're talking about things like corporate corruption, so there was only really *60 Minutes* and *20/20*.

Of course, the early 90s brought Maria Shriver and all the other big players that are still running the show today and with them came pap news. How to remove soap scum and how to put your children to bed replaced an hour with the mob and dinner with Yasser Arafat. Advertisers were no longer scared to get involved and dozens of news magazine shows appeared on every network.

As an associate producer for the biggest news show on ABC at the time, I was

totally unaware of how bad things were becoming and was determined to continue the tradition of biting news commentary.

The cold war was coming to an end and America was already desperate for a new enemy. For a brief moment it was decided that Nazi skinheads were taking over the country. Sensing that this was bullshit, I offered to go undercover to infiltrate hate.

I spent weeks researching hate groups and became an expert on the difference between the Neo-Nazis, the Aryan Nation, the National Alliance and, of course, the KKK. During this research I discovered that Pennsylvania was the hate-crimes capital of America and the KKK was trying to set up a chapter in a town called Yukon because of it. Before I knew it, I was on my way there.

Yukon is a working-class town that is very redneck and very prone to being exploited by the government. That means toxic-waste dumps, corporate pollution and very few social services; the perfect place for the KKK to recruit members.

My first stop in town was the local gay bar. There, the locals regaled me with stories about how homophobic the town was. The customers complained that the bar's windows were constantly being smashed and their cars were often vandalized. The strange thing is, in a town this dangerous, the gay bar was the safest place to be. Sure, the walls could cave in at any moment, but at least the person next to you doesn't want to rape and kill you.

Shortly after my arrival in town, a stranger on a white horse (I'm not kidding) came galloping down the main street making an announcement. The town was to come to a rally the next night to talk about the government's hatred for the people of Yukon.

The next night, following the horseman's instructions, I went to the KKK recruitment meeting at a nearby campsite. With me were two of my network colleagues, who were there as my back-up.

As I approached the gates of the compound (with a hidden camera in my baseball cap), I was a little nervous, but they waved me right through without so much as a second glance.

You see, the KKK is not hard to infiltrate. It is not a secret society. On the contrary, these are people desperate to get new members. The reason they are so pressed for membership is simple: These are the least articulate and charming people you've ever come across. They simply don't understand the concept of spin.

When the Republicans (the real KKK) say things like, "Tax dollars aren't the government's money—it's your money," people prick up their ears and take notice. It's a message that's easy to digest. If the Grand Wizard really wanted to recruit people, he could talk passionately about government corruption, corporate pollution and unmonitored immigration. He could rail against Reagan, shopping malls and Gary Coleman. Instead, that night at the campsite, all he talked about was...I don't know what he talked about, actually. He was an unintelligible and insufferable bore.

After what seemed to be an endless rant, most people got in their cars and went home. I told someone in a white robe I wanted to stay and find out more, and he directed me to a cabin where I'd be staying the night. I sent my two partners back to the gay bar but told them to stay by the phone in case there was a problem.

At this point, I have to admit, it was getting a bit scary. All the cabin had was a cheap-looking cot and an empty chest of drawers. I was told to wait there for further instructions.

An hour or so later a man walked in to my cabin, cordially introduced himself, and handed me a rifle. I was to put the gun under my thin mattress, strip naked and go to bed. I did as I was told (well, I kept my bra and panties on) and tried to get some sleep. Then rifle shots started going off. Apparently my initiation had begun, and that included a dozen men surrounding my cabin and shooting guns into the air. It wasn't as scary as it sounds. Like building a haunted house in your basement, it was one of those things that was so meant to be scary that it just wasn't. I should mention, however, that upon hearing the shots a mile away, my assistants jumped into their cars and drove back to New York, leaving me to rot with the KKK for an entire summer—thanks, guys.

The next morning I awoke at dawn, ready to complete the second half of my initiation. Two cars pulled up and we drove into town. I was handed a stack of "monkey money" (essentially Monopoly™ money with a monkey's face on the center of the bill) and told we were going on a drive-by.

As we drove by an old black man, everyone threw the monkey money at him and yelled "Here's your monkey money, monkey, now go back to Africa." The old man didn't seem fazed by us; I don't even think he could hear anything we were saying. He seemed more confused than scared—a reaction that was typical for the Klan.

After about an hour, they seemed satisfied and we went back to the camp. I'd like to tell you more secrets about the Klan. I'd like to write a tell-all about their immense white power and their horrible plot to take over the world, but I'm afraid there's nothing to say. The next two months were an excruciating combination of painfully boring lectures and pointless road trips.

We were taught about the cryptic symbols on our dollar bills, about the Jews' stronghold on the government. They tried to peer pressure me into getting a white-power tattoo that said, "I hate niggers," but I told them I was allergic to needles.

Toward the end of the summer, I wasn't even using my hidden camera anymore. I had my Betacam on my shoulder for every event and was never questioned about it. I brought it to the cross-burning pictured here thinking there would be some real action going on, but the whole night seemed like a pantomime of a cross burning. It was held in the middle of an empty field so as not to disturb anyone, and everyone was going through the motions, looking at their watches, and passing time. Lines like, "Do not turn your back on the cross" (which they all did) were spoken in the routine monotone of a high-school assembly. These people were not the personification of evil, they were the personification of low-IQ rednecks with nothing to do. Though the barbeques were tasty, that summer was a lifeless bore with very little to redeem it. My only solace was that I was going to debunk the myth of the KKK's power and have some of the most unique footage the network had ever seen.

Of course, this is late-80s TV, and we were embarking on a new epoch of newslessness. When I returned, I showed my boss some of the highlights and awaited my instructions. I got a phone call the next day and was told my summer in hell was a total waste of time. They were not running the piece because they were concerned that I had committed a hate crime by throwing the monkey money and that violated the network's standards and practices.

When asked what they thought was going to happen when they sent me to join the KKK, they told me that the real reason they killed the story was that the anchor who originally had wanted to do the story didn't want to do it anymore. Another explanation they gave me was that not enough people had been recruited by the KKK, so it wasn't newsworthy.

I knew the truth. My story was cancelled because TV news was over. 1990 was approaching, and infiltrating the KKK has nothing to do with the new fad diet or the problem with Mondays.

That was my last summer working in corporate television and, as I see it, the last year TV news really meant something.

**From Vol. 8, No. 10, December 2001

The original article featured the author flipping a bird the bird.

HOORAY FOR HATE

Why Tolerance Has Become Intolerable

by Gavin McInnes

A black guy, a Jew, and a Chinese dude walk into an Irish bar. The black guy says, "I'll have a Guinness." The Jew says, "I'll have a Stella," and the Asian dude says, "I'll have a Maker's Mark on the rocks." The bartender looks up from cleaning a glass and says, "What the fuck are you guys doing in here? Get out of here."

These days it's hard to tell if you're allowed to like jokes like that. All over the so-called free world, common sense and basic human rights are being smothered under a stultifying wave of censorship that used to be called "political correctness" and is now called "tolerance." Even at *VICE*—where we are committed to saying what you want, and where new employees are sometimes shocked that terms like *slut*, *paki*, and *faggot* are part of casual office banter—we are not immune to this insidious form of repression. In spite of the fact that I am one of the owners of this company, our lawyers suggested I undergo sensitivity training after saying, "I love fags," in the middle of an important meeting. During the training we were told that it is illegal to discuss anything personal about your coworkers under any circumstances. In other words, I could be sued if I went to the bathroom with a colleague, locked the door, and whispered, "The managing editor is Italian."

This magazine was once banned at Ottawa's Carleton University (my alma mater, I'm ashamed to admit) after we featured an ad that displayed a female model's pubic hair. The censors' rationale was that the ad had used "sex rather than sexuality" to sell the product in question. When a student at the school tried to organize a debate over the university's actions, the student council revoked the room that he had booked for the occasion. The school paper proceeded to print an article about the controversy and, as a result, was also temporarily banned from the campus.

Sadly, this sort of blatantly irrational hypocrisy has become the rule, rather than the exception, at most North American universities. At Wake Forest University, one of the few orientation events that freshmen are obliged to attend is an experience called Blue Eyed, in which whites are abused, ridiculed, made to fail, and taught helpless passivity so that they "can identify with a person of color for a day." At Michigan State University, where certain elevators and cafeteria tables are reserved for blacks and gays as a way to "counteract oppression," columnist Jason Van Dyke was dismissed from the school paper after he wrote a piece suggesting that the gay community may be intolerant. And sanctions aren't restricted to those whose ideas are deemed hurtful or offensive. When Dr. Richard Zeller, a sociology professor at Ohio's Bowling Green State University, proposed a course on political correctness that would offer students a chance to look at this integral part of university life from a conservative perspective, he was forced to resign. When asked to comment, Dr. Kathleen Dixon, BGSU's director of women's studies, said, in an admission that was as frank as it was disturbing, "We forbid any course that says we restrict free speech."

The irony wouldn't have been lost on tyrants like the late Chairman Mao Zedong. The Chinese communist leader and mass murderer once proposed a campaign of "thought reform and re-education" for university students that would not be complete until, as Mao put it, "children had denounced the lives and political morals of their parents and emerged as progressive in a manner satisfactory to their trainers."

This neo-fascist desire to control people's attitudes and language also makes its way into the legislature. If you are arrested after being involved in a street fight, for example, you can be charged with some form of assault. But in many states, if you used the word "nigger" or "faggot" during the fight, the incident can be labeled a hate crime and you will be subject to an additional or more severe sentence. Now, obviously a gang of racist skinheads deserves a harsher punishment than some drunken brawler, but problems arise when tribunals try to identify and quantify an entity like "hate" as defined under a statute. Arguably, there is a degree of animosity present any time one human being assaults another, but prosecutors have to determine whether this hate is the kind of hate they're looking for. And so, an accused can be grilled about how many black friends he has or if he's ever made any off-color jokes. Often the "proof" comes down to an offensive epithet uttered during the incident. But, as anyone who's ever called their partner "a dirty fucking slut" in the heat of an intense sexual encounter can tell you, context is everything.

Ultimately, censoring discourse only serves to send bigotry underground, making the task of exposing its inherent stupidity that much harder. After several officers on a military base in Texas were reprimanded for using the word "nigger" in casual conversation, soldiers simply substituted the word "Canadian." The euphemism spread to the general populace and led to some very confused Canuck tourists wondering why Texans were always going on about "lazy fucking Canadians" and the dangers of living in a Canadian neighborhood.

And often, hate laws end up hurting the people they were designed to help. When a coalition of Vancouver women's groups was asked to help set the Canadian government's guidelines for acceptable pornography, so many lesbian-made books and movies ended up being banned that two women's bookstores were forced out of business. Similarly, America's hate-speech laws have often ended up enhancing the societal imbalances they were designed to redress. In Michigan, more than twenty blacks have been charged with racist speech but not a single white person has. In Florida, the hate-speech law was used to throw a black man in jail after he called a cop a "white cracker." In fact, the only hate-crime case to make it to the Supreme Court involved a man who had been called a "white piece of shit" by a black man.

Just when it looked like things had come full circle, and our attempts to wipe out hatred and intolerance had created an intolerant dystopia of thought control and censorship, terrorism reared its ugly head and good old-fashioned hate has come back with a vengeance. All over North America, people are rethinking the live-and-let-live policies that may have contributed to the September 11 tragedies. More than half of the nineteen terrorists involved in the attacks on the World Trade Center and the Pentagon were here on expired visas. This situation is only now being addressed because prior to 9/11 anyone who discussed America's lax immigration controls was immediately labeled a nazi. Under the protective cover of multiculturalist policies, enemy nations and terrorist organizations have been allowed—and in some cases, encouraged—to openly install fifth columns in the heart of Western democracies.

After September 11, a group of Muslim demonstrators held an anti-American rally in Luton, England. When asked if they considered themselves traitors, they declared that they were not British Muslims, but Muslims living in Britain, and that their allegiance was to Islam, not "Britain's infidel government." Idiots like these may represent only a tiny portion of the Muslim population, but the fact is that nobody actually knows because anyone who raises the question risks being labeled intolerant. And don't even suggest that the protestors were assholes who should've been deported or thrown in jail. The same people who tell us that it is imperative to scour the intimate details of college professors' personal lives for signs of sexism, racism, or homophobia insist that any attempt to investigate Muslim extremists or enforce existing immigration laws is a violation of human rights and proof that we are living in a police state.

This so-called tolerance has brought us to the point where a man who tells a woman she has pretty legs can lose his job and be dragged in front of a kangaroo court, but a terrorist sympathizer who declares that America got what it deserved on 9/11 must have his right to free speech defended. It's time that we bid adieu to this ludicrous state of affairs and embrace the angry, purifying power of hate.

The fact is that throughout history, hate has been the impetus by which people have overcome the inertia of fear. From the Boston Tea Party, to the suffrage movement, to the fight for civil rights, progressive change has only come when people hated the status quo enough to actually do something about it. Hate is even a factor in the supposedly super-rational world of science. Journalist Charles Cross once estimated that 90 percent of scientific discoveries are made by stubborn and prejudiced researchers whose primary motivation is the desire to humiliate their competitors. In a 1983 article, he wrote: "The entire scientific community seems based on hate, on a bitter and stubborn desire to win the argument." He also noted that scientists regularly refer to each other as "sons of bitches" and talk about "nailing those bastards (their competitors) to the wall."

It seems that wherever hate is allowed to flourish, truth and justice will eventually prevail. Take the case of Mr. Death, a.k.a. Fred A. Leuchter, Jr., one of the world's most influential Holocaust deniers. Rather than being censored, Mr. Leuchter was encouraged to expound on his theories and debate them in an open forum. Motivated by hatred of Mr. Leuchter and his hateful ideas, researchers embarked on an intensive re-examination of the facts. This closer study led to the discovery of important new evidence that established once and for all the horrible realities of the Holocaust, and in the process, actually increased people's awareness of the atrocities.

Clearly, hate does a lot more good than its supposed counterpart. The warm and fuzzy stupidity of "tolerance" is a refuge for dull-witted bullies too lazy to think for themselves, or too cowardly to call a spade a spade. Rather than trying to twist the speech of all the unbelievers, it's time we embrace our inherent hatred. The Clash said, "Let fury have the hour. Anger can be power. You know that you can use it." All we know is we hate people that hate hate, and we have no tolerance for the intolerance of intolerance.

SPECIAL PEOPLE

**From Vol. 7, No. 6, July 2000

STOP IMMIGRATION!

Why Antiracism Is Turning Us Into Cockroaches

by Gavin McInnes

After hanging out in Beijing for two years and watching Chinese attempts at population control morph into decomposing baby girls floating down the Yangtze River, Craig Nelson started Project USA, a political group dedicated to "moving the immigration issue into the center of the national debate." Despite the fact that the group's policies are so logical they're almost boring, Nelson has been the target of censorship, protest rallies, and even death threats.

Although his supporters include Latinos, blacks, and immigrants like me, Nelson has run up against hundreds of pissed-off antiracist psychos since he created Project USA. "I moved away from my family in New York because the threatening phone calls were getting scary," says the forty-year-old activist from his new apartment in Queens. Somewhere along the line his "Immigration is causing the population problem" was understood to mean "Immigrants have to die and I'm going to kill them if you don't stop me." Within weeks of his group's inception,

Nelson was being referred to as a "cleverly disguised Nazi" by New York's *Daily News.*

"I don't understand it," he says. "Eighty percent of Americans want to see immigration slow down. The population explosion is destroying our environment, causing all kinds of social problems, and drastically reducing our country's quality of life, but the American establishment refuses to acknowledge the problem. We are not going to let political correctness scare us away from the problem."

It is surprising that people still cannot see the link between immigration and population explosion. As Peter Brimelow proves in *Alien Nation* (HarperCollins 1996), "the single biggest impact on the environment is the fact that the American population continues to grow." Now take a look at population growth since the immigration act of 1965. As Leon Bouvier (former Vice President of the Population Reference Bureau) points out in *How Many Americans?: Population, Immigration and the Environment* (Sierra Club, 1994), "Immigrants and their descendants make up more than two-thirds of US population growth." That's not *the majority* of population growth. That is *all* population growth. If we had the kind of population we had before the immigration act of 1965 we could spray Freon in the air, throw half-eaten turkeys in the garbage and drive Hummers all day and the environment wouldn't even blink but if you even alude to that fact, the liberal artistocracy is thrown into hysterics.

Project USA's first billboard featured the image of a six-year-old and a warning that the imminent doubling of the population was a bad thing. After seeing the way city officials dealt with the poster, you'd think it featured a gigantic swastika with "Niggers Beware" written in dripping blood below it. Within a few days, the sign was torn down on orders from the municipal government, as were others in Brooklyn, Queens, and other parts of the country. Nelson is taking the city of New York to court, but he admits he's facing an uphill battle. Even the American Civil Liberties Union has refused to acknowledge that removing his billboard was a violation of free speech. Nelson's attempts to resist this censorship have only resulted in further vilification by the press. Project USA has been subjected to the same hate-speech scrutiny that has seen universities ban gay magazines for homophobia and record labels denounce black language as racist. The same liberal fascists who believe that Mumia Abu-Jamal should be released immediately, that OJ was innocent, and that Lorena Bobbitt was acting in self-defense refuse to even consider Nelson's point of view.

"White people are scared to discuss immigration problems," says J.C. Hernandez, a board member of Project USA and Texans For Immigration Reform, "but I'll be damned if my grandchildren are going to suffer because the government was too worried about sounding racist to tackle our nation's most serious problem."

It's silly to worry about racists wanting to get involved anyway, because the subject matter is way too highbrow for them. Nelson's often confusing discussions on the complexities of population growth tend to leave white power people scratching their bald heads (don't forget the KKK barbecue last year, when the Grand Pooh-bah summed up all his views in a three-second speech that went, "I hate niggers. I hate Jews. *Sieg heil.* Let's eat!"). So yeah, Project USA's website does have people writing in saying, "Let's send the drug dealers home with no money" and "South America and Cuba are a brown plague," but when Nelson comes back with, "Immigration is creating an overcrowded, polluted aggregate of balkanized and contending factions," all the racists go, "Uh . . . what?" and leave.

Without the rhetoric and the hysteria there is one solid fact: America's population shot up at the same rate as India's and China's last year. If current policies continue, it will reach half a billion by 2050—twice what it is now—but American-born citizens will account for essentially none of that increase. Studies have shown that one of the reasons immigration results in exponential increases in population is a phenomenon known as anchor babies. Because an American birth certificate means instant citizenship, many illegal immigrants will have as many babies as possible as a way to ensure a secure future for their families.

"The situation is completely haywire right now," says a Chicago-based INS officer who asked to remain anonymous. "No matter who denies it, the immigration problem is going to explode over the next three years. Fraudulent passports are so rampant it's like we already have no borders."

There are, however, signs that the public's mood is shifting. Three weeks after calling Nelson a Nazi, for example, a front-page headline in the *Daily News* announced a "Human Tidal Wave!" of illegal Chinese immigration.

His experiences in China taught Nelson that trying to stop people from breeding is futile. A tenfold increase in the number of people leaving India, China, Pakistan, and Mexico every year would cause a decrease in their respective populations of less than half a percent. The hippie myth of a one-big-happy-family world with no borders is about to turn North America into a stifling mosh pit peppered with bad wages and dead birds.

Some of the biggest hypocrites in the chickenshit movement to avoid discussing "dangerous" topics have been environmentalists. In the mid-'70s, environmental groups went from discussing overpopulation constantly to totally dropping the subject because it didn't sound groovy enough. The focus switched to Band-Aid solutions like fewer cars and more recycling. The fight to limit immigration was left to a handful of marginalized activists.

Sierrans for US Population Stabilization is one of the few remaining environmental groups able to focus on the numbers. According to SUPS, if we had stuck to the immigration policies of the late '60s, the country's population would have stabilized ten years ago and would actually be declining by now. We wouldn't need cancer-causing pesticides to feed everyone, there'd be fewer erratic weather changes and less smog, and people wouldn't be freaking out about water shortages.

Everything from deformed frogs to the allergy epidemic can be attributed to overpopulation, but most environmental groups are conspicuously absent from the debate. In the '70s, when bourgeois students started talking about all the uninhabited space in Australia, Canada, and China, environmentalists were quick to point out the terrible effects of population sprawl on delicate ecosystems and the need for nature to have its own turf. Nowadays, it seems that all those bearded mama's boys are too busy wearing socks with sandals and smoking pot under a Bob Marley poster.

Through this enormous hurricane of bullshit, Project USA has become a well-established, tax-exempt organization with a paid staff and over 3,000 members. Nelson is hoping that his cause will be taken seriously before North America is turned into a giant sweatshop ruled by a tiny oligarchy of rich, white assholes. "No matter what I do, this is going to be one of the top five issues of the next presidential campaign," he says. "I just don't want to wait that long."

THE BASIC ARGUMENTS:

1. Your ancestors were immigrants. It's the history of this country.

Actually the history of this country is not constant immigration but intermittent immigration. Before 1965 it was: open the doors for awhile, close the doors and let them assimilate, open the doors for awhile, close the doors and let them assimilate etc. The recent past is historically unique because it has been non-stop open doors.

2. Immigrants built this country.

At some point, maybe we should stop "building."

3. We need immigrants to do the jobs Americans can't or won't do

Yes, there is a labor shortage for dishwashers who are willing to take $3/hr but is that the society we want? Between the years 1925 and 1965, there was very little immigration to North America and

during that time Americans and Canadians built great countries...and we still managed to get our dishes washed.

4. We're all immigrants. Only Native Americans are the true Americans.

"Native Americans" permitted mass immigration and look what happened to them.

5. Limiting immigration is mean. Everyone in the world deserves to come here and consume more.

Putting a lock on your apartment door is "mean," too. But you do it. While it is true that many of the world's billions would love to come to North America in search of higher consumption levels, it is simply a fact that in the world there exist national borders and there are such things as limits.

For more answers go to projectusa.org

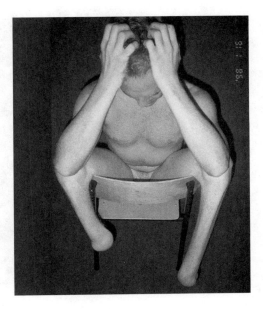

**From Vol. 4., No. 2, March 1997

A NEW LOOK AT THE POPULATION PROBLEM FROM THE CHURCH OF EUTHANASIA

by John Coinner

The Church of Euthanasia was inspired by a dream, in which Reverend Chris Korda confronted an alien intelligence known as The Being who speaks for the inhabitants of Earth in other dimensions. The Being warned that our planet's ecosystem is failing and that our leaders are in a state of denial. The Rev. awoke from the dream moaning the Church's now infamous slogan, "Save the Planet, Kill Yourself."

The Church of Euthanasia is a non-profit, educational foundation devoted to restoring the balance between humans and the remaining species on earth. They believe this can only be achieved by a massive population reduction, which they say will require "a leap in human consciousness to a new species awareness." The Church has but one commandment: "Thou Shall Not Procreate." Sounds innocent

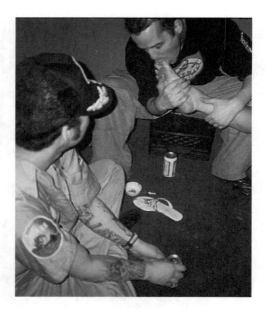

enough, doesn't it? I mean, any moron knows there are way too many of us assholes out there and it's starting to really hurt this rock we're living on. So what are we doing? Recycling programs, non-aerosol hair products, public transit. Hey! Pick that falafel wrapper up there, mister! The Church, however, does not see any of these as being even remotely helpful in undoing the damage we humans have caused. No, they see the only hope for the planet and the human race to be through steps that are a little more "hands on." This brings us to the Church of Euthanasia's aforementioned "Kill Yourself" slogan.

At the core of the Church's theology is the belief that every aspect of the deepening global environmental crisis, including climate change, reduction of biodiversity, topsoil erosion and poisoning of the water and atmosphere directly results from the overabundance of a single species: humans. Major wars or epidemics are not perceived as a viable means of reducing the population, as they would have tremendous environmental consequences and hardly make a dent anyway. It is for these practical reasons that Euthanasists support only voluntary forms of population reduction. There are four principal methods, the "Four Pillars" that the Church subscribes to: suicide, free abortion, cannibalism, and sodomy. The word "euthanasia" translated from Greek literally means "good death." There many means to a good death, however, they suggest the official Hemlock Society-approved method involving sleeping pills and a garbage bag fastened around your head with a rubber band. The rubber band enables you to hold the bag open in order to breathe freely until you lose consciousness. No fuss, no muss. They say those who want to be really hardcore can try skipping the pills. You down, bad boy? For those who may be a little timid the Church is currently in the process of setting up the world's first Suicide Assistance Hotline. Ya know, just in case maybe things are too good with you and you're not sure you can go through with it. They'll convince you that you're nothing more than a worthless sack of bacteria. But before you off yourself, become a Church member first and leave a note willing them whatever worldly possessions you may have.

The second pillar, free abortion, is pretty self-explanatory. However, it doesn't end there. Among the vast amount of literature churned out by the Church, mostly contained in the official journal, Snuff It, are some rather, er, interesting uses for the aborted fetuses. There is extensive documentation of doctors in state hospitals in China eating fetuses for their nutritional value. They suggest that fetuses be eaten as a soup, together with pork and ginger. Euthanasists find this a disgusting thought (the pork, that is). They are fiercely vegetarian, but if you insist on eating flesh then cannibalism is the way to go. Again, all the resource material you need is provided, including Bob Arson's step-by-step guide on how to break down the human body into serviceable choice cuts of meat. He also provides some very enticing recipes. I'm telling you, kids, you have not lived until you've tried the "White Devil Dinky-Dao Mothafucka Bobbacoo Sauce." It is also ideal for a "Bloody Leroy Mix."

The final pillar, the solution to avoiding the abortion issue, is sodomy, which the Church defines as any sexual act not intended for procreation. As Church founder Reverend Korda states, "Since we have all these angry men trying to get rid of their sperm, why don't they get rid of it in each other?" But what if a boy's back door isn't your preferred point of entry? "No problem," she states. "Women can oblige just as easily. Grease it up. If more guys were fucking asses instead of pussies, the population would drop. That's the bottom line." Indeed.

According to the Church doctrine, the planet is a living, breathing organism, and is capable of defending itself if necessary. The Church says we can avoid the planet"s wrath by using the methods outlined above. What are ya waitin' for?

**From Vol. 6, No. 4, May 1999

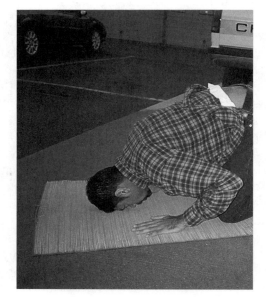

THE VICE GUIDE
TO EVERY RELIGION
IN THE WORLD

by Christi Bradnox

Religion started a very long time ago because people wanted a name for their gang that would seem all heavy and spiritual and everything. Today there are religions all over the world and they are each very unique and important for their own very important reasons. Here is every single one and the reason why it is very important.

CHRISTIANITY
Christians believe Jesus Christ is the Son of God. Jews and Romans killed Jesus, but he came back from the dead so he must have been a zombie.

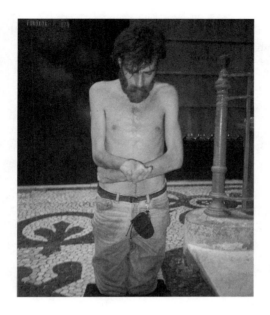

Roman Catholic

Now it's just mobsters and prostitutes, but Catholicism was started by the first disciples of Jesus (the apostles) and says the pope is the one and only king. No masturbating, no premarital sex, no anal sex, no condoms, and no abortion unless you confess, in which case it's OK, but you can't do it again. Unless you confess again, but then it's getting a bit out of hand.

Orthodox

These are the Russian guys with the big beards who left the Catholic Church in 1054 because they hated the pope. The Orthodox Church is radically unique because its churches can have two names like St. Peter and St. Paul, and they use a different calendar. This is why Orthodox Christians like the Serbs want to decapitate Roman Catholic Christians like the Croats and play soccer with their heads.

Rastafarian

Christianity mixed with animism. Rastafarians believe that they are one of the lost tribes of Israel, and that former Ethiopian emperor Haile Selassie was the Second Coming of Christ and therefore you should smoke tons of pot.

Protestant (there's around eleven of these)

Back in the 1500s, Martin Luther proved the Catholic Church was inferior at a debate called the Diet of Worms, and thanks to the printing press was able to tell everyone about it. This changed everything and Europe was no longer unified under one language and one religion. Protestants are not as decadent as the other Christians and the fact that they're so DIY means you get a lot of splinter groups like . . .

Lutheran
Old-school, Martin Luther Protestantism. Found primarily in Germany, Scandinavia, and Minnesota, Lutherans comprise almost one-third of the world's total Protestant population but we're not sure what exactly separates them from, say . . .

Presbyterian
There's tons of Calvinist Lutherans (more than regular Lutherans) like the Dutch Reform Church and the Swiss Reformed Church, but a scary-as-hell group from Scotland called Presbyterian is the biggest. Started by a tough-guy communist named John Knox who hated everyone posh and thought Lutherans and Anglicans were too "popish."

Adventist
A faith which is convinced that Jesus will return to Earth very soon as a real guy.

Anglican
Henry VIII started the Church of England in 1534 because he wasn't getting laid enough.

Baptist
Protestants that are heavily into baptism (duh) and live in the southern United States. The black ones sing gospel real well and like R&B.

Pentecostal
Usually born-agains (people who, like Jesus, died and then came back to life), Pentecostals are total fanatics who sing really badly and like the Holy Ghost way better than the other two guys.

Christian Science
People like John Travolta who realize it will take science to bring Jesus back to life. It would be funny if he came back and he had those bolts in his neck like Frankenstein, eh?

Jehovah's Witness
Like Adventists, but way more literal. They may be totally insane but you have to

hand it to them for fighting the Nazis in Germany, apartheid in South Africa, and Maoism in China way back when no one else would dare.

Latter-Day Saint (Mormon)
Started in the 1820s by Joe Smith, who found a book in his backyard that had been left there by God. Mormons made Utah and Salt Lake City, banished caffeine, had tons of wives, and showed really good commercials that made you cry.

Mennonite
They hate everyone, pray like crazy, have huge beards, and won't drive around in anything machine-made. They also live in communes and avoid inbreeding by paying outsiders for sperm. Whoa.

Methodist
Raver Protestants that do way too much meth.

Quaker
Pacifist pilgrims who follow their inner light and get burned alive.

SATANISM
Bad people who like Rob Halford even though he's gay.

JUDAISM
Eighteen million people who don't like Jesus. Moses was the first one and he said Jews are God's favorite. Kind of like Shintoism but with curlier hair and bigger noses.

Reform
After the discovery of science, a bunch of Germans started the Reform movement and saved face by saying you don't have to take the Torah so literally.

Orthodox
The opposite of Reform.

Conservative
Orthodox Reformers like former Israeli prime minister Benjamin Netanyahu.

ISLAM
Instead of God, he's called ninety-nine other names. We like: al-Mudhill (The

Humiliator), al-Basit (The Enlarger), al-Matin (The Firm), al-Rafi' (The Elevator), and al-Mu'akhkhir (The Retarder), but most use Allah. Their bible is the Qur'an, which was dictated to the Prophet Muhammad by an angel who thought Christianity was falling apart and had to be totally reworked. Being a good Muslim boils down to observing the five pillars of Islam: repeating the Shehadah, praying five times a day, fasting during Ramadan, charity, and a pilgrimage to Mecca.

Sunni vs. Shiite
After Muhammad died in 632, the Muslim community decided to elect Abu Bakr as his successor. Sunnis (85 percent of Muslims) think that was a good idea, but Shiites (Ayatollahs and Hujjatul-Islams, who want to kill Salman Rushdie) think they should have elected Muhammad's cousin Ali.

Sufi
Islamic hippies who wear tall hats and bell-shaped dresses and pray by twirling around in circles.

Nation of Islam
Believes that its founder, Wallace D. Fard, was God, and that an evil scientist from outer space called Yaqub landed in Africa and removed the pigment and goodness from some of the natives, creating a thing called white people. Besides the outer space thing, Elijah Muhammad's perversions, and killing Malcolm X, they're all right because they dare to acknowledge the Middle East as not completely evil.

HINDUISM
Hindu is a European term for billions of Indian religions that revolve around four collections of ancient Indian scriptures called the Vedas. Hinduism is 3,000 years of Aryan civilization and Indus Valley civilization getting together and deciding things like birth determining social status, reincarnation being based on karma, and cows being intense.

BUDDHISM
In the sixth century BC, a fat Indian rich kid named Siddhartha Gautama meditated under a tree so long he met a grunge band called Nirvana. The best thing about Buddhists is they like nature and don't use religion to decide how they feel about sex and abortion and everything, though they do occasionally pray for a new car.

Mahayana (Northern)
Use Bodhisattvas (celestial saviors) to get to Nirvana. Since Kurt's suicide, the Mahayanas are satisfied going to wherever Dave Grohl or Krist Novoselic are staying at the moment.

Theravada (Southern)

They are getting bored of resisting desire, passion, and ignorance and want to get to Nirvana, like, now.

Zen

White Buddhists who live in California and drink weird tea.

CONFUCIANISM

Confucius was a really Chinese guy who said you should be gentlemanly and educated and have spiritual politicians.

TAOISM

This is the yin and yang one. Taoism was started by Lao-Tzu, who, like Buddha, believed the closer you live to nature, the better. There were times when he would dress like a tree.

PAGANISM

Women in sandals who worship the Easter bunny and eat their mothers' placentas.

SIKHISM

People who were told by God that they're better than Hindus and Muslims. They wear the five Ks—kesh (uncut hair), kangha (comb), kachha (short drawers), kara (steel bracelet), and kirpan (sword)—and want a separate country called the Punjab.

SHINTOISM

Shintoism is the indigenous religion of Japan and it says the kami (natural and supernatural forces that control the universe) chose them as their favorite people on Earth. Extremist Shinto groups are making a lot of money these days by threatening to embarrass corporations by being rude.

**From Vol. 7, No. 10, Decmber 2000

AXE THE FARM

Who Would Win in a Fight?

by Marcus and Jen

A rabid raccoon or a goat?

Although goats have been domesticated for thousands of years, they've still retained some vestige of wildness. Unlike sheep, they can fight back—especially if they have their horns left on.

The raccoon, however, is also very tough and could kill a dog, for example, with relative ease. They have teeth and claws and can put up a great fight. Rabies helps too, because it gives animals a swollen throat and prevents them from drinking and makes them furious. That's why they go so crazy. They're enraged from not being able to drink.

If it was a female goat, it would be a very close call, but if it was a full-grown billy goat, things would be different. A male goat weighs close to 300 pounds. They can stomp and kick and ram it against the wall or whatever so, yeah, the raccoon would lose if the goat were male.

A cow or a ferret?
A ferret weighs, what—five pounds, three pounds? A cow weighs about 1,100 to 1,800 pounds for a full-sized bull. That's a lot of flesh to tear through.

A squirrel versus a chipmunk?
The red squirrel (which we have here) is a pretty energetic guy, and I think it would win. They seem to chase them away from food at our bird feeder. They are bigger and pretty aggressive and they can climb trees, where the chipmunk pretty much stays on the ground. The squirrels have bigger buck teeth and they sharpen them regularly, so they could hack a chipmunk to bits just like that.

A snapping turtle or a very young Jack Russell terrier?
A full-grown snapping turtle, which could have a shell length of up to sixteen inches, has too much armor for, say, a Jack-Tar Village Russell Terrier. They were bred as hunting dogs and they go down holes after rabbits and kill rats in barns. That's what they were bred for. They're a pretty good fighting little doggie, even though they're tiny and have short legs.

I would think that the turtle could probably defend itself long enough to get away, to crawl back into water or whatever.

Yes, but who would win if it was to the death?
I don't know. I don't want to do this anymore.

**From Vol. 8, No. 10, December 2001

Where are the malls? Yet another farmer's market right downtown. Where the fuck is the roof on this place anyways?

NEW YORK SUCKS—
SO WHY DID I MOVE HERE?

by David Cross

Until recently, I lived in Los Angeles. I had been there for a little under nine years. I love Los Angeles, to the extent that I've had a number of wet dreams in which I end up fucking the city. And unlike other wet dreams, there is no shame when I wake. Only regret that this dream will never be realized. Do you understand the depth of love I am talking about? Listen to me: When we were children, and someone would say something like, "I love Pixy Stix!" a popular retort was, "Oh yeah? If you love them so much why don't you marry them?" Well, I would marry Los Angeles in a heartbeat—if she would have me.

But then, but then, but then there was always the nagging contingent of people ("friends"?!) who would go on and on about "New York City" this and "New York

And what's with the four distinct seasons?

The neighborhood bars are open way too late. Plus, since I don't have to worry about driving drunk, I end up getting totally wasted. They MAKE you be tired the next day.

And what's with the friendly neighbors saying shit like, "How's it going?" and "See ya," all the time? Whatever. In LA people are so over the friendly thing.

Where's the silicone? The girls here don't wear tons of makeup and they're not even interested in hearing about your deal—booooring.

And what's with *the Onion*, free on every street corner? Just because it's funny it has to be in your face all the time? How about something useful like the Hollywood Reporter?

A fucking restaurant that specializes in grilled cheeses with eight different kinds of cheese, and it delivers?! That's fucking bullshit!

City" that. "Oh you've got to move to New York, you'll love it. It's perfect for you! You can do, and taste, and see, and hear, and participate in, and rent, and experience anything you want whenever you want!" etc., etc. After nine years of listening to their constant harping and verbal bullying, I had had enough. After a lifetime of avoiding New York and its so-called allure I said, "Fine, have it your way." I packed up and moved.

So, now I'm here. New York? Cultural center of America, the West, the world? Huh? Are we seeing the same place here? New York sucks! I can't believe people like this shithole. Where are all the strip malls? The affordable, two-story, pre-fab apartments built in the '60s with names like "Casa Del Sol La Tigra Dios" or "The Royalton Arms"? Three Blockbusters!? For the entire island? You're telling me that I gotta go to some weird coffeehouse/nursery/Indian sweet shop hybrid and slog through some guy's collection of 10,000 hard-to-find, out-of-print, underground videos just to be able to watch *Jurassic Park*? What the fuck's up with that? And where the fuck am I supposed to park my car? In one of the subway stops that's "conveniently" located every two blocks? On top of one of the thousand cabs that'll take you wherever you want? Come on! And what's up with Central Park? A vast expanse of land that's just going to waste. That place would be great for parking your car. It's HUGE! And another thing: How many fucking museums do you people need?! There's like sixty-three museums or some shit like that. You people should look at every unnecessary museum and think, "Shit, if I was in LA right now, that museum would be a Denny's. I could be having a 'Moons Over My Hammy' right now instead of looking at this bullshit." That's it. I'm going back to LA. I have television shows to watch and then make fun of.

New York is stupid.

**From Vol. 7, No. 5, June 2000

The original article featured the gay slob in question.

QUEER AND CARELESS

Gay Slobs Leave a Rotten Turkey Sandwich on the Neat Myth

by Ben Ewy

Regardless of how finely tuned you may think your gaydar is, a new breed of fag is slipping by. Unencumbered by the typical homo signifiers (elaborate bathrooms, expensive vacuums, lint removers), this new group is more like your average pothead shut-in than C-3PO. They are called gay slobs, and although they live in Manhattan's fiercely gay neighborhood of Chelsea, they don't enjoy hanging out on Fire Island and dancing to house music. In fact, they would much rather spend the night watching a Planet of the Apes *marathon while scratching their flaccid bellies and gulping down a Big Mac or two.* VICE *tracked down two specimens of this new breed of fags and woke them up at 3:00 PM to find out what the hell is going on.*

VICE: Are you gay slobs?
Slob 1: Sure. We're non-Chelsea queers of gay Chelsea.

Why is being a gay slob so huge now?
Slob 2: I think we are part of a significant proportion of gays who are not repre-

sented at the Big Cup/Big Cunt [a gay pickup joint in Chelsea] or at the local gyms. I get my porn near the Big Cup and I actually cross the street to avoid the place. It's filled with yuppie faggots and all their nonsense.

Do you hate that flamboyant gays get all the limelight?
Slob 2: No, I could care less about the limelight. I was a young little thing at one point so I had the limelight for a while. Now I'm too old and jaded to care about stuff like that.
Slob 1: Speak for yourself—I don't mind the limelight. It's just that the gays that are getting the attention are part of this weird reflection of mainstream straight culture that I don't give a shit about anyway.

Do you think all those neat-freak gays are trying to make up for all the societal pressure saying they are dirty?
Slob 2: Yes I do and no I don't. There are some deficiencies that the gym queens definitely don't have. They try their best to be good little American consumers, though, keeping up with the Joneses and all that: "We want to be the first gay couple to get married because all the straights get married, yadda, yadda, yadda." I don't give a shit about getting married, that's not part of my world view.

Is dick cheese a major problem with uncircumcised gay slobs?
Slob 1: Not any more than it is with straight slobs.

Do you have a network of gay slob friends?
Slob 2: We do, but we're trying to keep it very small and very underground. I think we are a small percentage of the total queer population, but things are changing fast. Soon you're not going to be able to open a fridge in the West Village without gagging from the smell.

Being a gay slob, do you find yourself having to hang out with straight people more?
Slob 1: Probably. I don't know for sure, though. I am not sure what the hardcore of Chelsea does, but we are at the fringes of gay Chelsea society.

Do you like Judy Garland, chest hair, house music, and that type of stuff?
Slob 2: A lot of the Judy Garland stuff I just don't get because I don't know all the references to the classic queer experience in cinema and all that. Like Esther what's-her-name. It's boring.

Esther Williams?
Slob 2: Yeah, I just don't know all of the names.

Slob 1: Recently we have been trying to see more iconic gay films, but we have not gotten that far yet, just up to the '40s.

You don't sit at home eating bon-bons while watching *Spartacus*?
Slob 2: I would love to see *Spartacus* because I've never seen it, but I would probably be like, "Ewwww." I don't know if I can deal with all of the stuff I heard about in high school.
Slob 1: It's a Kubrick film, though. It's great.

Are there any gay stereotypes that you do adhere to?
Slob 2: In our own ways, I think [Slob 1] is closer to a gym queen than he would want to admit, and I am pretty much a lesbian.
Slob 1: I don't spend enough money to be a gym queen.

Who are your idols?
Slob 1: Either Frank Zappa or Coil.
Slob 2: It's a toss-up between John Waters and Marianne Faithfull, I don't know which.

Who do you want to fuck?
Slob 2: I love Keanu Reeves. I love him because when he's not doing a $20 million film he's a total slob and has a big belly. I love him in his films, but I probably love him more when he's acting like a pig, smoking weed, and making terrible rock music somewhere in the East Village. I also love young, smooth Slavic boys.

How about you?
Slob 1: Henry Rollins.

Deep down, though, you want 2.5 kids, an SUV, and an AOL account, eh?
Slob 2: I may not identify with the 2.5 kids, but I do identify with 2.5 bumps of cat tranquilizer. I think the number of bumps of K that a gay person does is analogous to the number of kids a straight person has. I have always wished that there was a K patch, you know, like the nicotine patch. If you're at a dinner party, trying to enjoy your guests, and someone's kid starts screaming, or you're on an airplane and some crying kid won't shut up, how cool would it be to just slap a K patch on the back of their neck and they go into a K-hole and leave decent society alone? How wonderful would that be? You could get on to any airplane and not have to worry about anything, everyone is happy.

What does a typical evening of going out consist of?
Slob 2: We don't go out that much. We'd rather stay at home and play 8-bit Atari video games.

**From Vol. 5, No. 8, October 1998

WAS JESUS A FAG?

by Robbie Dillon

Blame it on St. Augustine. The seminal Christian philosopher is often pointed to as the source of the modern church's uptight sexual attitudes. Blame it on biology and rebellious hormones that even the most pious among us struggle to control. Either way, the fact remains that sexuality and Western religion have been bashing each other's heads in for millennia. Now, I'm not a very religious person. (As kids, my brother and I used to break into St. Monica's Church every Christmas and steal the money and toys that had been left as offerings on the altar.) But having said that, I have to admit that the thought of the Messiah, down on his knees, doing the Hoover on some guy's yardstick is not something I particularly relish. Like most people, I'm comfortable with an image of the Savior that presents a vague, illogical blank where his sexuality should be, kinda like Barbie or G.I. Joe.

But regardless of my feelings on the subject, Jesus was a man with a penis, and sooner or later it was bound to come up. Discussions of the Son of God's sexuality date back at least as far as the nineteenth century and George Eliot's English translation of *The Life of Jesus*. More recently, gay scholars have pored over the Bible

and other early Christian texts searching for signs that the Prince of Peace was, in fact, a cocksucker. This process is highly speculative and generally frowned upon by historians, but for gays who have seen Christianity used as the moral justification for their oppression, torture, and murder, the debate concerns their fundamental right to exist.

The arguments are compelling. Jesus was, after all, a thirty-three-year-old "confirmed bachelor" at a time when even the religious elite observed Jewish traditions of marriage and family. He lived in a time when male-male sex was widely and openly practiced, and taboos against it were nowhere near as virulent as they are today. His followers were mostly male, but although he forcefully denounced adultery and divorce (Matthew 5:27/32), he made no specific reference to homosexuality. Omissions like these (see also Matthew 8:5–13), which can be interpreted in many different ways, have been taken by gays as a tacit approval of their sexual orientation.

The New Testament refers to a "beloved disciple" believed by some to be John the Evangelist, author of the Book of Revelation. This disciple, "whom Jesus loved," reclined on the Lord's bosom at the Last Supper (John 13:23) and, in medieval paintings, is often depicted as a younger, beardless man asleep with his head in Jesus' lap. The Passover meal is itself historically connected to the symposia, all-male drinking parties that were held in ancient Greece and usually ended with older males lounging on couches in the arms of their younger companions.

Gnostic Gospels describe a secret baptismal ritual that Jesus performed on converts who came to him at night wearing only a linen cloth around their waists.

Scholars have suggested that the young man who ran away on the night that Christ was arrested (Mark 12:51–52) was one of these "special" initiates.

Okay, so Jesus may or may not have been a sword-swallower. But, hey, the guy's been dead for 2,000 years; does anybody really care about this stuff anymore?

Well, yeah. Rick Hinshaw is the communications director of the Catholic League for Religious and Civil Rights, a group that fights against anti-Catholic discrimination. "There's been a lot of speculation about a gay Jesus," says Hinshaw. "But none of it has any basis in Scripture. Our problem is with those who are trying to appropriate Jesus as a symbol or advocate of the gay lifestyle in spite of the church teaching that homosexuality is a disordered condition."

The NYC-based league is currently organizing a protest against the Manhattan Theatre Club's presentation of *Corpus Christi*, a play that relates the story of Joshua, a Christ-like figure who has sex with his twelve disciples. Hinshaw is expecting anywhere from several hundred to several thousand demonstrators at the play's opening on October 13. "For obvious reasons, we're leading the protest against it," says Hinshaw. "We would object to any depiction of Jesus as a hedonistic, self-centered, sin-filled person. The sins in this case happen to be homosexual promiscuity, but we'd be just as offended if he were portrayed as heterosexually promiscuous or as a habitual thief. This is a total distortion and defamation of what Jesus was about."

At a preview of the play, Franciscan monks held a prayer vigil on the sidewalk outside the theater and protestors carried signs reading "Don't support blasphemy" and "You call this art?" Ticket holders were required to pass through metal detectors and submit to X-ray searches of their belongings before gaining access to the theater.

A press agent for the Manhattan Theatre Club refused to answer any questions about the play, the controversy around it, or whether or not he was the worst press agent in the world. But, considering a large number of threats to burn down the theater and exterminate everyone involved with the production, including Tony-award-winning playwright Terrence McNally, the actors, and (please, God) the press agent himself, his reticence was somewhat understandable. Hinshaw insists that the league does not support violence and strongly condemns the threats. But he points out that there are lunatics on both sides: "We've received e-mails saying things like 'Gas the Pope' and 'Bomb the Vatican' and 'The Virgin Mary should have had an abortion,'" he says. "But we don't hold the Manhattan Theatre Club responsible for that."

And so the debate rages on. When it comes right down to it, Christ's sexuality—gay or straight or ambiguous—is nowhere near as important as his message, which is clear and unequivocal with no exceptions for blacks, Muslims, Republicans, or even gays and Catholics: Love thy neighbor.

**From Vol. 7, No. 7, September 2000

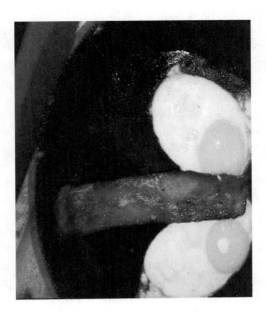

FREE THE SLAVES
AND YOUR ASS WILL FOLLOW

Abe Lincoln Was a Fag

by J. Bennett

It's true. Although the moral majority and the honky-tonk puritans of Bible Belt America would never admit it, political supernova Honest Abe Lincoln was guilty of sensitive crimes.

Just ask John Wilkes Booth, the male model who assassinated Abe Lincoln in 1865. A high-level bounty hunter for the Confederacy, his main claim to fame was that he was Abe's spurned lover. A member of the Richmond Theater Co., Booth was considered "the handsomest man in America," a reputation that attracted a healthy following of both female and male admirers. Lincoln himself was in attendance at Booth's performance as Raphael in *The Marble Heart* at Ford's Theater on November 9, 1863, where he reportedly sat in the same box he would be assassinated in almost two years later.

Before he married, the future sixteenth president of the United States lived with a man named Joshua Speed in Springfield, Illinois, for four years. In fact, the two young bucks even shared a bed together. Wasn't this considered unusual behavior for two grown men, even in the mid-nineteenth century? Some historians say no, but they sure sound like ass darts to us.

When Speed left to get married, Lincoln, coincidentally enough, fell into a deep depression. The two continued to exchange extraordinarily tender letters and apparently remained quite close until having a falling-out over slavery in 1855. Pulitzer-nominated playwright and gay activist Larry Kramer owns Speed's diary (discovered under the floorboards in the room the couple shared), which proves beyond a shadow of a doubt that Lincoln took it in the posterior. Kramer presented the following excerpt from the diary at a gay and lesbian conference: "[Lincoln] often kisses me when I tease him, often to shut me up." Speed goes on to say that Lincoln was "like a schoolgirl." However, Kramer also believes that John Wilkes Booth was not gay, but rather a staunch homophobe. He paints Lincoln's assassination as high-profile gay-bashing. Either way, Abe's fagitude is not in dispute.

Kramer is not the only one to realize that Abe preferred the company of men. Poet Carl Sandburg, in *Abraham Lincoln: The Prairie Years* (1926), referred to Lincoln's relationship with Speed as having "a streak of lavender and spots soft as May violets." Gore Vidal, who authored a book about the president, *Lincoln* (1988), also hints overtly at Abe's potential homosexuality.

In the spirit of historical revisionism, would it not be prudent to look to the Log Cabin Republicans (the homosexual faction of the Republican Party) for clarification? When Bob Dole refused to accept campaign contributions from the LCR in '95, the *New York Times* quoted Log Cabin member and Tufts professor W. Scott Thompson as saying that Dole should have had no issue accepting funds for his party, "given that the founder was gay." The founder, of course, was none other than Abraham Lincoln, whose image is featured prominently on the LCR's logo. Thompson went on to write a controversial essay on the subject entitled "Was Abraham Lincoln Gay, Too? A Divided Man to Heal a Divided Age."

It's entirely possible that Honest Abe wasn't born gay. His wife was, by most accounts, a more hideous first lady than Barbara Bush. Lincoln knew his future wife Mary Todd while he was shacked up with Speed, but the nature of their relationship was hazy at best. Eventually logic got the better of him. He could either lie with the warthog and feel her pendulous breasts melt over her sides like wet hams, or he could feel the soft caresses of handsome devils like Speed and Booth. Bestiality or fucking like a beast. What would Jesus do?

**From Vol. 9, No. 7, September 2002

The original article featured the author holding a bag of her pee.

NO SHIT

The Truth About Female Defecation

by Sarah Silverman

I have never gone to the bathroom. Sure, I have peed. I've tinkled like an adorable puppy, like a pretty ballerina. But never the other. I'm just lucky that way. I have never been mad enough to take it out on the bowl. What did it do to ever deserve such punishment? Why would anyone give a clean white porcelain friend such a beating? I wouldn't. I don't. My asshole is as pink as the day I came out of my mother's vag. You could eat off it, and some have—ew! Don't be a pig. I don't mean that in a sexual way. I mean hungry, homeless children. Did you know there are more homeless children in America than homeless adults?! That's what this piece is really about—that and my immaculate asshole.

MY IMMACULATE ASSHOLE:

Say I go out and have a big meal at a nice restaurant. I may have an appetizer, an entrée, often dessert, and coffee to make it complete. Maybe I'll unzip my pants. Undo my top button. I may even go to the bathroom and pee out that coffee. But anything else is the doing of the Lord. The food I eat may be digested, it may even turn to waste, but before anything turns brown, God or maybe Jesus himself magically takes it from me, and, I can only assume, brings it to heaven.

**From Vol. 7., No. 2, March 2000

  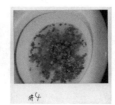

The Polaroids in question.

EXPERIMENT 36: CORN IN YOUR POO

Scientist: *MARK MAGEE*

After noticing how there's often pieces of corn and peanuts in your poo, scientists at VICE decided it was time to find out why. Our experiment: how long do you have to eat nothing but corn before you shit out a poo made up entirely of corn?

Procedure:
Purchased two big bags of Green Giant frozen corn (one "Niblets", one "Peaches & Cream"). Ate a bowl of corn for breakfast, lunch and dinner every day. Photos were taken of each bowel movement and examined closely.

Observations:
Photo #1: Day 1, 3:29 PM. Though corn-eating commenced at 10:00 AM, our experts were surprised to see an average, run-of-the-mill poo come out. 0% Corn.
Photo #2: Day 2, 1:09 PM. While half of this poo maintains the traditional 'log' configuration, the other, cornier half has dissipated into a crumbly, free-flowing shit. 20% Corn.
Photo #3: Day 3, 4:51 PM. This corn-heavy poo seems to lack the binding agents present in standard poos. A cloudy, structureless effort. 45% Corn.
Photo #4: Day 4, 3:17 PM. Corn critical mass achieved! Although there is brown-colored liquid discharge accompanying the corn, no tangible "shit" can be sighted anywhere in the bowl. 100% Corn.

Conclusions:
A pure-corn poo is attainable within 96 hours.

**From Vol. 7, No. 2, March 2000

This is the urinal Goiter Guy was using.

WHAT THE FUCK IS THAT GUY DOING?

The Mystery of Goiter Guy's Piss Plate

The other day we were at the $1.50 here in Williamsburg and this guy with a big goiter on his face took a plate to the bathroom to go piss. He didn't seem like a very nice man. He seemed like a mean old bastard. The couple next to him at the bar was saying, "Don't start, all right? Not tonight." To which he leaned back to an angle of 45 degrees and yell-slurred, "Oh excuuuuse me," before announcing to the bar that "we got a couple of geniuses over here." He has a big goiter on his cheek the size of a tennis ball so it must be pretty disturbing getting into a fight with him. But bad attitudes and facial growths are just the tip of the iceberg with our fifty-plus alcoholic pal. There is also a rather serious piss problem.

Here's the deal. Goiter Guy finishes being a rude person and grabs his ceramic dinner plate to go to the washroom. We follow him in there. Even though he's at one of those one-man stand-up urinals with a big lip on all sides to catch the spray, he puts the plate in between himself and the urinal and begins to urinate on it. It was hard to see what was going on after that, but there was a distinct piddling sound on the plate. Then he goes to the sink like it ain't nothing and rinses his dish before drying it off with a paper towel. It should be noted that he was cavalier enough to continue drying off the plate as he walked out of the bathroom, through the whole bar, and back to his spot.

Then he puts the crumpled paper towel on the bar, puts the plate back in a green plastic bag at his feet, and proceeds to order two more drinks before arguing again. *VICE* took it to the streets to figure out what was going on.

Theory 1

"Maybe his pee comes out at 90 degrees but in 360 degrees around. So it's a big spray that comes out like a sunflower, and he needs the plate to make sure the top of the spray doesn't go everywhere."—Roberta Chan, marketing list coordinator

WRONG: As we said earlier, the sound on the plate was a piddling sound, not a big spray sound. Plus, these urinals have a huge lip. They could handle a sunflower spray.

Theory 2

"I think his dick is bent like a letter C. His piss comes out in an arc and the plate redirects it."—Naomi Gallvin, boutique owner

WRONG: If you had a penis you would understand how malleable they are. You can bend it right and then left and the pee still comes out fine. You can even twist it so the bottom of the head is facing up and the pee still comes out straight.

Theory 3

"Maybe his dick is really small. Just a head. If he didn't have the plate, it wouldn't make it past his fly."—Rick Lynch, engineer

WRONG: Even if your dick is a tiny little mushroom, the jet still comes out at least a foot. Like all animal penises, it is designed to make the pee go far no matter what the size.

Theory 4

"Maybe the sound you heard was his piss hitting the drain, not the plate. He just brought the plate with him because he wanted to rinse it anyway and thought, 'Oh, I should give this plate a rinse while I'm here.'"—Darius Sillvan, newsletter editor

WRONG: If you were taking back a lasagna plate from a potluck, would you stop along the way to give it a wash? No, you'd wait until you got home. Besides, who takes back a normal white dinner plate from anywhere?

Theory 5 (The Winner)

"You have to leave the realm of what kind of penis he had. There is no penis that needs a plate to deflect a normal piddling stream. It cannot happen. Therefore, there is no penis. This man has some sort of prostate cancer that has cost him his penis and what he has now is a meager hole that only shoots the pee a few inches from his body. That is why he is so rude to the lovers and why he hasn't bothered to have his goiter removed."— Richard McLaughlin, illustrator

**From Vol. 10, No. 4, May 2003

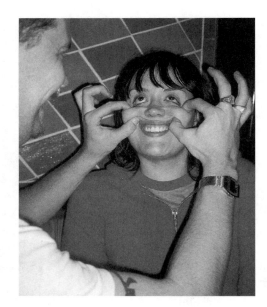

I CALL BULLSHIT

On Tons of Stuff

by Donna Deliva

This stewardess seems pretty and nice and everything, but why are we supposed to sit here and learn what to do when we go careening into the ocean? I already know what to do. Blow up into a thousand pieces and drown. Got it. Do you actually think I believe that we're going to ditch (that's what pilots call it) softly on the ocean and the inflatable ramps will come out and I'll take off my high heels and slide down to the not-freeze-me-to-death water? I guess I'll just use my seat cushion as a flotation device while the Coast Guard comes to take me to my destination (hope my luggage doesn't get wet). BUUUUULLLLLSHIIIIIIT. My dad's a pilot, and guess what he said. "You're right, Donna. It is total bullshit. Small planes and helicopters ditch all the time, but there has never been a single ditching by a US flag commercial airline." I fucking knew it! Those oxygen things that fall down, the inflatable life jackets, the little cards that tell you how to crash: all bullshit.

Thanks, Dad. I can almost forgive you for drinking your way out of me and Mom's life. In fact, that little familial affirmation has given me the confidence to call bullshit on a lot of things. I call bullshit on...

BIG BROTHER
Hey, Craig, stop calling pot "Al Green" and coke "Barry White" when you talk to me on the phone. The FBI are not listening. What kind of budget do you think they have? You'd need three hundred million people to monitor three hundred million people that closely. Is there another America in another dimension that's keeping tabs on us?

TERRORISM
Oh, and like a bomb is going to get you. Yeah, right.

If you were in the most dangerous city in America on the morning of September 11, the odds of you being killed were about .0125 percent. (There's 20 million people on the island and only 2,500 got hit, so that's one in 8,000.) We lost 80 times that many people to cigarettes and car accidents last year. All right, we should definitely fight to stop terrorism and it's really bad and everything, but as far as anything happening to you—fegeddaboudit. I call bullshit on terrorism.

SURVIVING ANIMAL ATTACKS
Have you heard what you're supposed to do when pit bulls attack? You're supposed to collapse under them, and as they jump up on you to bite your face, you're sup-

posed to grab them by the neck and strangle them. Sure, I can do that. Of course, I'll have to practice it ten thousand times so it's a natural reflex, but yeah, I can strangle flying pit bulls, no problem. I'm a female ninja.

Dogs smelling fear, punching sharks in the nose, covering a crocodile's eyes, playing dead when bears are around—bullshit. Bears can rip off your head the same way we hit a T-ball off that little post. Like I'm going to lie there and play dead while he sticks his wet nose in my ear and starts sniffing.

Shit my pants and start crying—that I can do.

FAKING ORGASMS

What guy insists his girlfriend cums every time? Andrew Dice Clay? An in-the-closet fag? I'm sorry, but that is bullshit. The majority of women always cum from being eaten out and *occasionally* cum from getting fucked. Guys know that. What, do you pretend to faint from ecstasy and roll your eyes back in your head like you're having a seizure, too? Outside of Meg Ryan in *When Harry Met Sally*, I call bullshit on women faking orgasms.

MASSAGES

I know a masseur (the degree is as hard to get as anesthesiology, but it pays about as much as a dishwasher), and he says most of his clients are middle-aged divorcées. Sorry, guy, but those are also the least-touched people in the world. That can't be a coincidence. I'm going to have to call bullshit on your whole job. It's just a tenderness substitute. Like ugly girls with pets.

And chiropractors? BUUULLLSHIIIIIT. You move around some muscle and all of a sudden my bones are aligned? Yeah, right. Forty-five years of my mom sitting in a shitty chair can be outdone by a few tugs of her skin? Why don't you realign the bones in your bullshit and try to make it less of a huge pile?

MEDICINE

Come to think of it, I call bullshit on *all* medicine. Everything from acupuncture to chemotherapy is total fucking bullshit. Like that *New York Times Magazine* special "Medicine and Its Myths" (March 16, 2003). Doctors have no fucking clue what they're doing. It's one big gigantic placebo. Chris Rock said it best: "They've been working on blindness for how long? And they still can't do shit for Stevie Wonder. Can we not get Stevie one peek? Just one peek!"

Oh yeah, and that whole thing where doctors say the antibiotics don't work if you drink. Hey doc, did you test that theory out? No, you didn't. You just say that because drinking is bad for you (which is another thing I call bullshit on) and you think that it's PROBABLY kind of bad to drink on antibiotics.

Go back to leeches and bloodletting, you fucking frauds. I call bullshit on you. This is fun. What else do I call bullshit on?

SEXISM

You heard me. I know things are bad for prostitutes in Southeast Asia and everything, but me and my sister Kate have had nothing but a gay old time here in North America since day one. And we grew up dadless in a shitty part of New York. If anyone in our family can complain about sexism it would have to be my little brother, Carl. He wants to be a fireman, but girls wrecked it. Used to be you had to lift 180 pounds to get the job, but women couldn't do that so they lowered it to 100 pounds. What the fuck? Why don't they lower the requirements for urinals so women can use those too? Now you have these 180-pound firemen scared shitless of going into a burning building with their female partner because they know she can't carry him out.

Maybe I'm just ignorant, but once you take all the bonuses of being a chick into account, whining about sexism sounds like total bullshit to me.

ART

Did you ever read Dan Clowes' *Art School Confidential* comic? He's making it into a movie. Basically, it calls bullshit on art school and points out that anything they teach you that isn't a specific technical skill or art history is totally subjective and a complete waste of time. Don't believe me? Ask an art-school graduate. It's a scam. Come to think of it, *art* is a fucking scam. Some Japanese millionaire gives you $400,000 to mount three hundred taps on a wall that exude hot rubber? Wow. You can come up with weird ideas and hire carpenters and engineers to spend three weeks carrying them out. Fuck artists. None of them can even draw hands. You know who does valid art? All those taxidermists that make walruses and wolves and cougars look real at the natural science museum. They may not wear leather jackets with one sleeve and fuck the Hilton sisters, but at least they are actually talented.

AMERICA IS RICH

BUUUULLLLLSHIIIIIT. I am flat broke and so is America. Sure, Bangladesh still uses mopeds from the 60s and we have twenty million SUVs, but that's still only 6 percent of the population. And how many of those people can actually afford to be driving them? The point is, most Americans' lives are like *Roseanne*. The average American owes $7,000 on his credit card. That's a lot of money when the median annual salary is $38,000 a year. Everyone thinks we are the richest people in the world and everyone else is starving, but that's bullshit. We only have the sixth-highest standard of living in the world. We're not just below all those hippie European places like Belgium, Norway, and Sweden; we're also below fucking Spain and Australia. According to the UN, it's Canada that everyone is tripping over themselves trying to get to. The only ones pushing down our doors are Mexicans that are dying of starvation. I call bullshit on us being so rich.

CONDOMS

I call bullshit on those things. Unless you're a total slut in a Puerto Rican neighborhood, you don't really need condoms. Especially in high school, when everyone is too inexperienced to have STDs. Oh, and AIDS (or should I say "SHMAIDS"). I call a huge fucking gigantic bullshit on that stupid disease. Sorry, but middle-class kids who don't have gay sex and never use needles (i.e. 80 percent of North America) DON'T GET AIDS. I know hundreds of people, even some who died of AIDS, but they were either gay or junkies. Do you know anyone who knows anyone who knows anyone who knows anyone who isn't gay or a needle user but got AIDS anyway? No, you don't.

And STDs? Big whup. The worst ones I've ever heard of anyone getting are herpes and venereal warts. Herpes tends to go away after the first two outbreaks, and venereal warts are taken care of with a few blasts of liquid nitrogen. I know that technically the virus is with you forever, but talk to someone who got herpes or VWs more than three years ago. They've probably forgotten about them. As for the clap and gonorrhea and the other bullshit STDs, they can be cured in an afternoon. Seriously. Doctors have us scared so shitless of sex that we won't let any guy come within a light-year of our pussies. I'm sorry. I like guys and I like doing it with guys and the guys I do it with are really cool to me. As far as my boyfriend not wanting to "wrap it"? Come on in, Craig! The only guys I ever made wear a condom were the ones who were too stupid to pull out. I haven't seen a condom since I called bullshit on those types of guys years ago.

PEDOPHILE PRIESTS

As The Rev. Richard John Neuhaus said in the *New York Times*, April 10, 2002: "The overwhelming majority of the sexual abuse cases involve adult men having sex with teenage boys and young men, and by ordinary English usage we call that a homosexual relationship."

Pedophile priests!? Um, I think the proper term is "horny gay dudes." Why doesn't anyone acknowledge the fact that 90 percent of the cases are homosexual priests hitting on post-pubescent boys, like they're supposed to. Shit, I would if I were them. Fifteen-year-old boys are hot! But everyone was so happy to find a cool bad guy that they made it a problem with Catholicism and celibacy and the church and blah, blah, blah. Look, gays in the clergy seemed like a great idea. It wasn't. Gays are too horny for that job. Next!

TRANSSEXUALS

Transgendered, transvestite, drag queen, whatever. You're a woman trapped in a man's body and you need to reverse it? What? Let me tell you something: If you think being a woman is something you can buy off a shelf, you don't think much of women. You think throwing on a pair of earrings and wearing some brown nylons makes you the same as me? Don't talk to me like you know me. You don't even know me. You think turning your penis inside out makes you a woman? Bullshit. It's called "being able to reproduce," you fucking lunatic. That's being a woman. Listen closely, what you're saying is EXACTLY the same as saying, "I am a bird trapped in a human's body." You can put all the feathers on your body that you want. You can even glue a beak to your face. But sorry, as they say in Britain, "you can't become a bird."

HUGE COMPANIES

One hundred floors of hard-working people that are generating tons of revenue for the company working 50 hours a week? Sure they are. How can you possibly monitor the work of all those Dilberts sitting in those little cubicles with their little Garfield posters and Monday jokes? Especially when the company's going through a boom and nobody cares. No wonder Enron got away with murder. You could probably surf internet porn and IM all your old high-school buddies for the rest of your life without being noticed. Big, huge companies are just a fancy word for welfare. Shit, I'm writing this thing at my job right now and I have a HUGE FUCKING PILE of purchase orders sitting next to me. I call bullshit on those, too.

THE WILLIAMSBURG BRIDGE

Speaking of make-work projects, how long have they been working on that fucking bridge? Thirty years? I know it's a little New York-specific for an international magazine, but c'mon. You probably have one in your town, too. You know how it goes: First they fix one side, then they fix the other. Back and forth and back and forth for decades. Shit, it only took seven years to build. Why didn't you just demolish it and start again? It would have been cheaper and faster. Oh, I know why. It's a make-work project. The city figures it's cheaper to have them working there than to have them at home on welfare. That means they are on welfare. That means whenever the construction workers catcall me, I yell, "You are all on weeeeellll-faaaarre!"

REPORTERS

"This is Carl Keegan reporting for CNN. Back to you, Barry."

"Thanks Carl. Coming up next, Bill Donaldson is going to tell us about Mondays."

Fuck reporters. All they do is read cue cards and we're supposed to care about them? Their job is as hard as being a celebrity guest on *Saturday Night Live* (but without the opening monologue). Why do they make us listen to their names all the time? We don't give a fuck who they are. "America's most trusted newsman"? What the fuck? What's he going to do, ignore the cue cards and start making shit up? This isn't *War of the* fucking *Worlds*, you know. I call bullshit on those guys and I call bullshit on them saying their names all the time. I'd also like to lump photography, acting, modeling, singing, styling, interior decorating, directing, and fashion designing in there under "easy-as-shit jobs that get way too much credit."

WINE

OK, you've had your taste—is it spoiled? No? Then fucking nod at the waiter and let's get this shitty date over with. Jesus Christ. The wine is either spoiled or it's not, and the odds of it being spoiled are incredibly low. Most restaurants I've worked at had about two or three spoiled bottles a year. It's like milk, you fucking moron—either it's gone bad or it hasn't. Stop looking at the waiter like it's OK but you've had better batches.

While we're on the subject, I call bullshit on wine. At the Marseilles Wine

Festival last year they did a blindfold test with France's top wine-tasters. The majority refused the test (I wonder why), but the ones that were foolish enough to accept ended up looking like total assholes. Less than a third of them could tell the cheap shit from the good stuff. So stop looking at the wine menu. Like you've heard of any of those wines before in your life, you bullshitter.

HORROR MOVIES NOT BEING SCARY
I call the mother of all bullshits on people who say *The Others* and *What Lies Beneath* weren't scary. What is your problem, you cynical piece of shit? Of course you weren't literally scared of the monsters jumping out of the TV and biting you. It's called suspension of disbelief, OK? Participate in life a little more, for chrissakes. You're invited.

If you weren't scared of *The Omen*, I call bullshit on you. You're not even trying.

SUFFOCATING SOMEONE WITH A PILLOW
Have you ever tried this? Maybe if it's your dying granddad and he's on life-support and he's basically in a coma. Maybe. But suffocating a healthy dude with a pillow? It is so easy to pull your chin into your neck and create a breathing space, there's no way you could suffocate. If someone was trying to smother me with a pillow I'd bend my mouth down towards my neck and then wriggle around like I was choking. Then I'd go all limp and hold my breath like I was dead (sucker).

PEOPLE WHO CALL BULLSHIT ON EVERYTHING
I lost my temper when my Mom was watching *Taxicab Confessions* with me and said, "That's not real." Of course it's fucking real, you big fat crazy British bitch! Truth is stranger than fiction. I am sick of everyone thinking everything is staged. *America's Funniest Home Videos* is real. Sorry if your life is so boring that zany things seem impossible. The only reality things that are fake are a few *Springer* segments (it's really obvious when they're lying, by the way, so that doesn't count) and dating shows. The reason I know the latter is fake is because they tried to have the same show in New York and Toronto, but because these cities aren't filled with people trying to get on TV and get ANY kind of reel together to show producers, nobody applied.

OK? Everything else is real. And I will do a hell of a lot more than call bullshit on you if I hear you calling real things bullshit around my house.

Ahhh, that felt really good.

**From Vol. 7, No. 4, May 2000

MONDAYS

by Sharky Favorite

We're not sure if you know this, but all office people talk about is how much Monday sucks and how they can't wait for Friday. It's considered a better conversation stimulant than sports because girls can talk about it too. For five days a week, all these people talk about is how they live for the remaining two days a week. In other words, they spend 71 percent of their lives wishing for the remaining 29 percent.

We were so freaked out by this phenomenon that we had Brooklyn country singer Sharky Favorite go undercover as "Dan Morrissey the office temp." He recorded the six most painful conversations ever heard and brought them to us.

Location: New York public school administration.
Temp position: Data entry.
People talking: Me and a mustachioed thirty-five-year-old named Craig who was into demystifying the whole concept of Mondays and Fridays. Craig was like a weekday commando who wasn't going to take it anymore. He wore funny ties on casual Fridays. One was of Buckwheat.

Craig: No boss here today. I shouldn't have come in. I could have stayed home and just chilled.

Me: Why didn't you just take the day off?

Craig: Too easy. You can't take off a Monday or a Friday. They can tell you're full of shit. The best day to take off is like a Tuesday or a Wednesday. Punch a hole right in the middle of the week. Break it up.

Location: Headways placement agency.

Temp position: Inputting employee evaluations.

People talking: This was a Monday morning in an elevator full of strangers, and I knew it was going to be good because it was raining out and morale was low. This guy got off on the wrong floor and before the elevator could close, he turned around all fast and made it back in while yelling, "Wait! Wait! Wrong floor!" Then he turned to everyone else on the elevator.

Wrong floor guy: Um, is it possible to forget what floor you work on after being away for two days?

Secretary: Depends on what kind of weekend you had.

Wrong floor guy (after the laughter in the elevator finally settled down): I did have a pretty good weekend, actually.

Location: NYU Hospital.

Temp position: Data entry.

People talking: Two secretaries (Debbie and Sandra) were in an elevator. Debbie was kind of the office slut and she wore tight, revealing dresses. Sandra worshipped the ground Debbie walked on but was plain. It was like Loni Anderson and Bailey, if Bailey wasn't so good-looking.

Debbie: Mond-a-a-a-y.

Sandra: You know, we have Friday off so it's more like a Tuesday.

Debbie: I guess you're right.

Sandra: And . . . and that means tomorrow's kind of a Wednesday, so we'll be over the hump by lunch tomorrow. Just think of it that way—we'll be over the hump by lunch tomorrow.

Location: SkyTel pager company.

Temp position: Administrative assistant.

People talking: Steve wore jeans and a dress shirt and was overweight. He seemed a bit confrontational and aggro all the time. I think he was single. It's worth noting here that my "Sundays" comment totally disgusted him. I came off as a total Mondays amateur and was not worth talking to after that.

Steve: Man, I love Friday.
Me: But you have to work on Friday.
Steve: I don't even mind coming to work on Friday because I know I got maximum weekend ahead of me.
Me: I kinda like Sundays.
Steve: Nope. Too close to Monday.

Location: Donaldson, Lufkin & Jenrette.
Temp position: Proofreader.
People talking: William looked like Biggie Smalls and loved Friday. He had a rich wife, but he went to work anyway because he was bored. In this particular instance Jasmine (the only other black person on the floor) came in for her daily visit and slumped into the chair next to him.

Jasmine: (sighs) Tired.
William: It's Wednesday, girl. We're over the hump.
Jasmine: What?
William: Hump day. We're over the hump. It's almost Friday.
Jasmine: What are you doing Friday?
William: Oh, you know, this and that. Getting my groove on.
Jasmine: When I get home on Fridays I get in the tub and I'm in bed by ten.
William: Oh, so you like Saturdays! I like Fridays. I *live* for my Fridays.

Location: Court TV.
Temp position: Fact-checker.
People talking: O.J. defense lawyer Johnnie Cochran was on the elevator, heading up to the eleventh floor to do his show. He was wearing what appeared to be a suit made of the finest silk.

Business lady: Ohhhhhh, check out Johnnie, smellin' so good.
Johnnie Cochran: Thank you, my sister.
Business lady: How you doin', baby?
Johnnie Cochran: Busy, busy, busy.
Business lady: Well, at least it's Friday. (gets off the elevator)
Johnnie Cochran (turning to me): You think I'm wearing too much cologne?

**From Vol. 10, No. 1, Feb. 2003

THE VICE GUIDE TO HAPPINESS

by Gavin McInnes

Hey, why the BUMMED-OUT FACE lil' guy? Are you cold? Do you have the February blues? I'm talking to you there, grumpy Gus. What's the matter? You're not happy? Why? There's no reason to be not happy. C'mon now, we can work it out. I can turn any frown upside down, just try me. You give me a reason you're bummed out and I'll give you a reason not to worry about it. OK? Look at that frown. I see those little corners turning upwards. There we go, I see a smile starting up, you little fag. Watch...

THE WORLD IS A GHETTO

A point that was first introduced to politics by a band called P.O.D. True, Sonny Sandoval, global politics does seem to be at a level of crisis we haven't seen since the 20s and 30s, but that's no reason to be a gigantic BMX track about it. In fact, I've got another quote for you, Captain Fucking Bringdown. It comes from that astute nineteenth-century political scientist Alexis de Tocqueville and it goes like

this, "Democracy is slow and sluggish and difficult to move but once the people collectively set their minds on something, nothing can stop them." Humans are essentially good, and so good will eventually prevail. Even if Iraq does get crushed, people will eventually see that Bush is an asshole and get over the infinite need for a finite resource like oil. Plus, immigration is getting handled, which is helping the environmental problems overpopulation has caused. We're in a heavy state of flux here that is not irreparable so chiiiiill.

Think of this global mess as a dirty bedroom. You just put on a tape and get to it. It's kind of fun getting it all organized anyway. Just look at Eric Schlosser's colossal bum-out *Fast Food Nation*. Even there we learn about hero stories like Jack in the Box, which is reinventing the way meat is processed, or In-N-Out, which never fucked it up in the first place. He also spends a chapter on ranchers like Dale Laster and Rich Conway who, if you believe Michael Pollan (the guy who wrote that cover story in *The New York Times Magazine* about the problems with animal rights), are better for cows than vegetarians. The book ends with Schlosser saying, "I remain an optimist despite all the evidence to the contrary." See?

NOBODY WANTS TO FUCK ME

Being rejected sucks ass. Trying to suck someone's ass and being told "no" sucks even bigger ass. Fooling around with some chick with a big ass and trying to go down on her ass and getting rejected sucks HUGE ass. Going out with some guy that's a big asshole and who has a fat ass and trying to suck his ass and having him go, "What the fuck are you doing? Stop that," sucks ass the size of China. Being a tiny African chick and going down on a Chinese guy's ass even though he's a total asshole and has a HUGE ass and THEN being rejected sucks ass the size of both continents combined! But that doesn't mean you can never get laid. Just be a gregarious loudmouth who talks to everyone and something will fall in your lap. And you can do your research first. Ask the friends' friends if you have a chance before you bust a move. If you do eventually go for it and get rejected, do this jokey thing (even though it's a bit Chandler from *Friends*) and go, "No yeah, yeah, no, I was kidding, yeah, I don't want to either, eww gross" and shudder jokingly. Keep that joke going all night and don't cry until you get home. If you keep getting rejected despite all this—start a club. Call it "The B-52 Bombers," and what you do is, you and all the club members meet for breakfast after every night out and the girl or boy who bombed the worst is known as King (or Queen) Bomber. The King, for example, has breakfast bought for him and everyone at the table is like, "Are you OK for coffee there, King?" as they top him up and he's the total hero of the meal. That way after you bomb you're like, "Cool, I'm-a be King tomorrow."

THINGS ARE SO FUCKING GAY

Yes, things like TV ads are so bad they can be infuriating. Right now a Chili's baby-back ribs ad is on behind me where this yuppie asshole in a Hugo Boss turtleneck is BEATBOXING and saying "barbuhquuue saaawce" in a James Earl Jones voice like a show-off from *Shipmates*—but I like it. You'd have to be a total

Peter Bagge to get pissed off at things that are that bad. How about, "Ah ha ha ha, what a fucking loser! Hoo hoo, oh shit, man"?

When *Vanity Fair*'s Graydon Carter proclaimed, "Irony is dead," he forgot about the part where shitty things are fucking hilarious. Am I not supposed to love it on *Cops* when the Vietnam-vet crackhead in an army coat gets caught with women's clothes in his house and uses "I'm starting a plastics museum" as an excuse? (He even adds, "Is there something wrong with a man trying to better himself?") I don't know if I'm being ironic or just plain cruel when I enjoy that, but I don't care. It's like *Showgirls*—once you realize that bad is good the world becomes a smorgasbord of fun things to check out. See you at TGIFridays! (I'll be the one in the cat sweat-shirt drinking an Awesome Blossom).

I HATE MY FRIENDS

So do I, little guy. So do I. They always want to drag you out when you don't want to go out and they want to stay in whenever it's party time. The secret to retaining good friends is dumping the stupid shitty ones. I, for example, recently had to let a guy go for saying, "I'm going to write it out in big letters but when you email me you have to make it in smalls."

Define who the keepers are. If you're straight, gay jokes are the best way to see who your BFFs are (if you're homosexual, everyone who doesn't care is a BFF). Men: Can you walk down the street with this guy holding his hand and lovingly call him Charles? Ladies: Can you fondle her tits in public and scream, "Tune in Tokyo—helloooo!"? That's a best pal right there. The rest are secondary; thirdary even. Here are the categories:

Gay-joke pals: People you look forward to seeing and talking to about outfits without kidding. This is the only person you tell about your cheats.

Dudes and homegirls: These are people who probably would be your gay-joke pals if they lived in the same town as you or had any time to hang out.

Table scraps: These are pretty fun people who you don't know that well. You may spend all night talking to them if you see them at a bar (prime potential to be bumped up to second tier—unless they say something idiotic when they're giving out their email address) but then, you may not see them for months.

The beauty of organizing your friends like this is, when you get a call from someone in the third tier going, "Dude, you never call me back, we have to get a beer," you can relax and quietly think to yourself, "Relax pal, I've got plenty of shit to deal with up in the top two groups. I don't need your guilt-trip bullshit right now, you fucking table scrap," and the stress is relieved.

I HATE MY FAMILY (MY DAD LEFT)

Assuming you have a good relationship with your family, all you have to do to beat away the blues is hang out with them (duh). Make them pay for the plane ticket if you live far away. However, if you're like most of us, your dad is a fuck-up who either took off when you were eleven or hasn't spoken to you in five years just because he found out you smoked (that last one's a shout-out to all the Asians out there). Here's the deal: If you have reached out and they have not been there for you for more than, um, three and a half years, they are Xed for life. Fuck 'em. Don't answer those emails that go, "I'm sorry I messed things up but I want to be in your life again." Mr. 57-year-old in a jean jacket was bringing you down, and like a shitty friend, you had to draw the line. See ya later, shithead.

I'M NOT WORTHY

In the words of Dr. Phil, "You are worthy." I know sometimes you feel like a total loser, but if it's anywhere near a Tuesday at ten p.m. why don't you turn on a show called *The Real World*? You're not worthy? Have you seen their bandannas? Have you heard them talk about being "scared" and "not being honest about needing things"? Ha ha ha ha ha. Just imagine how you would be on that show with your never-been-to-the-gym body and your balls-to-the-wall attitude. "Anger management!?" you'd yell at the black dude incredulously, "What are you, a fucking fairy!?" And get this, you low-self-esteem-having motherfucker: Those people are your average Western young person. Believe me. You're worthy.

I HATE MY JOB

Everyone hates their job. Jobs suck. Do you think I like sitting here at 10:43 on a Saturday night (January 18) trying to make your shitty job sound less shitty? Do you think the singer of Korn likes his job? Touring is the worst hell on earth. Do you think Jimmy Kimmel, now that he's about to be the new king of late night, do you think he likes his job? I know that dude. He works about fourteen hours a day. Plus, being famous is like owing every shithead in the world "personality" money. That's why models desperately foster those low IQs—their jobs are that boring. Just check out that book *Gig: Americans Talk About Their Jobs* by John and Marisa Bowe. The only person who really likes his job is either a total fucking idiot or a store manager with a small dick. The rest of us are in the same boat.

What you do is you zoom in on the good part of your job and bust your ass at that (yes, that means weekends) until it's more of your job than the shitty stuff. Then the magic rule starts to come into play. "The magic rule?" you ask. "The magic rule," I say (with my eyes closed). And that magic rule is this: If you focus on one thing and work hard at it for exactly ten years, you get a million dollars. Ask anyone with a million bucks in the bank. Twisted Sister? Ten years of shitty gigs. Huey Lewis? Ten years of bar-band bullshit. Even Henry Ford had to eat shit for ten years before the damn thing worked. Like the Ten Stairsteps say in "Oooh Child": "Oooh Child/ Things are gonna get easier/ Oooh Child/ Things'll get brighter/ In ten years/ You just wait and see how things are gonna be/ In ten years/ You just a wait and see-hee how things are gonna be/ bdddfffdddfff (almost a drum and bass, two-step garage level of drum beats)/ We'll walk in the rays of a beautiful sun/ Right nooooow/ When the world is much briiiighter." Etc.

**From Vol. 10, No. 1, Feb. 2003

In happier times: Lesley and Sam before they were institutionalized.

DEAR VICE:
OUR HAPPIEST LETTERS

Dear VICE,

Yo douche bags, what's the haps? I am literally writing from The Infamous Betty Ford Clinic. You would not believe this place. You just would not fucking believe it. It's been four days for me, seeming more like four months. People come, people go, some people run away and some don't ever want to leave. Two days ago my bags were pretty much packed and I was ready to bolt to LA and fly home, but I'm actually considering doing the 28 days now. I feel so far away from home. I get so sad when I think about New York and you guys and my mom. I realize my decision to come here was not a sober one, and the repercussions were a lot more intense than I had ever imagined. One thing that really bothers me is that the boys and girls aren't 'sposed to "fraternize," which is so different from the last place I was in.

The last place, South Oaks, was fucking awesome. Everyone there was mandated and had missing teeth and were hiding chicken in their bedrooms. Everyone there was a junkie.

Everyone here however was into booze + pills mostly, the occasional meth-head, a handful of coke heads. I think me, this dude Kevin, and this chick Lisa are maybe

the only Junkies. Can you imagine? You guys would hate it here. Everyone is normal. I'm still here. Haven't left yet. Wouldn't be opposed to getting kicked out but there is no dude who is worth it. My mom's heart is breaking and I really want to get better so I guess I'm staying. Yes. I'm staying.

I guess I just want to learn how to be happy + stop hating myself so much. Gavin, you are a hypocrite for doing dope with me at Christmas, but you're also an alcoholic so fuck you (J.K. – sort of). I want to write books. I wanna do stuff. I fucked Mark the night before I came. We got high 2gether. It was nice but I know when I'm not fucked up I think he's boring. I'm so bored right now. Withdrawing from dope w/out methadone SUCKS!

I know I'm doing the right thing though. It's beautiful here. I'm in the desert, there are mountains all around. The weather is in the 80s but it's dry and comfortable. I'm going to be starting a whole new life when I get back; a real one. That's going to be rad.

Peace + what not,
LESLEY
Betty Ford, CA

Dear *Vice*,

It's me, Sam Salganik. I'm in jail. I'm at Riker's Island. It's been about 4 weeks since I've been away from the world (that's what New York is called in here). I miss it dearly, my friends, and especially my Lil' Girl (you know who you are). Don't think I am writing this for a cry for help or pity. I am writing this because you need to know something about partying.

It's not important how I had gotten myself in this situation, that's irrelevant information. All I can say is be careful of the company you keep. Those who are reading this know who you are, and did me wrong. You live and you learn. It's not so bad. I will come out unscathed. I always do. I might have more muscle and more insight about myself, but I shall always be the happy go-lucky guy that I am.

This is for all your readers out there that are facing charges and are going to do a "bid." First off, the night before you go to court to get sentenced, you have to trip the life fantastic. What I mean by this is get your "son." This is what I did, which I recommend highly. You smoke weed? Great. You do coke? Great. Drink, sex, great. Plan a night of debauchery, not like your regular night going to the bar and doing coke in a dingy bathroom. I mean fucking live it up. Your anthem should be some Andrew WK song. Call up your closest homies: Charles, Cup, Sashas, Eric, whoever. Tell them it's that time. Next call your dealers. Make sure you call your weed dealer first. Those guys are usually bigger stoners than you, so they take their time. Next is the coke. Make sure you tell your dealer you want his best shit. You know that shit he keeps for himself and doesn't cut with baby laxative (I never got that by the way. Don't babies shit non-stop? Why do they need laxative?). I'm not even mentioning the booze. If you're like me you should have been drinking since you hired a lawyer.

The most important thing, and I can't stress this enough, are the bitches and hos (lucky for me I got a girl at home waiting). You gotz to getz laid son. In the big house the only ass you'll be seeing is the guy next to you in the shower.

Now it's time to party. Every bar you go to make sure they know it's your party and you'll cry if you want to. This party does not stop till the fat lady sings, or till they drag you into a cell. Remember you're going away so it's okay to come into court high & drunk. Even the judge is OK with it.

When the party is finally over and your sentence is confirmed you say goodbye to your family and friends and say hello to your new friends, Africa, Pop, Oh-Boy, Streets, Mexico (pronounced Me-hee-co) man, Angel (there must be like 400 Angel Nunez's in here), Dread (even if you don't have them they call you that, you just need a Jamaican accent) last but not least me, "Professor." Yes, that is what they call me in here. They think I killed my assistant or something to get in here. Great, just builds my rep. To quote 50 Cent, "I ain't no Gangsta, I ain't no pranksta, me just me".

"I'm going to keep to myself and just stay in bed. Sleep my bid away." Wrong. I was told by Big Mike: "If niggaz see laying in bed, niggaz gone think you scared. You gots to be social, walk around, watch TV, play chess." That's not a bad idea, I thought, I haven't played chess in years. Let's try my skills. I mustered all the energy I had. "Life's a bitch and then you die/ That's why we get high/ Cuz you never know when you gonna go." That line ran through my mind.

Damn it I lost. This was a blessing in disguise. Later I found out that the guy I played against was a murderer. The last guy who beat him went to the infirmary and never came out. Beware of inmates that wear red tags on their ID cards.

Jail sucks—no cable (unless you're in the State pen) no VCR, no sex (unless you're gay), no freedom, no alcohol but fuck it. You get a lot of reading done and there's always drugs.

Weed, shuttle (crack), dog food (heroin), ecstasy. Ecstasy is pretty popular in the Afro-American community nowadays. I don't have the slightest idea why anyone would pop E in jail. Nothing but guys. Wake up in the morning with balls across the nose. I smoked weed once in here and it wasn't worth it. I had bought it for a brick (a pack of smokes). By the way, the only cigarettes you can get here are Kools. You can also get drugs from a psychiatrist. Adorax, Depprecol, Paxal, Mapersol. These are your variety of uppers and downers. If you're really down with the system, your best source for drugs is from One-Time (cops). These guys have the Golden Ticket to the drug factory. All you have to do is hit them off a little more. Drugs help pass the time.

Don't believe all the shit about niggaz getting raped and shit. I'm not saying it's a resort or anything like that. You always have to watch your back no matter how cool you are with your peoples. Point is, it's not all that bad and if you have the memories of a fucking killer going away party, things are even better. Be happy with what you got.

SAM "PROFESSOR" SALGANIK #1100200715
Rikers Island, NY

CELEBRITY LETTERS
Okay, now on to a whole new and exciting part of this very special letters section.

You see, since *VICE* is all famous now and we hobnob with the stars and everything, we called on our most popular peers and our most popular peers' peers and said to them, "Dude, can you write us an optimistic and honest letter about what makes you happy? You don't have to deny any political truths or be blissfully ignorant or anything stupid. Just give us some hope."

Here's what they go, they're like...

Dear VICE,

Everybody has problems but as a celebrity it's really hard to live under a microscope. I never used to want to disappoint anyone, but if you start off like that as a young artist and record companies see that you're willing to do an album a year, they'll milk you dry. It's the nature of the job. And last year I was burning the candle—forget both ends—basically it was just the wick left! So I've changed the way I live my life now. If I need to take a break, have some fun, take a nap, I'll do it and I'm very happy.

Before my father died of cancer last year, he said to me, "There's only so many really happy moments in life, and I feel that we have shared most of those together." It was an amazing thing to say but I don't know if he had that much fun. So for me life should be a party when it can be. No matter what happens, you have to turn a negative into a positive and press on. A lot of people don't realize that I have a sense of humor, but laughter is what gets me through. We only have so long.

 MARIAH
CAREY
R&B singer

Dear VICE,

ABBERRAXAS AND I HAVE DOLLAR SIGNS......TAPES, ORIGINAL POETRY....MESSAGES TO YOUTH......LETTERS TO THE WALLS AND THE HILLS. HAVE YOU SEEN THE MASTER PUPPETEER? WE'VE FINALLY REALIZED ALL SANCTIONED PARAMETERS....HISTORICAL BAG-MEN BUT AFFORD THE USERS OF OUR MENTAL SUBSTANCE A SOFT SPREAD ON THEIR SUBLIMINAL SANDWICHES. THE ALLURE OF OUR CRYPTIC CRAP NO DOUBT EQUALS YOURS. THE CRISP FOLDS OF YOUR FEALTY FRACTURES ALONG THE SHEARPLANE OF SHARING.....BUT WE'VE ALL BEEN BROKEN BEFORE....WE'RE INSISTENT UPON HAVING PEACE....ARE YOU SPREADING THE RIGHT INGREDIENTS? We must buoy the young in the river of no return lest we all drown (as if we aren't drowning already).

In the circles of empirical thought I've already been cast as a "sexual deviant" by those who maintain that they do not subscribe to the thoughts of the mediawingers. It's funny that they would choose to buy into a ragged thought process. But ecological news was my beginning and it looks to be an end in itself. Nothing's changed since the inception of my conscious thoughts....22 years in prison prior to my release last time taught this writer that their spell had to be broken by a new spell and a new spelling....Admittedly, I'm not the most astute person. Perhaps I'm still just a blue-ridge mountain poor-booy.....you know, kinda like a dumb Okie.....but put the money on the books!

 CHARLES
MANSON
Renowned loony person and mass murderer

We had to contact Charles again after he sent this and ask him, "Yeah, but what makes you happy?" to which he replied simply, "ATWA. Air, Trees, and Water."

Dear VICE,

I don't foresee a cataclysmic future, although I've just finished reading an article which suggests that we only have 500 million years to go, at which point the sun explodes. But I absolutely do consider myself an optimist. There was a French writer, his name will come to me in a second, who said that his only reason for not committing suicide was that he wanted to see how the next elections came out. There's always something to keep you going, whether it's finding out who will be the next mayor, or the next writer who comes out with something that makes you startle, or the Boston Red Sox winning the pennant next year.

I had a tremendous backhand yesterday in tennis. Really one of the best shots I've ever hit in my life. I'll treasure that for maybe another month or so. I like the little things like that. Like when you make a quip at the dinner table and you think, "Gee, that was a pretty good one." My father once said that life is worth living for the surprises that come along, which is a nice way of putting it.

 GEORGE
PLIMPTON
Notorious American icon, intellectual and guy that invented Edie Sedgwick

Dear VICE,

I'm optimistic because after *Hedwig* I was offered lots of money to be a Hollywood bitch-for-hire but I got scared and decided to work on a film I really wanted to do with hard-core sex for no money (www.thesexfilmproject.com). I ran out of money last month, but was offered a job on IFC introducing "indie" movies that I haven't seen. I don't have room for a desk in my apartment but a new café opened a block away with good coffee and nice Eastern-European girls working there where I can write for 10 hours if I want so that's pretty fun. My boyfriend may be kaput but I've met a lot of nice boys lately who weren't told "Gay Is Evil" and like to say howdy with a healthy-minded blowjob. Maurice Gibb and Peggy Lee are dead but Dolly Parton and the Breeders are going to do songs on our *Hedwig* charity album. Bush is leading us all to hell, but people I know and like are moving back to New York anyway.

 JOHN
CAMERON MITCHELL
Guy that did *Hedwig and the Angry Itch*

Dear VICE,

Family has gotta be number one. I'm always happy around my family because you can be as silly as you want. Y'know what I'm saying? You don't have to worry about the way that people perceive you. It's just you with your guard down. Anytime you around family it's cool. Other people, with their codes and their sayings and their intentions... you don't know what they want. With family, it's such a relaxing feeling. You can take it for granted. When you're an artist, it's very rare that you're around people who like you genuinely. You don't know the reason why they like you. My family is my mom, my two sisters, a brother, all my nephews, my niece Deeana. My sister is Mickey, all my nephews, they don't have individual names, they're just known as the Carter boys, they're just one group, the Carter boys. There's four of them. My brother got another two. They look like me and everything. All of them are taller than me.

They come over on Saturdays and we have family breakfasts and from that we go to a bunch of competitive stuff, from pool to basketball to cards to Playstation 2. None of them can beat me. Every week they come over like, "I'm gonna beat him this weekend!" But I don't let that happen.

My favorite game is the basketball because we go heavy with that. Football too.

I'm a sports guy. I usually just play football and basketball and baseball, but football and basketball dominate. I play with everybody.

My pop was a Dallas fan. Don't ask me how he got to be a Dallas fan. I grew up watching Tony Dorset, Danny White. I was a big Cowboy fan. I knew why my dad liked the 76ers because of Dr. J, because he had an Afro and they used to call my dad Dr. J.

The happiest moment of last year was when my Mom retired. She used to work in investments, the city of New York, One Center Street. I don't remember a time my mom wasn't working. Y'know what I'm saying? Like, my ma was always working from 15, 16, 17 years old. We had a party when she retired. All the family and all the people from her job came and it was great. All her childhood friends came and they did a whole speech about what they used to do.

Drinking Boone's Farm, sneaking off, smoking weed. She ain't going to want me to tell you this, but I'ma tell you anyway.

I got a lot of new challenges. I'm WRITING my first album, because the first album that I write is going to be my last. I've never actually written down a word. I've been doing rap for seven years and I've been getting too comfortable with it. I want to have passion and fire about it. I know I have a gift. It's not even like an accident. If I tell you what a song's going to do, it's usually going to do it.

 JAY-Z
Rapper and
hip hop mogul

Dear VICE,

For me I'm happiest when I go to Africa, I give thanks and praises to the Most High, Jah Rastafari, for being on the land at that time. That I can even speak and say I have been on the land in Africa. It is beautiful. Very beautiful. And I see love and righteousness in abundance. Yeah, when I walk along the shores and see the sand beneath my feet, betwixt my toes, and I walk way out to the sea, and it still doesn't pass my neck, and I'm way out.

And it's entirely different from when I'm out in Jamaica; you go out a certain distance on one of our little beaches and it becomes deep. In Africa, it's not, the slope is so perfectly calculated by the Most High.

Food in abundance. The people greet you with love. And they're willing to learn. It's just that it's so large and so vast, such a vast continent, you've gotta be rugged. So I get rugged. The hotels are beautiful, the streets are beautiful, the people are so beautiful whenever they smile, their teeth so white. You know, gold, and being in the presence of the Most High.

 SIZZLA
Ragga / reggae guy

Dear VICE,

We're at an important juncture. We've seen the great ability of a broadly defined civic community in New York City to throw a monkey wrench in the "business as usual" approach to the revitalization of lower Manhattan. The first six plans for rebuilding at Ground Zero were resoundingly vetoed, and I can't remember another instance where something the assembled financial and real estate community were largely in favor of didn't automatically roll through to completion, whatever the consequences. That's all well and good for the moment, but these guys have long-term staying power. The question now is, do we?

From my perspective, the nine plans that came out next are wildly irrelevant to the questions that are on the table. They are architectural solutions to a problem which hasn't been agreed upon yet. The notion that we should be debating between those nine plans is a colossal red herring. What we should be debating are the various earlier proposals, which ranged from doing very little down there in terms of building commercial space, all the way up to stuffing millions of square feet of office space into that area. In fact, there is right now more vacant office space in lower Manhattan than there is commercial office space in all of San Francisco.

My penchant in the question of the restricted 16-acre area is that less is *considerably* more. We should cover much of the space with grass, put a shard in there from the original buildings, and say, "We're going to wait for 10 years now to figure out how we really want to approach this thing." It took 50 years for Pearl Harbor and I feel like people aren't going to allow this thing to be rushed through. After all, what's the rush?

 MIKE
WALLACE
Not the *60 Minutes* guy but the Pulitzer Prize-winning author of the amazing books *Gotham* and *A New Deal for New York* (among others)

Dear VICE,

Our optimism is a little bit different than others. At the moment, we take a position of "worse is better." Almost everything that's going wrong is supporting what we're looking for. What other people cry and moan about, we're happy about. The imperialist nature of the government of the United States is leading it into a situation where it's not going to be able to keep the people happy. Like Rome, it will gradually disintegrate.

We are very anti-system, combining the left and the right, although our number one issue of course is race. Our optimism on the racial front is guarded because of the tremendous amount of immigration that is taking place and the tremendous invasion of the third world across our borders. However, we are optimistic that we have to go through this before radical change can take place.

The white man is the most aggressive and dangerous beast on the face of the earth and when he really, finally, figures it out and has his back to the wall, he will come out swinging. In terms of the war with Iraq, we're totally against it. Our war is here. We tell all our people, "Don't go joining the military unless you are going in there to learn things that will serve our purposes." We are totally against meddling in other countries' affairs.

All in all, we're optimistic. We don't see the need for us to do much physically because the American government is eating its own tail. Remember this old quote from Napoleon Bonaparte: "When your enemy is making a very serious mistake, don't be impolite and disturb him."

TOM
METZGER
Notorious white supremacist

Dear VICE,

I'm just an average guy that's been blessed by God. I'm trying to write more songs about world peace and love, something to take my mind off all the bad stuff. K-Ci and myself can't wait to go on tour. We love touring. Hopefully I'll see the same people I see this year next year, you know?

Happiness is something that's brought out of you. It's inside you, but it needs to be brought out. If I'm in an environment where everybody is having a good time, smiling, hell, that's gonna bring my smile out and I'm gonna start having a good time. That's where happiness comes from, your surroundings.

 JOJO
R&B singer

Dear VICE,

I think that this is an optimistic country. Notwithstanding whatever reservations a particular public might have about the US as it has to do with Iraq, for example, there is a general appreciation of an American quality that is optimistic. It's certainly something that I agree with. The last century was an American century and there's no reason to believe that this one won't be as well—not in a sense of domination, but in a sense of giving opportunity and voice to a range of creative endeavors. The general climate of America is optimistic regardless of who's president or economic times. This is more unique to us than any place in the world.

If ever there was someone whose essential view of life is optimistic, it is me. I'm a man who ended up with this rather remarkable thing that I get to do every day. For me not to be optimistic would be a failure of sensitivity and imagination. I have reason to be optimistic, and I am.

I have lived more than half my years, and yet I see the best ahead of me and not behind me. There are things in the realm of possible that excite me as much as things did when I left college. Even though I'm in the autumn of my life, I look at it with great enthusiasm and optimism.

 CHARLIE
ROSE
Talk-show host

Dear VICE,

I became very fascinated recently by the growth of the commercial housekeeping industry. It's really zoomed up in the last 20 years. Most of the women who do this work are recent immigrants. The same holds true for nannies. It's interesting to think that the upper middle class in this country puts so much emphasis on a good upbringing, but nobody comments on the fact that their children are being raised by nannies from the Philippines or the Caribbean. That's like, not mentioned. For some of these women it's a big break, although there are negative consequences for the families they had to leave behind.

More generally, what makes me optimistic these days is the living-wage movement. It's a lot of local campaigns to make city governments pass legislation that says that any company that does business with the city or has any kind of tax breaks or subsidies from the city has to pay a "living wage." New York City passed one recently. The minimum wages, if you look at them, are pathetic. They simply haven't risen anywhere near as fast as the cost of housing has. Everybody knows that the minimum wage doesn't do it. The living-wage movement figures out what you would need to live in any given city or state at some kind of barebones level. A lot of resistance to this movement is coming from the hotel and restaurant industries. So far, though, 80 cities have passed living- wage legislation. I really think that the idea is getting out there that people are busting their butts to earn a living, working two or three jobs, and not being able to make it on six, seven, or eight dollars an hour. Getting back to nannies and maids, though, this legislation won't affect them yet, because they're obviously not employed by large companies that do business with cities. Their conditions are often invisible but things are changing.

BARBARA
EHRENREICH
Activist, writer and the genius behind *Nickel and Dimed*

Dear VICE,

Happiness. I'm having a hard time figuring that one out but I will. I like my car. It makes me happy. It's a hybrid car. I got it in March. Before I bought it, I had a big gas guzzler. One day I just figured that I'd make myself happy and get a hybrid car. It has a gas engine and an electric engine. Whenever you're coasting or breaking the electric engine runs backwards and acts like a generator and keeps itself charged up. It has a screen in the dashboard that has different modes that tell you different kinds of information about the car. There's one screen that tells you how many miles to the gallon you're getting at every given moment and in five minute increments. It's called the consumption screen. It's always on but I've become addicted to watching it and accelerating real slowly. Then I'll see that two blocks ahead there's a red light and I'll try to coast for a while until that red light that's two blocks ahead turns green. It's getting really dangerous. It's like a video game. I've gotten addicted to trying to get better miles to the gallon. It's not a safe way of driving through LA. So I go through periods, a week or two where I set it to the other screen that shows you in which way the energy is flowing throughout the car. It's called the energy screen and it doesn't tell me the mileage. But of course I get curious and eventually I switch it back to the consumption screen and then I'm like, "Oh shit, I haven't been paying attention. It's gone down to 42 miles per gallon." Then I feel sort of guilty I guess. Maybe it's that I'm ashamed. Well, negative in general. Not happy. I feel that I could be doing better, better than 42. So I punish myself for that and then I figure, "What? I shouldn't really punish myself for that. I'm being too hard on myself." So I punish myself for punishing myself. It's hard having this car. It's a kind of "you-can-do-better machine" and sometimes that can be a bit much. But today I feel pretty good. For the last 84 miles I've averaged 45.3 miles to the gallon. I feel pretty good about that. But I should just keep it set to the energy mode. That seems more positive to me, to focus on where the energy is flowing around the car instead of the mileage. But you can get addicted to that too. As you watch it and you accelerate or brake, or turn, or whatever, the arrows change directions and so does the color. You can get mesmerized by it. "Oh, now it's flowing from the batteries, now the gas is running." I guess this car makes me happy, but I'm going to stop thinking about it.

SPIKE
JONZE
Film guy

**From Vol. 7, No. 2, March 2000

LETTER FROM FRANK

by Darren Clark

Dear *VICE*,

"The sexually dimorphic expression of androgen receptors in the song nucleus hyperstriatalis ventrale pars caudale of the zebra finch develops independently of gonadal steroids."

So the other day I was looking to get my yup-mobile washed cuz of all the salt and stuff. There was a lineup so I got a video instead. The video I got was Pushing Tin. It was your basic Hollywood vid about air traffic controllers and their crazy antics. I was enticed by the mention of a sex scene that gave the film an R rating. Imagine my fury when a half nipple (not a full nipple, mind you, a half nipple) was the torrid sex scene mentioned on the box.

Did I mention that I am a big fat lazy pig? I was lying on the chesterfield (a Canadian word) eating my gourmet pizza and drinking orange pop when I noticed that my feet were cold. I always wear big heavy woolen socks, even in the summer. I don't know why—I just feel better about myself when I do. Sometimes I envy those people who never wear socks and go around barefoot all the time. Oh the freedom! Anyway, like I said my feet were cold. They get cold because they get too hot and get all sweaty and then they get cold. So I took my socks off and turned them inside out so they could dry out a bit. While I was sitting there I decided to deal with my toenails. My wife complains about me scratching her in bed at night with my razor-sharp foot fangs. I was too lazy to get off the couch and get clippers so I did what I always do: I ripped them off. This can be dangerous, as sometimes I start at the edge and the nail rips down instead of across and I wind up taking the nail off the part of the toe it is attached to and that really hurts. I'm okay this time; everything goes great. Still too lazy to actually get up and put my toenails anyplace civil, I put them on the plate my pizza was on. I was going to put them in the orange pop can but I had a slurp left. I eventually got hungry again and got off my butt to get a slice of lemon pie. And I still had my pop to wash it all down with ("Heaven, I'm in heaven" sung to the tune of "It's Too Mellow" by the Dead Milkmen.)

On Saturday I was at a conference of librarians and Dr. David Suzuki spoke to us about the environment. I was feeling very "save the environment" so I decided that I would save some energy and not use hot water to clean a new plate (I'd put it on my pizza plate). I was happily eating my lemon pie when I saw an ad for a new TV show called *Malcolm in the Middle*. They were showing a scene where mom is shaving dad's body hair at the breakfast table with a voice-over that said something about them definitely not being your average family when I noticed that there were toenails stuck to the piece of pie I was about to put in my mouth. What a fucking pig. Anyway, could you please send me a copy of your magazine? Every time I go to the VICE store, the magazine is never there and I keep hearing snickering behind my back and things like, "There goes the Don'ts poster boy." I think they are making reference to my Nikes, heavy wide-welt corduroys, Bill Cosby sweater, purple-and-black ski jacket (with a ski hill tag), and brown dressy suede gloves. If you do this, I have some good stuff about fat kids. Pound for pound I've got the biggest class in the school. There are five kids who are pushing or topping 200 lbs. These are 13-year-old grade-eight students. I have this theory that all fat kids are dumb. The other teachers here think I'm insane, but they can't come up with one smart, fat kid to prove me wrong.

One of my students is Fat Albert. HEY! HEY! HEY!

EDUCATION

ILLUSTRATIONS BY MIN KIM

**From Vol. 3, No. 12, December 1996

SUSPENDED FROM SCHOOL

by Kyle Strachan

After getting suspended for bullying, twelve-year-old Kyle Strachan was sent home from his junior high school in South Jersey. So he wouldn't sit around picking his ass all day, VICE had him write a comprehensive essay on being suspended.

I got suspended for fighting, and the teacher caught me after two seconds because they patrol around the schoolyard with walkie-talkies. They say, "KKKKKHHH, there is someone by their locker and I am going to bring them to the office, KKKKKHHH." Getting suspended is a big deal because they send you home and make your parents or guardian or an adult stay with you. They keep calling home to see if my mum's there and ask if I'm busy enough, because if not they'll send a huge pile of work, like, the size of China. I got suspended because at my school there's this "no tolerance" rule, which is really annoying because they suspend

both guys (even the victim) because "it takes two to tango," which is what our principal said. Here are six true stories about getting suspended at my school.

1. Lee Gratton's dad is a gym teacher and was so mad at him for being suspended that he made him do fifty push-ups after every meal. Now he always has to burn off all the calories when he's done eating and, even though he does it, they still sent him to fat camp. Lee Gratton got suspended because he went totally insane on these guys who were calling him fatso. He took Blair Jessup's hair and smashed his head against a brick wall until his nose was all bloody. It (the nose) looked like it got run over by a truck. He has a right to be mad, I think, but he got suspended anyways. These kids who are really fat can use all their power to smash your head through a wall.

2. Girls never get suspended except for Lara Dowley, who wrote "This school can go fuck themselves" in lipstick on the office window. I was there when Mr. Hamilton saw it. He was yelling, "This is appalling! I will not tolerate the destruction of school property," and got her suspended. Mostly it's boys though.

3. There were these two grade eights (I don't know their names) who were chewing tobacco on the bus. They kept spitting it everywhere and when the bus driver kicked them off the bus they laughed at him and spit tobacco on his shoes. He

picked them up by their shirts and threw them off in the middle of nowhere, and then they got suspended.

4. Another time on the bus Mark Hinckling got up and sat in the driver's seat. Our bus driver, Paul, was waiting outside the bus. He used to drive an ambulance, and he says, "I've seen brains and guts before, and I don't wanna see yours so get your bloody heads in the bloody window!" So anyway, when he sees Mark in the driver's chair, he goes, "Uh, excuse me, do you realize it is against the law to sit in that chair?" And Mark gets up like he's going to leave, but he slams the door on the bus driver, which pushes the bus driver out. Then he locks it, sits in the seat, turns the bus on, and starts driving back and forth. All the kids were going, "Yahoo! Way to go, Marc!" and "Testify!" When he opened the door, the bus driver tried to grab him, but he escaped out the emergency exit in the back. When he came to school the next day, he was supposed to get suspended, I think, but he got expelled.

5. There were two eighth graders who got suspended for pretending to smoke hash, but it wasn't hash; it was pencil shavings. Mr. Gunther thought it was really hash because after he got them he said, "What is this?" and Kevin Pearson goes, "Hash." He was only kidding, but they took them to the office anyways, and the RCMP said it's a federal offense to even pretend you have hash. They said they were just kidding, and one of them started to cry, but they got suspended anyways.

6. At the dance these kids were moshing. They had a bunch of people, and they would make guys crowd surf. They pushed this grade seven onto the stage, then someone would run behind him, shove him onto the crowd, and if he tried to get off, they'd punch him in the back. These kids are the really big grade eights (all the people that I talked about were grade eights), the ones that play basketball all the time. Anyway, they carry him all the way to the end of the line where there's no crowd anymore. Then they flung him over, and he smashed his face on the ground. I didn't see his face, but I saw blood all over the floor in the boys' change room later on, and they all got suspended. I could probably think of a bunch more stories because getting suspended happens a lot, but those are the biggies.

**From Vol. 8, No. 1, February 2001

HIGH SCHOOL CONFIDENTIAL, PART I

The Only White Girl in New York City

by Jill Borri

Every day I enter the dark cesspool that is the New York City public school system. My school is as ghetto as they come. We share this big old decrepit building with four other schools, which are all equally ghetto in their own right. Ahh, how lucky we are to be young—the joyous high school years.

We have so much. We get six lovely teachers, 150 kids, one security guard, five different gangs, and an entire floor of an old building. The student body is very diverse: 40 percent black, 50 percent Puerto Rican and Dominican, 9 percent

Asian (not one Japanese person), and 1 percent Indian. I'm white so I don't fit into any category.

On a typical day you hear screaming and yelling coming from every classroom. All the black kids, Puerto Rican kids, and some of the Chinese kids cannot stop yelling and cursing. The teachers sometimes curse the kids out, but the more passive ones tend to fear them and are overpowered.

We have this thing called Family Group. In Family Group all these really thugged-out kids have to sit in a circle while a nosey social worker forces them to talk about their feelings. What ends up happening in Family Group is one really loud black chick takes over and starts yelling at everyone. Sometimes the black guys will try to join in but she always out-yells them. All this yelling scares the shit out of the Chinese kids. The black girl usually yells at the Chinese kids, saying, "Say somethang!" The Chinese kids are too afraid to go back into Family Group.

Every day something entertaining and obnoxious happens. One day I was sitting outside the school and this Zulu (gang) breakdancer said he saw one of the Latin Kings fucking with this Chinese Dragon member kid outside a Chinese restaurant. The workers in the restaurant saw this, and out of the restaurant came this Chinese guy with all his boys and this ass duck-choppin' knife. The Latin King saw how fucked he was and ran.

This little incident happened when our school was on a floor of the Chinese

Community Center in Chinatown. An acquaintance of mine who was the assistant principal's daughter and the English teacher told me why the school was in Chinatown. They said that our Chinese principal had to make a deal with the Chinese mafia. Since the Chinese mafia owns almost everything in Chinatown, there was no other way. We ended up getting thrown out of the mafia-owned building partly because Chinese people do not like loud black and Puerto Rican kids. Nothing good ever happens when you put those kids in an all-Chinese neighborhood.

Now that we moved, there is enough room for a nursery so that all the teen mothers will have a place to dump their kids during school. Almost all the black and Puerto Rican girls have kids, but not one Chinese girl has a baby. You frequently hear people say, "I gotta go visit my baby's mom, yo," or, "How's she gonna bring her kids ta class?" or the ever-popular, "My man's a deala." Shit. I thought all this was a stereotype, but it's true.

Sometimes people may rise above the stereotype of thugdom. For example, there is a thugged-out Dominican guy in my history class who just happens to be a Dominican Conservative. He said he voted for Pat Buchanan. Sometimes he gets into these really heated debates with the teacher on campaign finance reform, welfare reform, and abortion.

A few days ago this fat black girl came into class yelling, "That white bitch!" repeatedly as she parked her fat ass down right next to me. Once she was through with her "she-white," "she-devil" tangent she turned to me, the nearest white girl. Shit. I gave her the "I'm white, so what?" look. Then she said, "You're white! How come you don't go to a private school?" I told her that I couldn't afford private school. Suddenly this really dark black girl in the front of the room added her two cents into it and snapped, "Not all black people are crackheads."

The fat black chick felt embarrassed hearing something so stupid from one of her own team members. She went up to the front of the room where she saw a leftover Chinese cake one of the Chinese boys brought for the English teacher's birthday. She stuck her finger in and tasted it. The next thing we heard out of her mouth was, "Why these Chinese muthafuckas gotta make they cakes so fruity?"

**From Vol. 8, No. 1, February 2001

HIGH SCHOOL CONFIDENTIAL, PART II

Fighting for Weed, Screwing for Virginity

by Rob Roan

Things have been going pretty good for me these days. I didn't get caught for having a huge party at my house. My mom and dad just found out that I drank some of their expensive whiskey but whatever, they drink too much anyway. I made out with this girl who was there called Anik and I know it won't get back to my girlfriend Genevieve, because Anik hardly knows her and they've never spoken and Anik wants to keep it a secret because she doesn't want anyone thinking she's a slut. So I'm in the clear!

Yesterday was really cool because my friends Paul, Peter, Nicky, JF, and I were sitting down waiting for my bus and this guy from my school called Gaston White and his friend Frazhad came up to us and asked us if we had any weed.

Gaston and Frazhad always jack people at our school because they've got a lot of friends and they just beat the shit out of you if you don't give them what they want. We've never been jacked by them because they've never come up to us before, but they did last night. So Gaston comes up to us and he's like, "You boys got any weed?" and we said, "Nah, we don't have any, we just smoked our last gram," and then shit started to get heated. He was like, "Fuck you, I know you boys always have sacks of weed, give us the fucking weed!" So we told him to fuck off (we actually didn't have any weed). Then my boy Paul turned to me and was like, "Rob, there's your bus," so I ran up the street and caught my bus.

Ten seconds later I passed them on the bus, looked out the window and saw Frazhad punch Paul in the face! I told the bus driver to let me off, then I ran over as fast as I could and smashed Frazhad in the face with my deck and punched Gaston in the face. Then we all ganged up on Gaston because Frazhad was out crying on the ground (HE WAS CRYING, THE LITTLE HOMO!). We fucking trashed Gaston!! We kicked him in the face and shit and punched him so many times, it was great. I got punched in the jaw and it hurt like a bitch and Peter got a bloody lip and nose but we definitely won. Then Gaston stumbled off with Frazhad and we yelled at them—calling them bitches and shit as they left. Now Paul and them all have so much respect for me because I was the one who got the fight going. I'm still hyped about it. I don't know what's going to happen when I go back to school. I'll beat him up again if I have to, though.

**From Vol. 5, No. 10, December1998

KIDS ARE STUPID

A Teacher Goes Snap and *VICE* Is There to Pick up the Pieces

by Anonymous Teacher

A retired schoolteacher who asked to remain anonymous wrote the following article. After thirteen years of teaching grade eight, he's decided to cash in his 179 sick days, take a stress leave, and retreat into the forests of Ohio.

I just couldn't take it anymore. Last year, for example, I had the stupidest class I've ever had. Most of them couldn't speak English, and the ones that could were so thick I almost wish they hadn't (at least that way I could pretend they had a future). What really horrifies me is these people are going to be the leaders of American society in twenty years. I've often told them of this fear I have and to my utter disbelief most of them agree with me.

Witness a conversation I had with a student after reading a paragraph entitled "Birch Bark Canoes":

Me: Orson, could you tell me what kind of tree the Hurons used to make their canoes?
Orson: Spruce?

That's a good answer. They used spruce sap to repair leaks in the canoes, but what was the main building material?
Spruce?

No. I just told you that wasn't entirely correct. There was another type of tree they used. They used the bark of a certain kind of tree. What was that tree?
Spruce?

Stop saying that. I'll give you a clue. The title of the section we just read was called "Birch Bark Canoes." Now, what kind of tree did they use?
I don't know.

I'll give you another clue: BIRCH BARK CANOES.
Spruce?

I just told you the answer. It's birch bark. They made their canoes from birch bark.
Oh. The next day I asked Orson the same question again and he had no idea. I did

not lose my temper with him, nor did I insult him. I'd like to see you practice such restraint.

When report card time came, I had to decide what to do with Orson. How do I tell his parents what they must already know in their hearts but have a hard time admitting to themselves? Orson's mom told me all he needed was encouragement. I think I said something like, "Orson works with enthusiasm in class but at times is a bit too social. Regular review of class work wouldn't lead to more success." He wasn't even one of the three students who failed that year. It looks very bad if you fail too many kids. You have to explain what you did to prevent the situation, etc.

This year, as first-term reports were due on Monday at 9:00 AM and I was struggling to come up with bullshit the night before, I said, "Fuck it!" and wrote what I felt. After thirteen years of bullshitting, I came to the end of my rope and wrote the honest-to-goodness truth about each student. I was shocked at how far the replies were from what their parents would eventually see and decided to quit my job.

Jason is still a goofball. He never shuts up. It drives me crazy. He is a loud, obnoxious little shit. His father replied with, "Who the fuck is this?" when I called about his son's behavior. He remained unconvinced about who I was until the end of the conversation and said goodbye with, "All right, if you are who you say you are, I'll have a talk with him."

Nicholas has been acting like a goofball lately. I guess he is entering puberty and his hormones have gotten the better of him. Not to worry, he will be as normal as he possibly can be in about four or five years.

Veronica's only problem is that she's not very attractive. However, once she gets those braces off and starts to blossom, I believe she'll get along fine in life.

Yoon is not doing too badly for someone who can barely speak English.

I'm not sure about **Martin**. Sometimes I think he is okay and then other times I think he's retarded.

Teresa has got a shitty attitude. This, coupled with the fact that she is really stupid and greasy, doesn't bode well for her future prospects.

Bita takes up good air that someone with a chance could be using. It would be a good idea if she found a place to live that was close to a beer store and a bingo parlor. This way she won't have to walk far when the check comes in.

Sophia is a bit too eager to please. If she was halfway attractive, I might let her blow me for extra marks.

Lisa is closer to legal, and therefore a safer bet.

I don't really know anything about **Muhammad**.

Nicholas is a fat little Greek boy who looks like an Arab. He has a constant hard-on for Susan. I get a kick out of watching him do little things to annoy her so that she will pay attention to him.

Sean's mother thinks he's a genius but he is barely literate. With his dirty mop of hair, zits, funny Southern accent, and the growing realization that the only friend he has is his mother, I just hope he doesn't off himself too soon.

Justin is borderline retarded, but his mother thinks he just needs encouragement. What he really doesn't need is for her to do all his assignments. How much of an idiot does she think I am? The kid can barely string two words together but somehow he managed to hand in university-quality essays. DUH. [For Justin's report card I was forced to write something like, "Justin would be better suited to working in a more autonomous manner."]

Aryan (apart from his unfortunate name) is an okay kid. He is really smart and nice, but he prints like a four-year-old.

Jack is stupid. The most difficult thing about this is that he doesn't realize it.

Michael is a nice kid who seems advanced because of his classmates.

I don't know anything about **Matin**. She doesn't speak English and I don't speak Persian, so there you go.

Susan is an ugly girl but there is something about her. Despite the fact that her nose is the size of my elbow, she exudes a sexuality that is all the more attractive because of her ugliness.

Rufus is a miniature version of Chris Rock. He is very funny and very, very dumb.

Joanne is one of those Asian girls who completes every task with perfection.

Ricky bugs me.

Bruce has been identified as "educable mentally retarded," but you wouldn't know it.

Nena is the sexiest girl in school. I have bad/good/illegal thoughts about her.

Orson has the amazing ability to do nothing all day long. He is, without a doubt, the weakest student in the school. He has never done his homework and has never completed an assignment. The highest mark he ever got was 6/25. Zero is a more common mark. He will fail this year without a doubt.

Johnny participates in class activities with enthusiasm. He enjoys working with computers in class. His time could be spent more wisely if he would just shut the fuck up.

Daniel is a nondescript, boring Asian boy who I keep calling William.

Byron keeps getting kicked in the nuts.

Wing Wing has a funny name.

This is the truth, what I really wanted to write in the "Strengths/Weaknesses/Next Steps" box. After thirteen years of fighting bureaucracy, insolent parents, and classrooms full of people who don't want to be there, I'm not sure exactly what went wrong with education or why it happened. I don't know exactly when education in Canada went from world-class to world's worst, but to tell you the honest to goodness truth, I no longer care.

Jonathon's obit   Charles as VICE boy   Sanjay

Jonathon, the first VICE boy   Colleen   Charles' obit   Gordon

VICE OBITUARIES

4 O.D.s, 4 suicides, 2 murders, 1 accident and 2 heart attacks

Back in the mid 90s we had a column called "Vice Boy and Vice Girl." It was like an early version of the DOs. We'd feature a local personality that we wanted to support. It could be a local business owner, an artist or just someone we liked hanging out with. In March, 1995 we had our friend Jonathon as the VICE boy. He was addicted to heroin and hanged himself two years later. Then, in October of that same year we had punk rock legend Charles Kenny as a DO in that same issue we wrote about our friend Colleen MacIntyre. She had just died of a heroin overdose. Then Charles died two years later on June 6th, and again, it was thanks to heroin. In June of 1996 we managed to get our friend Sanjay in the magazine shortly before he died of a heroin overdose (we can thank his "friends" for that) and there was still one more to go. In March of 1997, a month after we announced the death of Jonathon, VICE boy Gordon Nyeste overdosed on heroin.

Five heroin-related deaths in a magazine that was started by a guy who almost died from heroin overdoses at least as many times. In fact, the only natural death we've had since we started was a severely handicapped kid named Max. He did a column called "Special Reviews by Special Kids" with his sister Didi and his fatal heart attack came as a complete shock. Fuck all the PC assholes that didn't approve of Max doing what he loved.

Wait, we're not done. We lost two graffiti artists in 2001. On April 21st, Hector Saul Ramirez (featured in V8N4's graffiti column "Steady Bombin'") was struck

Max on his death bed   Hec pissing   Jerry in the DOs

Max and Didi in the mag   CHILD flashing   Clinton   Coinner's obit

and killed by the subway while bombing the tunnels between stops. Two days later, CHILD took his own life. We featured his puke pictures in the V8N6 edition of "Steady Bombin'".

Most recently (March 15th, 2002) we lost Jerry Bacasa Jr., one of the DOs from V8N9. He was shot and killed during a botched robbery in Brooklyn. Six months later Clinton, the Jamaican dude on the cover of our July, 2002 (V9N6) photo issue, was murdered in prison. It was around that time an old staple, our "News Bites" editor from early 1994 , killed himself. Then, on Sunday December 27th , 2002, Joe Strummer died. Besides being one of the most influential musicians in the world and the only guy that could do the DOs and DON'Ts better than we could, Joe was a really personable and funny guy. He wouldn't want us to go on about it so we'll leave it at that.

One of our worst losses was of our good friend and punk reviews editor John Coinner. John hanged himself sometime between November 20th (when he was last seen) and November 24th (when his body was found) of 1999. We suspect he had some horrible disesase like MS but, all we know is that he wasn't a junkie and he didn't have AIDS or hep c. Aside from giving us incredibly ballsy reviews he wrote a lot of features for us. Always about death. He did our first article on the Norwegian death metal scene and he did a hilarious piece on The Church of Euthanasia (see p. 259) which includes the lines, "I mean, any moron knows there are way too many of us assholes out there and it's really starting to hurt this rock we're living on."

Being the least sentimental man that ever lived, John probably wouldn't want to hear how sorry we are that he's not around anymore but we're really sorry he's not around anymore.

From left to right: Terry Richardson, the book's editor Sharky Favorite, and Ryan McGinley

ACKNOWLEDGEMENTS

VICE would like to thank: the Alvi family, the McInnes family, and the Smith family (your support is 100% of why we're here), punk rock, Richard Bisson, John Reid, Patrick Gavin, Yani, Matt Sweeney, Walter Hooper, La Belle Province (best poutine in the world), Mirko, Bud Light, Derrick Beckles, Colin and Brigid and Anna Maria at Warner Books, Dan Morrisey, Nadia Uddin, Terry & Jenny at Rockstar, Craig Kallman (Atlantic), Mike Caren, Nadine Gelineau, Robbie Dillon, Terry Richardson, Andrew W.K., Jesse Pearson, Sharky, Eddy Moretti, Uncle Monty, Ryan McGinley, heroin, John Coinner, Richard Szalwinski, Patrick Lavoie, Le Grand Prix, Josh from Malathion, Erik Lavoie, Adam Berger, Sara & Sarah, Joe Moallempour, and the rest of the VICE staff, Dave One, Devon, 'Ol Curly, Joseph Patel, Jon Caramanica, David Cross, pot, Russ Hergert (you bought ads when nobody else would), Carleton University (for banning us), Maxx condoms, all the people we forgot to pay, Seth, Inkubator, Bruce LaBruce, Andy Capper, Andrew Creighton, cocaine, Markus and Jen, Brian Stegner, Austin (Texas), advertisers, and all the forgotten VICE contributors (writers, cartoonists like Fiona Smyth, Dave Cooper and Marc Bell, illustrators and photographers).

And of course the people that fucked us over: Jonathan and the rest of the old gang (your back stabbing spurred us to go on just to spite you), Kevin (for screwing us so badly we were forced to reinvent how magazines are distributed), Alix (for being so cheap we had to leave), all the advertisers that pulled out because of our content (you helped us define "us" from "them").